Winning and Influencing Customers

Customer Relationship Management

Winning and Influencing Customers

Customer Relationship Management

TEXT AND CASES

U. C. Mathur

Director, MDP

Professor

Integrated Academy of Management and Technology

Ghaziabad (U.P.)

I.K. International Publishing House Pvt. Ltd.

NEW DELHI • BANGALORE

Published by
I.K. International Publishing House Pvt. Ltd.
S-25, Green Park Extension
Uphaar Cinema Market
New Delhi–110 016 (India)
E-mail : info@ikinternational.com
Website : www.ikbooks.com

ISBN 978-93-80578-95-8

10 9 8 7 6 5 4 3 2 1

Published by Krishan Makhijani for I.K. International Publishing House Pvt. Ltd., S-25, Green Park Extension, Uphaar Cinema Market, New Delhi–110 016 and Printed by Rekha Printers Pvt. Ltd., Okhla Industrial Area, Phase II, New Delhi–110 020.

Dedicated to the biggest influence in my life

Bina

my best friend and wife

PREFACE

The title of the book has been inspired by the world famous book, "Winning Friends and Influencing People" written by Dale Carnegie. As an all time best-seller it has influenced generations. It is surely an ideal book for persons in business, dealing with the customers and is the motivating factor for writing this book.

The entire game of business revolves around the customer. There is, therefore, a crying need by the corporate world for exhaustive research, learning and continuous updating in locating customers, influencing them and finally winning them, now the buzzword is, "Customer Relationship Management: The CRM". The theme runs on the lines given below:

- Locating or prospecting for the customers
- Finding out their personality types and psychographics
- Buying behaviour of individuals and groups
- Products, their types, their utility and benefits for the customers
- Buying decision process in different customer groups
- Customer segmentation
- Product positioning
- Possible customer motivations and buying catalysts
- Customer communications
- Theories based on needs, impulse and other criteria
- From satisfaction to customer's delight and what next
- Future of corporate world, business processes, stimulations, incentives
- The final frontier-making the customer loyal
- The critical success factors
- The balance score card
- Customer-corporate interactive audit

Customers, we all are at one time or the other, we buy things we need or to satisfy somebody else's needs. Usually, there are two basic types of persons, the extroverts and the introverts. However, these terms need to be understood, refined and fine-tuned for making them useful to the sellers.

Today's market theme has become "Relationship Marketing". However, companies who primarily look to Customer Care end up building sustainable customer relationships. A few examples given below will prove the point:

- A lady comes out of a retail shop carrying a few bags in her hands. Suddenly she loses grip on one bag and out comes a bottle of ketchup that spills and breaks on the road. Without thinking about it the owner of the shop picks up another bottle and hands it over to the lady free of charge. He later informed that the lady became his permanent customer till she stayed in the town. And got a large number of her friends to shop too.
- A restaurant owner heard some discussion going on, in the restaurant between some guests and the bearer. The owner intervened to find out that the guests were not accepting the food brought by the bearer, as they believed they had ordered something different. The owner rebuked the bearer and asked another bearer to bring the best and costliest dishes on no charge basis. Needless to add the group of guests became the restaurant's permanent customer.

Marketing managers find it the most difficult task of creating and then keeping their customers. With competitive overtures customer loyalty has become a thing of the past, dead and gone. And yet companies need to survive and thrive. Customers, old and new are the only anchors on which the company's ship can remain steady. Considering the importance of winning and influencing the customer the author has tapped usual and unusual resources to bring about a comprehensive book on the subject.

The author owes special gratitude to Ms. Punam Dayal, Mr. Viresh Dayal, Mr. Sanjoy Mathur and Mr. Pankaj Mathur and Mr. Mayank Dayal for the support and encouragement provided by them during the time the book was being written. Thanks are due to the publishers of the book for the support provided by them.

U.C. Mathur

CONTENTS

CHAPTER

1

What is Business–Customer?

The question often asked is, what is business? The answer is, business is the customer and it follows that the manager's job is to create customers; prospecting for customers, motivating the customers and then retaining them. Besides, the manager must plan for reaching the goals and objectives of the firm. A manager has to organize resources of the firm, like human, capital, information and technology. The manager has to be a role model for the team. He must keep control points with him to ensure that as the team members get authority they are kept within the strategic framework by having the control points, like comparing the actual results with the budget.

At times the manager takes the role of only crises diffuser. This happens more often in unplanned firms where work goes on between one crises and the other. Managers need to become trainers, communicators, motivators and should shed the role of a figurehead.

Managers need not become people pushers and schemers, plotters of intrigues as had been happening in the last century.

Hence, it becomes necessary at this juncture to provide some guidelines for the salespersons.

The Right Way

Never over-sell yourself or your product:

Keep certain margins on timely supplies, if you overshoot you will be pushed out. But if you supply within the given time frame you will be applauded.

Customers or for that matter everyone appreciates praise if it is genuine and people do not like flattery. You can always find something howsoever small to praise. Shun flattery.

Have a caring attitude towards the customer or prospect. At times small gestures can win customer goodwill where even big discounts will not help

Play the game in the spirit of fairness. There may be times of shortages of products and playing favourite will be a sin. The better paymaster, bigger buyer should get better deals.

A good genuine smile, respect for the customer goes a long way.

The Way to be Left

Do not push the customer into action. Take him on the route you want him to take but preferably at his speed.

- Do not question his motives.
- Do not underestimate his knowledge of the product you are selling
- Never make a joke that he may dislike and get offended
- Always be polite even if he has become your best friend
- Never try to be extra friendly or flirt with his or her emotions

Never criticise competition. Even your customer asks you about any competitor the best answer usually is, "please ask me about my company and you can surely ask the competitor salesperson about his company". You never know you may be representing the competitive company next time around.

Management gurus have given so many paths to success, to salvation and yet success remains illusive to most of the managers. The chaos starts with the information super-highway, which provides information to the manager in quantities, which cannot be assimilated by them. It is carried on to the complex competition shifts and the business environmental changes, so the need for enlightened managers!

You need to prepare yourself for a holistic approach to your life, be it company's work or personal. Howsoever you may try it is well neigh impossible for you to place your official and home life in two separate watertight compartments. If you are good, intrinsically, you are good at home and also in office. Any one trying to act a goody-goody role, can do it only for a little while only. The façade is always short-lived. However, a charlatan in the business world can change gears to become a respectable businessperson, although it needs great efforts.

Management is teamwork. On the top it starts with the Board of Directors and the CEO. It has become extremely important to understand the enlightened method of corporate leadership, which is their task.

Corporate leadership (also being talked about as the **Corporate Governance**), tasks have been defined by several management experts and have been debated at various forums, including the Cadbury Committee. Its findings regarding the reporting on both financial and non-financial aspects of business of the firm have undergone hectic discussions where various groups have expressed contrary views.

The positivism of a person helps him in performing to his optimum level. If you are going to meet with your leader and have a preconceived notion that the leader is going to be unreasonable with you, then be assured your thoughts would definitely reach the leader and he would act as per your thoughts. Next time when you are meeting someone have positive thoughts about the meeting and see for yourself the positive results coming out of the meeting. You go to a restaurant with the idea that the food there is not good at all. It is as certain that on that particular visit you will never enjoy your meal.

As a manager you should delight in your actions, should be content with what you have, should rejoice in your work and you will find no action of yours as fruitless. On the other hand, if you neither enjoy your work, nor your actions and you are committed to personal gains only, you live in vacuum.

Your work should be without any personal profit or gain and your inaction should also not be for personal gain. Your dependence should be only on your team and no one else, otherwise others are ever ready to set up traps for you from where you can never come out unscathed. You must be aware of the traps of suppliers, buyers, financiers, which have lured business managers over the years. You should remain unattached and carry out your work in a manner worthy of your position in the firm and in society. Such actions will keep you on the road to sublime happiness always. The only word of caution is that your success should not get into your head, which becomes bloated with ego.

As you perform action, to achieve greatness as well as great success you should direct your action for the good of as many people as possible. Once your work gets appreciated it would become the benchmark for others to follow. It is, therefore a fact that your tasks are extremely important and carry a lot of weight in the minds of your team and others around you. It is your actions as the CEO, which help the firm achieve results and attain its goals. Without your proper action, which is unsullied and pure, the firm will never be able to attain the heights it wants to reach. It must, however, be understood that the achievement oriented actions are always selfless and for the common good of other people, your stakeholders and your firm. As the CEO you should inculcate similar action orientation in your team with full knowledge of its outcome and the fact that the actions from the team members are also selfless in nature. Actions must be considered the right actions and not the wrong, unlawful actions meant for personal benefit or even personal glory. You should, in the ultimate analysis believe in team action, removing the 'I' part and exchanging it with 'WE'.

Firefighting Managers

Managers are busy in firefighting operations most of the time. Things keep going wrong and then only the managers are called to find solutions to take the firm out of the problem areas. You must remember that it is difficult to solve problems by looking at them only. You must find out the cause of the problem, its genesis. You need to look at the roots. It is important to keep watering the roots of the firm, which would help you in not letting the problem get on to your firm. In other words, keep fostering the core competencies of the firm. Defective planning or incorrect execution of the plans causes problems. It is therefore, extremely important that you take great care in the planning process and the team's ability to execute the plans. The training of your team in the plan execution process needs careful handling. The team members need to be good listeners for effective communication, which is the basic part of good training programme.

Training Programmes

Training programmes should go beyond the basics to include confidence-building measures. When a person faces stiff competition, he is likely to lose confidence. It is a daily occurrence with new competition coming into the market and sure enough these can be disheartening, especially to the weak minded. The training should take a cue from the epic *Gita,* where Lord Krishna bolsters the confidence in Arjun by showing his real worth as a warrior in the battlefield. The team members must understand their true potential before they are asked to fight competition. The best way is to make a conscious play with the emotions of the team members, citing their prior achievements and their prowess as team members.

The training programme should be conducted on three levels as given below:

- Man or mind level, where the employee gets to understand the theory of your planning and he is able to internalize the same with the help of meditation.
- Articulation level where after having assimilated the plans and policies the employee is ready to discuss the same with the other employees and can ensure that each one of the employees gets committed to the same.
- Karma or action, where the actions of the employees are totally in tune with the plans as only then can the firm be sure of achieving its goals.

It must be clearly understood that anything less as commitment would never get you the desired results. Most firms are falling short of their goals and targets and the CEOs keep wondering the reasons for the same. If you analyze the commitment level of your team you will get the answer to your dilemma.

It must also be stated that in this world no one is perfect. However, if people do not even try to achieve perfection then they cannot blame any one else for the sorry state of their firm. The CEO and his team must stay in constant pursuit of perfection all the time, as there is just no other way for continuous success.

The marketers know the ever-changing nature of the market. It starts with the introductory stage, moves on to growth and then to maturity and decline. It can be compared with the stages of a man's life. The clever marketer therefore prepares himself for the changes taking place in the market. As new products get introduced old ones get relegated to some extent. The product life cycle is dependent on the research being conducted in that area. Hence, instead of crying on losing market, you need to be alert on the stage of life cycle in which your product is at any given point of time. The distinction between markets and products must be understood as the markets are there forever, while products have a life and they disappear once they reach the decline stage. As you appreciate the realities of marketplace, you can rise above the petty minded approaches of fighting competition in unscrupulous ways. The mainstream strategies and plans would be fully effective, if these are implemented with alertness, and speed then no underhand tactics would be required.

In an oligopoly situation, if one seller reduces the price of his product, he may gain temporary advantage. As the competitors get to know about it they go a little extra mile in price reduction and then see to it that the parity is restored. The ways to gain competitive advantage on a more permanent ways are given below:

- Differentiate your 4Ps
- Have cost advantage through economies of scale, experience curve or through better technology
- Have quick response to market needs
- Focus on a particular market segment rather than dissipate your efforts everywhere.
- Build brand equity to the extent that your product sells even at a higher price than the competitive product.
- Differentiate your service in a manner that no competitor can copy it.

You must understand that competition is a natural phenomenon and it has great value in keeping the firm on its toes. Without any competition, firms would tend to take things for granted, including customers, which no body likes at all. Competition is good for the customers as they get a choice of products, competitive prices and the best service.

The manager has a number of roles to play in the firm. He is the decision-maker, motivator, communicator, role model and disturbance handler. For abiding success in each of his roles he must make a conscious effort to remain rooted to the noble ideals. Only a good father and husband can become a good manager. His vision for improving the home should be followed by that of improving the firm and he can plan to make a difference in the community life. He would be making an impact on the country's life in this manner. You can not plan to lead a life compartmentalized, keeping home and firm totally segregated. This would also have the desired effect on his thought process for keeping his own goals in line with the goals of the firm.

The manager, who strives with zest to achieve the state of equanimity is devoid of sinful thoughts has mastered the art of keeping temptations away shall surely attain the blissful state from where his performances become exemplary. Such a manager becomes a superior performer and a great goal achiever, except when he gives in to his ego, without fail he loses all he had gained earlier.

Value Chain—Organizational Culture

The corporate leadership has the major task of building a cultural ethos in the firm, right from the beginning. Once the culture, which is an intangible entity gets permeated in the firm, the leaders can expect to get its fruits almost immediately.

A firm may have every thing known to for it to become a success and yet result of excellence slips away from it. The best of the product, technology, people, structures and systems do not guarantee that the firm would become a super achiever. It boils down to one intangible element called the corporate culture, which brings the super achiever tag to the firm. While the ingredients of culture remain esoteric the following would give the essence of what is called corporate culture.

- Action and plan implementation and not just decisions
- Result orientation, meeting the goals, objectives and targets, as planned
- Faith in innovation, training, experimentation and self analysis

It may not be easy to evaluate a firm on these areas unless an in-depth study is done through full cooperation of the top management.

Task Orientation

Firms believe in action, "Do it now", "Finish on time" are the buzzwords in the corporate circles. Besides, top managers also keep asserting that: (a) they believe in quality, (b) they are market driven or (c) they are technology driven. And yet the action with speed is the hallmark of values generated by the corporate culture. It transcends the boundaries of selection of one, from the different paths available for achieving the goals. It really defines the personal management virtues. Peter Drucker, the management guru has defined management as achieving things, which underscores the basic need of action, because without it nothing can be achieved.

Many firms in India believe that planning, conceptualizing, thinking and evaluating are far better intellectual activities and they need greater attention. However, even it is conceded, who would go to a doctor for treatment who has the degree but is not practising as a doctor. Strategies, plans, procedures and business philosophies are only as good as they appear after they are implemented. The Indian elitist manager believes that his work is acceptable only as long as it is concentrated on strategizing and planning. The role of staff functions like finance, administration and planning are accorded higher status than the mundane functions like manufacturing, marketing, purchasing and logistics.

However, there are several successful Indian firms, which are action driven and they consider planning, evaluation and analysis as necessary adjuncts of the line functions. In successful firms time becomes the most important dimension in which success is measured. They do not believe in rationalizing failures; they would rather concentrate on the action to reach their objectives and goals. They are not even bothered about the deft handling of situations, skills displayed while negotiating a deal. An international organization's CEO circulated copy of a ten million dollar purchase order sent by his travelling salesman enclosed with a scribbled note on a torn old envelope. The postscript said, **"it is nice to receive orders enclosed with properly typed letters on the memo pads, however, I have enjoyed this order, because it shows the urgency of the salesman to reach us the order as fast as possible."**

When the things are easy and going smooth, the managers are not even required. It is only during emergencies that the skill, acumen and resourcefulness of the manager comes into play and this happens only when such action oriented skills are part of the organizational culture. It is manager's job to find solutions to the tough problems and train his team to find solutions to problems related to their own areas of operation. This leads to a culture of transparency and experimentation at all levels; and in such cases failure of experimentation is not considered suicidal for the person doing the experiment.

In fact the failures of all experiments including those of the top management are discussed openly to ensure that such failures do not recur, and there is no adverse effect on the individual's future in the firm. In case the failure is attributable to lack of resource support by the management, the team member is supposed to bring it out much before the time deadline to enable the management take corrective action. It is not enough to say that 'sorry it could not be done because I did not get *xyz* from the management in time.' If in the end the manager is not able to provide the resources, then it is he who takes the blame for failure and he does not pass it on to the team member. The team member employee has to relentlessly ask for, what is required to succeed and it would prove his drive for action.

Stress on Achievement

While in Indian context, the ways of doing things are more important than the end results. They believe that as long as they have worked hard the other aspects of productivity and results would be automatically taken care of. People believe that they should be rewarded or their hard work and the poor results should never come in their way of success in the firm. They happily rationalize the exchange of results with hard work and several Indian firms suffer from **work supreme even against results** syndrome. It can however, be seen from the successful Indian firms that they are managing the results. The additional corollary to this theory is that while means are not supreme and only ends are, a large number of firms resort to using unfair and at times illegal means to achieve their goals. This, as they find in the not so long run, is only counter-productive, as can be seen from the number of frauds committed by them.

Results come from resource mobilization, countering constraints and impediments, coordinating with internal and external agencies, which happens only if the manager believes in action, is self-driven, innovator, organizer, planner and a motivator by example for others to emulate for achieving the results. The manager does not take credit for a windfall nor does he blame the employees for any shortfalls in results due to any unknown circumstances, like the act of god, recession. The firms believe that the output and results can define and assess the team's achievements, under the prevailing environmental conditions.

Self-analysis and Experimentation

Most firms believe that once they have achieved success using a particular strategy, plan, policy and methodology, they should stick to them and not think of making changes. However, in their thought process it is implied that the competitors would be just spectators in the marketplace, while the fact remains that the competition is ever ready to not only copy the success formula but also to upgrade it, which would leave the winners of the first race stranded. It is therefore imperative that even the most successful firms keep introspecting their shortcomings to chart out new routes to success. The wise would question even the basic status of the firm like its structure, procedures, strategies, systems, style the entire 7 S Model and plan innovations, which would take the firm to greater heights. It is important for the top management to respect such innovations and even experimentations to support deviant views to motivate the innovators. Even persons playing the devil's advocate, questioning the wisdom of moving on the highly successful but beaten track should be encouraged or else the management remains surrounded by the usual sycophants, the YES MEN who ultimately do more disservice than good to the firm.

It is the person moving with the times who can keep modifying the winning model with innovation, foresight as also by learning from other firms worldwide. The firms, which become the benchmarks of excellence, have to keep raising the bar, upping the standards, which would be good not only for them but also for the competition and the marketplace too.

Value Chain—Changing the Firm's Culture

Firms, which want to progress have their culture based on certain values. These values are not only the guiding factors for the firm, they also determine what the firm would do and would not do. Each firm has its own shared values and beliefs and these form the culture of the firm. It can be described as, "**the way we do things around here**"! As people just walk around the floor of a firm they may find a lot of useful creative activities going around or they may find people just lazing about. Since these values are shared and deep rooted in the psyche of the employees it is an uphill task trying to change the culture of a firm!

Cultural values of a firm are mostly unwritten undercurrents, which start from the fountainhead or the leader. It is the leader who sets the tone of the firm's culture. These are mostly transmitted down the line by either example or through the word of mouth. Culture and value based management are soft numbers and it is not easy to quantify the same. Culture of the firm can be felt, rather than described. However, since it has a major impact on the firm's results this need to be well defined and understood by the employees. If the CEO finds the culture too laid back he can plan to change the same as per suggestions given below.

Some of tried and tested methods of making successful cultural changes are given below:

- Understand and make a written statement on the existing culture
- The time frame for making the changes should be kept flexible
- Since the existing culture is also a shared one, employees would feel threatened if the effort for making the change were abrupt and confrontational in nature.
- If the top management has become part of the effete culture, it may be a good idea to replace them with management with a view for a different culture.
- While the firm's vision statement can do a lot for the success of a firm, it is not enough when cultural changes are needed. It is basically important to slowly but surely demolish the existing culture.
- In order to start the cultural evolution, it becomes important to take note of even small successes and then to get them spread out on the informal structure. These stories of success would start building confidence among the employees and would

definitely bolster their morale. Creating stories of success and putting them before the informal teams would generate a snowballing effect.

- Each firm has some symbols, the logo, may be a mascot. If these represent a laid back culture and the firm wants to introduce a culture of dynamism, it may be a good idea to change these symbols and get new more vibrant symbols for the firm.
- Firms need to have patience and should wait till some tangible results can be seen. Perseverance becomes a positive virtue in this matter.

The most powerful type of thrust area is the organizational culture. It determines what an organization would or would not do.

Management operate in the following manner if they want to keep the firm's culture as it exists.

Work with logic, caution, in an orderly manner.

For changing the culture they operate with:

- Innovation
- Participation
- Creativity

Organizational structures are not regarded as change agents as they are in the background always, while they have a positive effect on the making strategic changes in the firm. There are several forms of structures, each has their plus and minus points and each firm must decide about its structure from the viewpoint of best fit in the times of making changes. However, for the day-to-day operations firms need to have the formal microstructures, the teams. Care needs to be taken regarding the interplay of team members to ensure the effectiveness of the teams. Each firm has informal groups, which can provide a vital link between the management and the employees as they inform, advise but also help in changing the firm's culture if it needs to be changed through the stable long-term network. The firm's culture should be action oriented, should support result-oriented action and should keep innovating and modifying even the successful formulas in order to remain in the top position they have carved for themselves.

Trust and Confidence

The main focus of the manager, therefore, should be on action, ethically and morally correct action. The sermon of action must be given to the entire management team and to other employees as well. When you perform action with the confidence of being right you keep reinforcing your trust in your firm and its goals. When you are focused in trust of your goals and are committed to them, you are free of doubts about your success and hence you stop finding excuses for failures and stop blaming others for their faults, real or imaginary. Once you stop finding faults and placing blames you become an instrument of successful action. On the other hand if you keep finding faults and blaming others you become equally responsible for their wrong doings and sins.

Their bad influence keeps affecting you all the time as you keep dwelling on their dubious actions.

The philosophy of apportioning blame has a basic disadvantage that it stops further activities for which you are responsible. However, if you stop finding faults you gain a lot as then you concentrate on your work and perform the same with devotion. A lot of people give only lip service to the idea, while it needs to be practised in daily life. If you have to find fault, please make sure that they are yours only. In fact if you are practising meditation, *pranayam* and *yoga* you need not even do that, as it saps your confidence and energy totally, when you are on a personal fault finding mission.

To judge others, your employees, you need to know them fully, their knowledge base, energy levels, motivation levels, family circumstances and their commitment to the firm's vision, mission and goals. If you have been a motivating leader, the best way is to let the employees judge themselves. If they are not committed to the welfare of the firm their own purpose in being with the firm is lost and they cannot see any future for them in the firm. Those of the employees who have tried only to exploit their stay in the firm can never find fulfilment in their work anywhere and shall always suffer on that account.

Reach for the Stars

If you were to understand the greatest surprise of them all, you would notice that it is the fear, which people have when they face competition. In fact competition is what keeps you on your toes, all the time. Similarly, it is the pride and ego, which makes the competitors complacent. Pride can be your strength in the marketplace, your strategic planning and in your leadership abilities.

When the mind is confused, the inspiration is lost, the person is sad and worried, and he tends to become extremely keen on the outcome of his efforts. The desire for the result makes a person stupefied to the extent that he ceases to care for anything else, except the results, which he wants to obtain in any way, right or wrong.

The only truth in getting over the predicament is constant struggle towards the goals, without any expectations from the efforts.

The physical impediments in performing the tasks are several as given below:

- Strength of the competition, which causes fear of loss
- Ego, which makes the person believe that he need not put all his efforts, as he is too good for the opposition, the competition.
- The fear of winning as many persons do not know how to accept success with grace and humility
- Their own shortcomings in the marketplace
- Competition is for the competent and the persons should gain confidence before they start on the route to the marketplace.
- Working within the laws of the land with integrity are two essential requisites for success
- Never to be cowed down under competitive pressures, but to work with patience, courage and proper planning.

- At the cost of repetition it must be said that the marketplace is an ever-changing one and change is its basic character. You need to keep abreast of the changes taking place on a continuous basis, which would enable you to remain proactive in the market always.
- Wrong action can be due to inadequate knowledge, nepotism or personal agenda like bribery and corruption. At times it can also be due to overconfidence that you cannot do any wrong. The first tenet to get out of such situation is to become fearless, knowledgeable, balanced, without favour or prejudice and to acquire a positive attitude. This is the sure mantra for success if you couple it with ethical behaviour and positive work ethics.

The adverse conditions should never disturb you. Instead you should have forbearance, and patience to keep attacking your target till you succeed. This becomes easy with self-belief and confidence in your team. You get your mind, heart and your soul to work in unison.

When you work towards your goals but without any ambition for yourself, you rid yourself of ego, your desires of the senses, envy, anger and ignorance. The right type of work is the biggest giver of knowledge.

Selfless work frees you of the bondages of life like, fear, anger, sadness, and excessive happiness, lust. Freedom contains peace, contentment and fulfilment. Both the right knowledge, and selfless work from life for you as a successful manager. The very idea of selflessness is greatly enlightening and provider of knowledge.

In the ever-changing business environment, it is the alertness of the manager, which helps in imbibing or understanding the nature of the market, as also the stakeholders' concerns amidst the changes occurring all the time. The confusion, which emerges because of the changes, can be cleared with an alert mind. Besides, you need determination to succeed.

There is great dilemma among the managers about staying with the successful practices of the past or bring in major paradigm shifts in their working by taking the new environment into account. You have to understand the wisdom of the past and combine it with the new realities to remain on the success track. The most important element of success therefore, is your **curiosity** to learn about the market shifts and new trade practices. The knowledge base thus acquired becomes the solid foundation for success.

Good deeds, bad deeds or no deeds are all manifestations of the mind. Good deeds are of three types, the daily routine tasks, the symbolic tasks and the tasks wilfully taken on by you. As a manager you have to be performing all three types of tasks. The better manager knows the tasks and does them with his own motivation and he does not need any prodding for the same.

As a manager you need to keep time each day for introspection to know your own SWOT. You can get out of the schizophrenic tendencies, which keep surrounding you, as you may be a docile parent and husband and yet could be a tyrant in your workplace. You have to remain the same positive, calm, helpful and an ideal person in both homestead and at the workplace. You can take guidance from gurus, peers, and seniors and yet the ultimate responsibility rests squarely on you.

The following are the major traits of character of a good manager:

- He is unruffled even in adverse circumstances
- He is disciplined, has sense of justice and foresight
- He is without any desire for any thing, as the desire will surely derail his success plans
- He believes in the intrinsic goodness of his fellowmen
- He should NOT merely follow the leading competitor, as his success could be built on early entry and it may be without the idea of changing business environment.
- He should NOT copy a success blindly
- He should NOT chase competition when it is severe.
- He should NOT do anything without the environment consideration
- The time has come when you need to be transparent with your stakeholders. The ideal situation is when you involve them in your decision-making process, because then you can never go wrong. For example, if you supply products and services as per joint decision taken with your customers you just cannot err.

There is a lot of discussion on the accountability of managers. It is said that it was only due to no accountability of the managers in the government firms, they have not shown the desired results. The theory of manager's accountability has been misused at times in the private firms as a means of getting rid of managers not liked by the boss. A purposeful fine-tuned accountability plan must be made and linked with performance to be of real value and relevance to the firm.

Balance Accountability and Enterprise

It is the main task of the CEO to show results in quick time. It also means that he has to act in the age old structured manner and deviations could cause losses and therefore his ouster from the firm. The element of risk involves taking decisions, which could be iconoclastic, breaking away from the old mould and these could go either way; bring a lot of profits or huge losses. It is essential that a proper value judgement is made before such decisions are taken.

Search Competitive Advantage

The CEO has to constantly strive for gaining and maintaining the firm's competitive advantage, through differentiation in the 4Ps—product, price, placement and promotion. You can also use cost leadership; quick response to market needs for gaining competitive advantage. The firm's success starts and ends with the sustainability of its competitive advantage.

Accountable Entrepreneurs

The entrepreneur's task is to provide the right product to the customers at the right price with the help of right distribution channel and promotion. As he is the risk taker, he must also consider himself accountable to other stakeholders. The right decisions taken by them provide the impetus to the entire team for performing to their best ability.

A professional manager plans and acts in the total interest of the firm, always keeping his own interests subservient to the firm's goals.

The managers take initiatives and deploy resources to actively pursue operating objectives. They must enjoy the freedom and independence to produce results. And therefore they are justified in expecting rewards.

In light of their independence, the managers are required to provide accurate and timely reports to the Board.

Customer Orientation in Retail Trade: The product portfolio in retail is governed by the customers who visit the store. Half the success of a retailer comes from his correct inventory; he keeps products what the customers want. A few examples are given to prove the point.

Bata's own shops have been in the Indian market covering even the remote areas selling shoes, for nearly eighty years. The stores sold shoes only, till the management realized that located at prime sites in each town, visited by the majority of inhabitants of the town, the customers could also buy socks, shoelaces, shoe polish and brush. Later, the management added on an entire complement of leather accessories, tracksuits, T-shirts, cardigans. On a visit to the store the customer has the option of buying his entire need for fitness attire.

Petrol pumps, in most part of the last century sold petrol, diesel and engine oils. At best they provided with servicing facilities for the vehicles, tyre repair and compressor for tyre inflation, and water for filling the radiator of the car. Today, the prime location petrol pumps sell tyres, batteries, car air-conditioners and other accessories. The latest trend is seen in the metro towns where the petrol pumps have shops attached selling gift items, cold drinks, and items of general merchandize. These air-conditioned shops have given a new meaning to product portfolio management in this case.

Usha shops sold only Usha fans and sewing machines till 1970s. These shops also are located in the selected markets and were under-utilized till the customer almost drove them into selling a range of consumer durables, white goods and the like, making the shops a better shopping experience for the customers and more profitable ventures for the shopkeepers.

Brands Decisions

Brand identifies a product and differentiates one product from the other. A lot of selling rides on the brand, which is the product image in the customers' minds. Firms consider their brands as the most valuable asset because it is with the help of the brand that the firm is able to establish certain rapport with the customer. Brand symbolizes the product, gives the product its characteristics like Maruti 800 car focuses on the customers on a well made (with Japanese technology) economical car as given below:

- Product characteristics as stated above
- Product benefits for the customer

- Brand gives the product its significant personality, like Maruti 800 is known as a sleek car with good economical mileage for urban markets.
- Brand distinguishes its buyer from buyer of other branded products. Maruti 800 buyer is a conservative, town dweller with limited resources, who does not want to spend money on large cars.

Brands of FMCG Products do not ensure brand loyalty of the kind available for consumer durable products because the switching cost for FMCG products is not a large amount and customers love to experiment; they buy one brand of soap in one month and soap of another brand in the next month.

Brand loyalty in FMCG products is being achieved today by almost continuous promotional activities for the product in the marketplace. However, there are some loyal customers of brands who would refuse to buy another brand if Coke is not available in the shop.

For consumer durables, since the cost of the product is relatively high (switching cost), and customers do not buy these every other day brand loyalty can be assured unless the product fails to provide the benefits it had offered on sale.

Brand and trademarks are the visible identification of the product and its seller. In case of problems in quality or tracing dispatches these help.

Trademarks protect the seller against fraudulent sale of their product.

Brands help in attracting the customers and making them loyal to the seller through his brand.

At times brands become so strong and well known that the firms selling them get to be known by them. Hair dye and Godrej have become synonymous.

Brands sometimes due their popularity become generic names of the products, like mobil oil was considered as the engine oil, while it is the brand of Mobil company. Dalda became the common word for cooking oil while it is the brand name of Hindustan Levers in India.

Brand names emerge from either the family names like Godrej in India, Usha for sewing machines and fans.

Brand names can come from the town from where the product is emanating, like, Rampur textiles, Lucknow kurta.

Some firms like Hindustan Levers keep separate brand names for each of their product, Lux soaps. Surf detergent, Lipton tea.

Firms try to keep brands easily pronounceable, having a meaning significantly close to product attributes and then they advertise the brand to make it popular and try to increase the brand value—the brand equity.

Tasks for the Students

Pick up five brands common in India, define their market segment and discuss the firms product portfolio how the firm is promoting the same in the respective market segments.

Product Portfolio: It is the list of all products a seller has on sale. For example, HLL has a large product portfolio, including, soaps, shampoo, detergents, vegetable cooking oils, tea, coffee, cosmetics. The advantage of having a large portfolio is that even if one product does not show good result, others help the firm to show good results.

Product brand depth is the variety of models the firm offers for each brand. TV firms keep a large variety to suit different tastes. Kwality brand gives a large variety of flavours in ice creams

Connected products are those dependent on each other for usage, like, PC, UPS, and printer, modem. Sale of one affects the sale of other to an extent. Software products are also connected to computer hardware in the same way.

Selection of product portfolio is carried out by taking into account the following parameters:

Stages of product life cycle: The firm can plan divestment for the products in the dog quadrant unless they are support products used to help sell other products.

Market strength vs. market share of the firm, which can be assessed on the BCG Matrix.

Market trends, growth potential, profitability of the product

Level of competition in the product, today and expected in the near future.

Entry barriers and exit barriers

Market extensions through catering to up market segment with a new package or down market segment by reducing package cost.

Branding generic products till the last ten years, salt, sugar, wheat flour, rice were generic products and customers bought them from retail shops by giving the generic name. Today most products have brands and they sell according to the brand appeal they have in the market segment they sell. Same wheat flour could be sold at Rs. 100 for five kg as premium package, at Rs. 80 per five kg as medium package and even at Rs. 60 per five kg in lower segments with least attractive, just functional package as given in the matrix shown below. Change of venue or selling place can also help change in price; same Coke bottle, which sells with roadside vendor for ten rupees, sells for fifty rupees in a five-star hotel the charges ostensibly include the five-star ambience cost as well.

Increasing the range is attributed to the demands from the distribution channels, which insist that unless the firm matches the product spectrum of competition they will remain at a disadvantage in the marketplace. The concept of one stop electronic shop, which deals in TVs, radios, stereos, speakers, and similar products, helps the dealer in satisfying the customer who comes to buy an electronic product. The risk of non-saleable products, or slow moving ones which jack up inventory levels has to be understood by the firm.

Product innovations, new designs, technology updates viewed in customers' perception and fitting into customer mindset, is not only required but in today's world essential to keep ahead of competition.

The market dynamics ultimately decide what will sell when and what will not. In case of simple assembly line operations, dropping out of a product may not cause huge losses as with minor changes the same assembly line can produce other products. However, in case of process made products, like chemicals changing of product would entail scrapping up of the entire manufacturing equipment.

The matrix giving same product with different quality standards and their resultant prices is given below:

	Economy pack	Standard pack	Good-looking pack	Elitist pack
High price				For elitists
Above average price				For upper class segment
Average price		For middle income segment		
Low price	For low income segment			

Demand Forecasting

Firm's sale of a product is also its market share, a percentage of the total market. In specific brand resilient products, their demand could just be what the firm can supply in the market and therefore the restrictions come only from the manufacturing units. Maruti could sell as many cars it made till the arrival of Santro, Matiz and Indica in the market. In case the product differentiation is not marked or pronounced, another can substitute one brand if the seller can convince the buyer of the better benefits available with their product. In case of vastly different products, the demand remains with the manufacturers until they are unable to meet the same.

Total product demand can be divide into different market segments as follows:

- Travel by businessmen or by tourists
- Cement for house construction or for constructing dams.

In monopoly conditions, the firm's supply could be regarded as the industry demand. However, in perfect competition, which is the case in most products today, the total market demand has not much in common with individual firm's demand. Therefore it can be assumed that in perfect competition, brand image, price and the consumer behaviour of the market segment decide the firm's product demand. The firm's demand is defined as its market share for the product. The definition works well in similar product competition and stable markets. Market share, is the most important asset of a firm and the firms are trying their best all the time to increase it even by fraction of a percent. Product innovations, channel motivation, price manipulation are ways of keeping the share parity or for increasing the market share. Price reduction, going in for penetrating prices can increase the market share, at least in products where the demand is price elastic.

Market Share

It is possible to retain or improve firm's market share by the following means:

Product differentiation should make the product visibly better but without adding a huge amount to its cost. Gold plating the interior of a TV set will not bring any additional business but will surely increase the cost of the product.

Price reduction for price elastic demands of the product, low price can increase the firm's market share. But try to increase market share by reducing the price of Mercedes car by one thousand rupees would not make any difference whatsoever to the sale of the product except it would reduce the profit picture by that amount.

Advertising and promotion help increase in sales and hence in improving the market share.

In case of price reduction in price sensitive products, the firm indulging in the reduction can gain additional market share, but it could at best be a temporary increase as the competitors is likely to reduce the price and bring parity of market share back to the original.

In case of non-price elastic products, it is the brand equity and the product-usage fit that counts. The Maruti van with large sitting capacity has been accepted as a means of transport for office workers and hence a moderate price increase may not affect its sale. While increase in price in Santro by the same amount may divert customers from it to Maruti 800 car.

Demand forecast can be divided into two segments as follows:

Short term forecast time period is dependent on the total life of the product. For example, fashion garments life can be considered as that of maximum of six months. Hence, the demand forecast cannot be of more than six months. In such cases both short and long term forecasts remain the same.

For other products, short term forecast is usually of a year. Short-term forecast helps the firm in establishing production schedules, purchase and inventory management, reducing material costs by 'Just in Time' technique, manpower planning, arrangements of finance for production, selling and advertising promotion activities.

Long term forecast helps firm in augmenting production resources, buying additional equipment, increasing manpower on a permanent basis, increasing geographic coverage in marketing, arranging long term finances, or doing the reverse if forecast shows a decline in market demand.

Demand Generation of FMCG Products

The FMCG products like soaps, shampoos, ice cream, petrol, detergents are purchased by a large number of persons. The purchase is dependent on the factors given below:

Increase or decrease in disposable income of the target market segment. With cost of living index going up, if the income does not increase in the same proportion, the purchase will reduce. People will buy less of ice cream, use alternatives, washing soaps instead of detergent powder, tooth powder instead of toothpaste. However, in case the income rises equally or more than the cost of living, than the purchase will automatically increase.

Price is a major factor, which determines the purchase or the quantum of purchase the price is compared with like products, substitute products. In case of small price differentials, customers tend to buy either more reputed product or the one they have been using for long.

Demographic profile of the geographic segment-income, status, life style in the area, age levels—number of children in different age groups, number of senior citizens for toys and health products respectively, define the purchase levels in the area.

Demand Generation of Consumer Durables is dependent on the availability of cash in the market. During festive seasons like Deepavali, when most people get bonus from their employers, there is a sudden spurt in demand of consumer durables. Leasing and hire purchase options also give boost to sale of the consumer durables as also the following:

- Prestige value of the product, keeping up with the Joneses
- Exchange offers from firms, get new product at a discount by giving the old one
- Extended usage, for example more TV channels
- Increase in number of households with the slow disappearance of joint family system.
- Decision of purchase done jointly by adults and teenagers
- In addition to new owners, there is a regular replacement demand of consumer durables.
- Price dips, credit or leasing facilities help in increasing the demand.

It can thus be surmised that the demand of a consumer product is a function of, disposable income including hire purchase option, price and demography.

Marketing Conscience

In the race of achieving the sales targets, the firm's salesmen, at times forget that selling must be carried out within the legal and ethical framework of the government and the society in which we live. Profit making leads to satisfying the stockholders of the firm and the other stakeholders. However, profiteering, as different from profit making, does not satisfy anyone except the greed of the person indulging in the same. With competitive forces keeping prices in check, the methods available to the dubious marketer are, supply of substandard goods, spurious material; even food items and life saving drugs are not excluded from such activities.

The sellers therefore have to abide by certain rules and regulations. Some contraventions are legal and punishable, others could be ethical or moral and from these too the customer must be protected. Following is a basic list of the Do's and Don'ts for the seller.

Dos for the Seller

- Supply goods as per specifications given by the seller
- Keep quality of goods and service uniformly good
- Supply products in correct weight, volume
- Announce the product price on the container/package
- Announce the ingredients of the product where necessary
- Supply only the product ordered, not its substitute
- Provide proper training in correct usage of the product.

Don'ts for the Seller

- Do not adulterate the goods to be sold
- Do not supply inferior quality goods
- Do not exaggerate product's virtues, do not over sell
- Do not give incorrect delivery date
- Do not use puffery in advertisements by giving false information on the product
- Do not refuse to give service, which is part of the product sale.

Any business, which starts with in some way cheating the customer, is not likely to succeed in the long run. Short-term benefit could also prove costly as violation of country's laws can lead the seller in serious trouble.

Consumer or the buyer needs protection from unscrupulous sellers, and this need has given rise to the consumerism or the consumer movement, which provides the information about the rights of consumers and also ways of redress to the victims of unfair practices of the sellers.

All along the book has emphasized the fact that the customer is the king. He must be treated with kindness, dignity and must never be ignored. The seller while dealing with customers must keep his benefits paramount. However, the ideal situation is never there and hence there is a need for consumer protection against the unscrupulous sellers. Ideal situation imagines the following:

- The consumer is well aware of his own requirements
- The seller knows the needs and tries hard to fulfill them with his product and services
- The sellers are all the time communicating with the buyers, telling them about the products. Their benefits, service, which go with the products and terms of business
- The products purchased by the buyers meet their needs and expectations

Consumerism

However, the ground reality is quite different from the above stated premises. Consumerism has become a force today to combat some sellers dubious plans and the task undertaken by it is given below:

- Informing consumers of their right of getting a product of good quality of acceptable price.
- Helping in fighting against the seller in getting the redress in case of buyer feeling cheated.
- Focusing on existing laws meant to protect the consumers and telling the government the need of more such laws
- Forming consumer groups in each city to fight against the malpractices of some sellers.

In India, the consumer is facing the problem of self-created shortages by the sellers, who can then increase the price, hoard products forcing the consumers into buying the offered product without recourse to fair treatment. Ignorance of the laws and long drawn out legal proceedings deter the wronged consumer, who just bears the brunt of the malpractices of the seller.

The above stated malaise can be considered a mirror of the times we live in. However, the marketing fraternity must take the cudgels on behalf of the consumers to protect their own market from these fly-by-night operators, who are there only to make quick money and then decamp. The regular sellers owe it to themselves as also to the society they cater to, as also the society they are very much part of.

While discussing the need for fair practices one can hardly forget the story of a seller of dubious medicines who was enjoying his newly created wealth with a gala party at his house with friends, wine and music when his servant came running to inform that his own son was dying after taking the medicine of his own firm. The business, the society the government are all part of us, the citizens of India should never be taken apart. The social responsibility of the business, the ethics involved is part of our heritage and a consumer movement, like the juggernaut, gathering momentum can bring back the sanity in our business dealings. For this purpose the consumers have to be made fully aware of their rights, the way they can get redress without cumbersome legal procedures. It is therefore the duty of those in power to ensure that there is proper legislation in this regard.

Consumer's Rights

The consumers have the rights on the issue of protection against dubious sellers as given below:

Right to know the product in detail, its quality, purity, size, weight, package, brand, and its price before the purchase is made. For many products in India it has become mandatory for the sellers to provide the information on the product package or label if possible. Food products, medicines, toys for children must follow the norms strictly. How the local application medicines need to be used must be given on the container.

Right to have safety products, which are substandard, (electrical goods which give shock), unhygienic food products, can cause unimaginable damage and the consumers have a right to get the correct products.

Information on consumer protection and the rights of the consumers must be made known to all the consumers through widespread advertising.

The consumer also must have the right to select the most appropriate product amongst those in the market. Advertising gives this right well in its own way.

The consumers have the right of getting redress in case the seller has cheated them. If the product carries a guaranty then the seller must replace or repair the defective piece, otherwise also the seller of bad product must compensate the buyer for selling him the bad product, or product not exactly like the one promised or advertised. In case excessive price has been charged then the seller must refund the extra amount charged.

The government of India has passed the Social Welfare Legislation for consumer protection, with ample safeguards against consumer exploitation. Special courts have been instituted in states to deal with consumer cases. These consumer courts deal with only the consumer cases and hence are quite fast in passing judgment.

The government of India has also created a commission to check monopoly business and unfair trade practices under the Monopolies and Restrictive Trade Practices Act

(MRTPA). Under this act price consortium are not allowed as these give advantage to the sellers.

The objectives of a firm can now be redefined as follows:

The firm has to meet its obligations towards its stakeholders including, buyers, sellers, vendors, employees, employers, trade bodies, the government and public at large. For this purpose the firm must ensure proper utilization of its financial, manpower technological and human resources. The firm must offer value for money products to its customers. It must standardize its operations on fair trade practices. It must treat its employees with consideration of a genuine friend. It must also conform to the national objective of increasing exports. Profit as an objective cannot be denied as only with adequate profit comes survival and growth besides the firm need to satisfy its stakeholders can be met only by making profits. Besides, the firm should actively espouse the social causes like literacy, healthcare to the extent it can. (Many firms have opened hospitals for its employees, also used by the general public living in the area).

Firms should run their operations in socially and ethically acceptable manner, as given below:

- Fair price for the products
- Correct weights, volumes of the product sold
- Pay taxes to the government
- Should ensure that products sold are not adulterated in any manner
- Not sell contraband goods
- Give weight, volume, price, ingredients on the package of the products
- Make supportable claims in advertising campaigns
- Hoarding of goods to create artificial shortages should never be done
- Firms should never bribe to get orders
- Firms should assist the customers in proper usage of the product, if required, by training the customer in the proper use of the product.

Tasks for the students—discuss the role of marketing considering the firms, legal, moral and ethical obligations to the consumer and the public in general.

Business and Manager

Managers need to focus on both the expected as well as the unexpected. Lateral thinking, out of the box thinking are the catalysts for innovation and creativity, the two mantras for success. The targets are normally kept slightly out of reach unless extra efforts are made. Managers competence can be measured only by understanding his imaginative thinking process, his ideas on innovative technology, marketing, HR and MBO. He should have bold imagination, he needs to be inspired with intrinsic urge to lead the company to prosperity. In most of the companies heavy financial outlays for leading the innovation field are difficult to find while competition always seems to surmount this obstacle. The manager as the leader must motivate the team members towards the organic, dynamic organisational culture that would create the right work ethos enabling the team to perform optimally despite resource constraints. Let us examine the following in this context.

You and your firm exist because of the customer. There can never be any dispute on this and therefore, you have to not only like your customers but enjoy their company. The ideal situation is when you send positive friendly vibes all around you, even to the passers-by on the road; they are your potential customers. And even better is when your customers start liking you and your firm, not just your products. You may find some customers not entirely to your liking and yet they are the reason for your existence. You cannot be play acting all the time in a make-believe world that your customers know the depth of your surface liking of the customers. You should be genuine; remember, a mother likes her children, howsoever ugly they may be. Your real love and adoration for your customers will become visible to them and that would be the starting point of a long lasting relationship with them. When you have achieved such empathy with your customers, no amount of hurdles of snakes would deter you from reaching your goals and that too well in time. Make that your goal today!

The talk today is of "customer delight" instead of "customer satisfaction." There will be times when you may have to sacrifice a lot for even a slight pleasure of your customer. You may think that this is an absurd theory as no one ever does that. However, you need only to apply the same yardstick for yourself. Suppose when you are a buyer, someone goes a long way to give you the delight while he is highly inconvenienced and he does it with a smile, you will like to continue your relationship with him. Now, you can decide about your actions towards your customers' delight in positive terms. This works especially well, when you have a customer who is in a problem situation. As you relieve him of his tensions by going an extra mile you earn not only his gratitude but also his friendship. The only caution is that you should have a genuine caring approach and not just a business attitude.

The corporate world today needs as many public relations officers as they get. In fact ideally each member of the firm should be its PRO, and leading the way should be the CEO. It means that good deeds of the CEO should not stop with customers alone as the general public is part of the grand customer prospect.

The moral of the story is, "if the customer is the king or God, you can serve him best by serving the masses."

The greatest gift of the God to mankind is the right to be of service to others. The other species in the world look after only themselves and they leave even their young ones as soon as they are ready to move out. The task as the PRO therefore, is to provide service to the people, who are your potential customers, without any obligations. You should put your body, heart and soul in the service of the mankind, without any reservations and make it a part of your daily itinerary. As you plan your time management in one slot place the PR job and you can see the firm's progress and the faster achievement of goals, one after the other.

If someone like a customer comes to you for advice, take it as a god sent gift. As you show him the right direction, be sure that you will automatically be correcting your own direction of movement.

Idea Management

Most managers get good ideas for serving the customers. However, implementation of ideas, managing them happens through the team and hence Idea Management becomes an important area for the manager. The **Idea Management** can be achieved through creativity, which results in diversity of ideas, views, and opinions and arranges these diverse items in the best possible orderly manner. Thus you can conclude that perfect management is a phenomenon based on two diverse values, the single entity coming from combining of the multi-factors and the multiplicity coming from the myriad of ideas. In simple words, the organization has one vision and yet it may have several goals. These goals emerge out of the vision and hence while they are separate entities, they also merge into the vision statement. In such an event, rest assured your organization can attain great heights with minimal efforts by you and your team, with a salutary effect on customer delight and resultant retention.

Hurdles in Your Path

The main hurdle in your path is, that you have divided yourself in different roles you play in life—the role at home and at workplace. You may be a devoted husband, father at home and at the office you could be tyrant, a person who uses a whip on the staff to get them to work. If you are like this, even if you do not readily admit it even to yourself, do not be alarmed because you belong to the majority of people in the corporate world in India. Most managers run their organizations by keeping their employees under stress, in dread of losing their jobs. Since the employees are mostly people with families, they keep succumbing to the stress, falling sick, even losing track of their work, and on quality of production, and meeting deadlines. As manager your task, in such a situation becomes doubly difficult and yet if you do not come down from your high horse, you are not likely to produce the desired results even by the most arduous effort, and the customers remain illusive to your overtures.

You can now start appreciating the way you can make your work easy for yourself and your team. First you define yourself. You are an Indian (or whatever), having an identity like name, personality, a mind, heart and a body. While you think from your mind, feel from your heart; look for body comforts, pleasures and happiness. This I-ness, takes you on a selfish trip, where you can think of only yourself and can harm anyone else for your benefit. Ultimately as your team members start alienating themselves from you, you start losing out on their cooperation and teamwork. This body and I syndrome with which you define yourself, takes you far from your goals and the customers.

Success brings pride and with it comes the downfall. The downfall is caused by the following reasons:

When you are proud of your achievements you lose focus on your job of locating, influencing and winning the customers.

You start living in the past glory, which can be short-lived, as your customers are too fickle to stay with you unless you continue to serve and care for them.

Your sycophant friends push you up, which in fact puts you down.

Where the Greed Resides

It the modern times greed is the omnipresent dweller in practically every person, every home. Organizations are no exception to the greed. Greed has devastated individuals, organizations, societies and even nations. In organizations, it could be the greed of individuals or of the organization itself. Personal greed manifests itself when the individual cheats others including his organization for personal gains. Organizational greed emanates from the managers, takes the shape of profiteering. While profits are the legitimate right of any business organization, as profits are required for satisfying the stakeholders and growth, profiteering could become self-destructive in the long run. Profiteering invites competition as also the wrath of customers. It works well only in monopoly situation; but these never remain as monopoly for long and sooner than you can imagine the organization comes to grief.

Greed is unending as once you have gained the desired object of your greed, you start aspiring for something else. The strength of gratifying greed increases in arithmetic proportion, while the strength of greed increases with geometric proportion. When you become happy and satisfied with gratification of your greed, some one else, the customer, is becoming unhappy. The happiness you gain by making others unhappy can never be long lasting, as it takes the very essence of the firm's existence to the customer.

Information as Unifier

The propagation of information and knowledge in the team does the following for the team:

- Make them more committed to the organization
- Make them loyal
- Make them feel important enough to be told the vital information
- Motivate them for achieving the goals
- Build the team, as all its members have the information and have a common goal
- The team believes in the fairness in the management's treatment towards them
- The information base makes the team members more analytical and sharp focused

The difference between management and the employees diminish with wider knowledge base, the working of the organization becomes smoother. You also build leaders from your team members, who can be delegated important tasks and portfolios, leaving you free to do your task of planning for the future. Ultimately, when you retire or are ready to take up a higher position, some one will be there to take over from you, and the organization work will go on smoothly even during the transition phase.

When you operate with such unified goals and one vision you get spontaneity in your decision-making and you remain ever fresh and clear-headed and highly creative, self-starting and self-sufficient for all your activities.

Do You Like Your Job?

You must answer the question asked truthfully, because your entire future depends on the answer. Suppose you always felt the job is just a job nothing more to you, a nine-to-five part of your existence, please understand you are in the wrong job. If you like the job then it ceases to be a chore and if you actually enjoy your job then the job is only enjoyment for you, howsoever taxing it might be. When you start your career you must take time to know and understand the culture of the firm you want to join. In case you have no choice, you should yet not make compromises on ethical issues even if your superior wants you to. If you sanely analyze you will realize that you have only lent your services to the firm and it does not own you.

When you find the job market is getting tough, please understand that it is the doing of unscrupulous people who keep contaminating the job market. If you stick to your fundamental honest work nature, you may have to wait before you get what you deserve. Ultimately, however, good firms are always on the look out for such persons and you may get inundated with offers of jobs from good firms, which honour good people.

In the final analysis, you can like your work, but the better situation is when you are doing the work, which you like doing.

What is the purpose of your stay in a firm? Have you ever thought on this aspect of your life? The purpose of life and work should always be "to get happiness and spread happiness to people around you. The happiness is an inner mindset, the conscience or your soul, which is the guiding factor in everyone's life. You create happiness around you with the help of task fulfilment and evolving as a better manager and a better human being. The purpose of business life is the same that of personal life, only its sphere of action differs. The functions of a manager are the basic source of its getting the competitive advantage, as they serve the customer community first and then of course the firm itself. The service of the firm should be directly related to the service of the customer community.

The manager faces the ever-changing marketplace with such efficacy with his unflappable accuracy, which is never changing. Your mindset, your discussions with your team and your personal actions hit the success trail with uncanny accuracy. Even as the manager has to have two types of activities, one at work and the other at home, he accepts the changing relationships in both places with perfection.

A firm may have every thing known to for it to become a success and yet result of excellence slips away from it. The best of the product, technology, people, structures and systems do not guarantee that the firm would become a super achiever. It boils down to one intangible element called the corporate culture, which brings the super achiever tag to the firm. While the ingredients of culture remain esoteric the following would give the essence of what is called corporate culture.

Action and plan implementation and not just decisions.

Result orientation, meeting the goals, objectives and targets, as planned.

Faith in innovation, training, experimentation and self analysis.

It may not be easy to evaluate a firm on these areas unless an in-depth study is done through full cooperation of the top management.

There are certain factors, which protect and nurture the organization. They are knowledge, skills, correct attitude, transparency within the organization, and generosity towards the weak. Organization should be considered sacred as it truly looks after the present and the future of its stakeholders. The organization consists of top brains, the average persons and the mediocre person, and they are allotted the tasks accordingly. However, as each of the persons interact with the other, these categories should be forgotten and they should live in friendship, unity and harmony. The organisation provides the opportunity, a platform to use and enhance the talent to the employees, to enable them to achieve their goals, fame and money. Your intelligence blossoms in the organization.

The skilled and the learned persons do not while away their time, if you have to achieve your goals and that too with minimum efforts. Each one puts his best efforts and the result is that the organizational goal is achieved. Achievement of goals increases your energy level and strengthens the influence of the organization in the marketplace.

As you plan your business strategies, the environment affects you. In the same way, your strategies can affect the business environment. Business related environment issues, like demographic, social, cultural, political, legal, macroeconomics and global impact the business, as the businessmen are aware of. However, good business strategies can have impact on governments' political will, which affects the environment. The latest government policies in the telecom sector have been influenced by the business organizations. The good strategies affect the right way, and the reverse is also true.

The nature of good management is always progressive, always evolutionary and therefore your vision, your perception, your activity naturally desires to be on the top. You keep going for more and more until you find the supreme value-based management for success. The other important aspect of management is the management of change as through change only, you evolve and if you do not change you forget about evolving into a successful manager.

The manager operates through feelings, intuition and his ego and then his mind, intellect take over, he learns through his aspirations and desires what are his priorities and goals, which propel him into action. He is a discerning thinking person and as long as his ego does not interfere, he achieves his goals easily.

A leader (manager) is the mirror of the collective consciousness of the followers (employees). As the followers are trained to succeed, the success story gets reflected in the leader's mindset. No man is isolated and has to operate in teams. This is the quintessence, the summary of the laws of nature. Once understood, it imparts infinite creativity and organizing power to its practitioner. And this knowledge is the basis of right action.

Market and Organization

Market is the essential, basic necessity for the organization. The organization, however is attuned to its own creativity, and fails to appreciate its true nature. It is important for the CEO to understand the changing nature of the market, as it controls the organizational activity, its life and dwells in the core of the organization.

Overdrive Gear the CRM

A number of software packages are now available in the area of Customer Relationship

Management (CRM), but ultimately it is the soft skills of the manager and his team that will work in CRM. Organizations need to develop a friendly relationship with the customers. While it is possible rather easily in the service industry and in industrial marketing, even FMCG firms have innovated their marketing efforts to build relationships with their customers to develop relationships leading to customer loyalty. Scratch cards; find gold earrings in the soap cake package are some of the methods employed in this direction. The entire business paradigm has shifted to the overdrive gear to make business transactions as friendly to the customers as possible. The box below gives an example of the shift in banking process.

If you want a bank draft made from your bank account you can get it in the following different ways:

- Go to the bank, get the requisite form, and fill it with your cheque for the amount and bank commission. Wait for the bank to clear your cheque and prepare the bank draft before it is given to you
- Go to the bank where the concerned person completes the formalities, takes your signatures and hands over the draft to you
- Telephone the bank, declare your password, and inform your need and then the bank does the needful. In a short time you get the draft couriered to you.
- Call the bank who sends a bank employee to you, who completes the formalities at your place and hands over the draft to you
- Go to the bank on the Internet bank site; give your password and the instructions regarding the draft you want. You can view the draft online and it is sent to you by courier.

The five methods given above are possible transaction modes. The actual method will depend on your needs and the facilities available with your bank. The ultimate aim in the grossly competitive market is to be friendly with your customer by building relationships with him.

As the CEO, you form teams for specific goals, train the teams, enunciate the goals in clear terms and motivate the teams, by a variety of incentives. The teams, in their turn support you with their efforts. As the teams live in harmony, the organization becomes great. It attracts the best skilled and talented persons, who help you in combating competition. The organization keeps moving forward, enriched and prosperous.

Breach of Trust

Organizations, which rise after trampling over other organizations, gaining success through non-ethical illegal means do not belong to the real civilized society. Search around you and you will find several organizations indulged in such acts. Bribing to gain favours, paying money to get their jobs done quickly, out of turn, has become a significant part of the business life in India and in most countries around the world. The businessman has made the bureaucrat and the politician corrupt. Politicians, seeing the personal benefit make such laws, which help them sponge the businessmen.

Bureaucrats being the executive branch, who process the laws become conduits for siphoning money from the businessmen and (naturally?) the conduits are not foolish enough to not take their share, before they pass on the rest to the politician. This tripartite arrangement serves all the three parties, the politician, bureaucrat and the businessman, to the total disregard of the interest of the common man, the customer. The deep-rooted malady has become part and parcel of the country's business paradigm. To add to its strength, the consumer movement in the country is weak. Therefore, it now appears that the bubble may be ready to burst and the public anger, through a new vigorous consumer movement may catch up with the culprits, sooner than you can imagine. The answer appears in a mass movement against the demon of corruption. It usually starts with one or a few individuals, who take up the cudgels of fighting corruption without fearing the politicians' or bureaucrat reprisal.

Long-term success of an organization can be predicted by knowing the strengths, intensity and focus of its leaders, their understanding of the business, the reliability of their structures and the depth of their talent. The best training for the manager is to be taught to develop the success mindset, which must be made to descend to the next generation of the leaders, when the transition time comes.

The manager has to be creative, with a sense of urgency and fully alert to the changes in the business environment, to value the following resultant gains:

- Increased profits and customer satisfaction and delight
- Stress-free operations
- Full of vitality
- Better health
- Better planning process
- Competitive edge
- Ever increasing success with least efforts on your part
- Knowledge and skills

The strangest quality of knowledge and skills is that as you use them for the right purpose, and properly these will improve and increase in geometric progression. Theoretical knowledge can bring you kudos as you give speeches and may bring more such opportunities of making speeches. Other than that you will not become any wiser. If a person claims to be knowledgeable, of good character, he also wants to be well known in his circle. Such ignorance only brings ego, which is difficult to leave behind.

When any organization fails to achieve its goals, the blame is usually given to lack of resources needed for success. In most cases this would be only a lame excuse, as the problem lies in deployment of resources. Proper utilization of resources can be achieved in the following manner.

Human resource get the right people, train them and place them according to their suitability to the tasks and not as per some preconceived notions about demand and supply ratios. Human beings are not mere employee numbers; they are having their individual needs, aspirations and skills and should be treated as such.

Financial resources usually you have enough. You should make proper use of it. There is ample time and opportunity. You must only make optimum use of all your resources and you will find no dearth of anything. The only criteria for having enough resources is that your requirement should be genuine and just enough. If you ask for more than what you require the chances are, you may not get even your just needs. It is like asking for an easy life, with all the comforts and achievement of goals, without any proper planning for the same.

Success and failure are in your hands. It is the ultimate reality of business today. The vicious mind, untrue thoughts and illegal actions bring failure and resultant sorrow.

What about the misfits and the criminals.

In spite of the best effort and care of the manager, at times, misfits and criminals join the organization. They may come with recommendations or fake certificates of good conduct and work. Initially they will try and out do other team members showing honesty, hard work and efficiency. It is only later, when they have gained your confidence that they start their nefarious acts of squeezing the organization at places where detection is not easy. They can adopt two different tactics for the purpose, one they can gradually milk the organization and secondly they can kill it in one stroke. Such persons are highly intelligent, smart, knowledgeable and yet evil minded. They can do immense harm to the organization before they are caught. Without your knowing they start creating their own evil sphere of influence, with temptations to the gullible team member. They try to destroy the culture base of the organization with irretrievable tenacity. As manager you have the following tasks to perform to rid the organisation of such persons, as you learn to improve your selection process, which would preclude such persons from joining your organization.

- Get the act of throwing out such persons, completed smoothly without any rancour with the outgoing employee, as disgruntled employee can do a lot of harm through bad word of mouth publicity.
- Better screening of the employees entering the organization, cross-checking their antecedents, their references.
- Have close control points for newcomers at all levels, especially the senior levels
- Train them in both hard skills like skills for the job, processes, and procedures, and soft numbers like the organisational culture, ethics, motivational skills and team spirit.

It is extremely important that such persons are apprehended quickly, allowed to change their ways, if you see signs of desire for change for the better or made to quit in good grace. However, very few persons change their characteristics for the better, if they are given a chance to do so. Some do play acting only to stay on in the organization, to do further damage spoil the team by luring others to their trap. Once you decide to throw such persons out of your organization, it should be done with positive vibes only, so that they do not cause any harm from the outside, later on. For die-hard culprits, a public denouncement with or without legal action is required. The organization is not a correction house and as the saying goes, "tigers do not change their stripes."

One major ingredient of success recipe for the manager is catholicity or breadth of outlook. He should be above the close binding rituals of procedures, without in any way denigrating them. When the manager's thinking is shackled with procedures, he tends to operate in a closed loop. He should be a thinking, living and vibrant entity, which fosters lateral thinking, thinking on absolute and on abstract, and then only he can be a good planner. Historical benchmark in process, strategic planning make no reference to the present. Only a broad all encompassing outlook of the CEO can keep analyzing the vagaries of today's market, which makes him a better planner. Distortions in thought process clouded by the lurking fear of the past lead to systematic dismantling of the manager's confidence and the goals start receding into oblivion. It is best to learn from the past, plan for the future and live in today's world.

New Paradigm

Let us discuss the new paradigm, as the time is just about right for it. Most government rules and regulations concerning business have been removed and today, the business is free to carry out its operations as per its own plan and the dictates of the competition and the market dynamics. The role of bureaucracy has become nominal, except for the inspectors like, the factory inspector, income tax inspector, and boiler inspector, excise inspector, who keep showing their muscle to the businessman to extract their pound of flesh. Business government transactions need to be transparent and the rule of self-assessment the duties to be paid, as a rule to be followed should become extensively accepted. Only surprise checks by senior trusted and known to be honest officers should be kept as deterrents for the wrong doers. Only then a truly open business environment can prevail.

If all the managers including you just accept the principle of doing business as per the laws of the land, come what may. You will see increasing success coming your way in no small measure. This can be proven scientifically. As you walk on the right side of the law, you walk without fear and you do not seek favours from anyone. You get the right raw materials; have good marketing plan, product and profit. The profits you share with your stakeholders, the customers, employees, the suppliers, employees, the government (by paying the taxes), the trade bodies and the community in which the business operates. You have good product. You get good market share, brand equity and naturally great growth prospects. As a good corporate citizen you earn goodwill, which helps you in the following ways:

- Get larger share of the market through customer goodwill.
- Get better employees
- Larger market share
- Easier finance at lower cost
- Government support for infrastructure
- Goodwill of the community

You can bring about a sea change in your organization provided you are ready to be bold, radical and a stickler of ethical legal business, you will be surprised to find your actions and policies have a snow-balling effect with more and more organizations falling in line with the principles of honesty and ethical business behaviour. You can start the desired revolution. This would in turn prepare a level playing field, where only merit will prevail, the hush money or speed money will not have any say in it.

These words, hush money and speed money will become extinct from the dictionary of Indian business and hence from the Indian society and the nation. Tough tasks, yes, but you know great successes come out of such tough tasks and decisions. Moreover, you do not lose anything, and yet you gain the following:

- Self-respect
- Confidence of the employees
- Loyalty of your customers
- Gratitude of the community
- Support of the government, with no strings attached

The path of righteousness is filled with initial despair, loss of face, monetary losses and yet when you look closely, you find that all you are doing is following the tenets of your childhood, the teachings your parents gave you. The demonic vices have for long taken a stranglehold on the psyche of business, the bureaucrats and the politicians, which must be defeated, sooner the better.

One more reason for leading an ethically correct life is the onslaught of international competition in India and opening up of the international markets or you. You can never prosper in the international arena with a tarnished image. The brand equity you must have in the international business will come only when your organization remains overboard all the time and is known for its straightforward business deals the world over. Caesar's wife should be always above suspicion.

Just imagine how would you react; when you come to know of a foreign firm, which has been cheating the customers, the government and other stakeholders. You will run miles away from it. You can imagine the reaction of foreign firms on Indian organizations, which are having a bad name in their business dealings. Even a minor blemish is enough to have the Indian firm thrown out of he international market. Not only the reputation of the organization but also of the country is at stake!

The only remedy, therefore, is to cure yourself of the major ills of corruption, malpractices, and GET RICH QUICK techniques. Otherwise the firm is ready to sell mother India's reputation for a song through its nefarious activities. Is it too harsh to equate people indulging in such acts as international pirates?

Present Business Scene

Imagine an organization where there are orders for supply of 150 units of the product in the month. The manager has given the target of manufacturing 150 units in the month and till 24th of the month only 120 units are ready. The production manager can make the balance 30 except for the fact that the quality assurance manager has rejected 30 numbers of vital components. The production team gets a special bonus if they can complete the target. They are ready to share the bonus with the quality team if they let them use the rejected components.

The production manager meets the quality manager and says, "look here, let me use the rejected components and complete the scheduled production. This will make the boss happy and we will share the extra bonus with your team. The chances are that even these components will last for 2 years, taking the product beyond its guarantee period. If a few fail within the guarantee, we can always replace them. At least for the present our target will be met. Furthermore, even our boss will be happy as he has too given 150 as the target production figures to the board of directors. And any lower figure will lower his credibility in the board".

Who, is bothering about the most important person in business–the customer.

Now the question is, should the quality manager succumb to the pressure in the interest of production or should he stick to his decision. If the matter is referred to the boss, he may even agree with the production manager.

The above is not an isolated case, such situations keep coming in every organization often. As the boss what is your solution to the problem? Let us take both the scenario as given below:

The quality manager agrees to the suggestion and production touches the 150 mark. The best case is if all goes well with the 30 units and they last not just through the guarantee period, but live much longer like all the other products. The other scene is when the 30 fail and the service engineers get busy for entire year changing the parts and setting the units rightly aligning the units with the new components. The time and money spent takes away all the profits coming from the 150 unit sales. Besides, each of the 30 units makes you lose 100 more orders by way of negative word of mouth publicity. You can see much more harm can come to the organization because of the decision, which could even prove fatal for it.

In the second scenario, the quality manager does not agree to the suggestion and only 120 units get sold, each proving its worth. You can expect the positive word of mouth publicity getting you at least ten orders per unit, totally 1200 units.

The moral of the story is quite obvious, the customer/market acceptance, word of mouth publicity is most vital for the organisations and its decisions should be focused on these issues only. Bad quality not only does not sell, it cuts down the organization size, which may lead even to its closure.

As the manager you have to keep your control points in place so that you are aware of the possible mishaps and can take timely corrective steps. As you keep your ideas and ideologies clear to your team, they will not only understand the same, but also subscribe to them. Your simple words and activities can bring about massive revolution in the organization.

Help from Core Advisory Group

Good management ensures highest returns with lowest investments. For this purpose, you need to have courageous, knowledgeable, strong-willed persons with high emotional quotient as your senior team members. Faced with complex problems, the decisions should not be taken unilaterally or in consultation of too any persons. That is why you need an efficient core group. It is better to have one wise man, sincere to the organisation than even a hundred mediocre, as the wise will ensure prosperity even during recession. You should have tested and trusted persons of integrity for strategic positions, who will be secret weapon against the strongest of the competitors. The persons should be well paid to make sure that they stay with you and remain loyal. They should be allowed to work in a transparent atmosphere, where they can obtain any information they may need and their grievances must be settled promptly.

Profit and Growth

Companies exist for the basic motive of profit and with it the growth gets associated. Companies need to make legitimate profits. Those indulging in making a fast buck through profiteering are more likely to fail than others. Companies need profit for success, growth, security, expansion, innovation and a healthy bottom line. They can then look after the stakeholders' interests and successfully create double bottom line. Managers have to keep improving the productivity of men and machines plus management—and to be a role model. They need to be balancing quality, quantity, cost and market demand with price acceptability.

Planning

Managers must plan the following for achieving success:
- Resources—HR, capital and information
- Time management
- ABC Analysis of tasks and available time
- Managers must understand that meetings take lot of time and yet substantial success is achieved through delegation of tasks as success comes from work, leisure, time management and less or no talk.

Managers need to work out their time table as follows:
- Time/work analysis
- Prioritise work
- Stop wasting time on phone calls, chatting
- Stop doing other person's tasks

Managers must be good and they need to show that they are good as follows:
- Know your tasks well
- Be sincere, hardworking, systematic
- Work with integrity, set good example
- Reprimand in private, praise in public
- Induct team spirit
- Be a good listener
- Listen, not to reply only but to understand first.

Managers must understand themselves as manager on the following lines:
- Self as manager, employee
- Product and terms of business
- Competition
- Coordination through personal contact

- Mutual trust in team work
- Good communication
- Conflict resolution-divide the cake or increase it

Managers need to work with their teams and yet on the level of individuals as follows:

- Self selected teams
- Multi tasking teams
- Team leadership
- Individual excellence rewards
- Team rewards
- Team objectives vs. individual targets
- Work redundancy in teams

Managers need to ensure harmony of team work as follows:

- Cooperation vs. individual work
- Development of teams vs. individuals
- Maximise team outputs
- Calculate costs, productivity, profitability of teams
- Keep contingency plans ready
- Analyse failures even your own

Managers have a major role in establishing the budgeting as given below:

- Capital and revenue budgets
- Balanced budgeting
- Availability of resources including funds on time
- Stakeholders' interests in budgeting
- Training costs
- ABC Analysis—priorities

Managers need to be in every stage of planning as follows:

- Short-term and long-term planning
- Optimising utilization of resources
- Controls
- Bar chart, Pert chart
- Your business? Is planning in line with it?
- Investment in success or in ego
- Input/output or process control

Managers need to understand MBO status as follows:

- Purpose of MBO to help them relate to the company's objectives.
- Communication failures—reasons
- Barriers to communication with the team members due to differences in perceptions, language

- Communications types are upwards, downwards and parallel and each one of these need to be taken care of.
- Listen to understand

Managers have to take decisions all the time as given below:

- Decisions—accurate, timely, legal, objective and impartial. These happen when the managers are not parochial, biased and strongly attached to the company's goals with no personal agenda.
- Fair in dealings with the team members without prejudice and ready to take calculated risks in the interest of the company.
- Speedy-time is the essence of success. Urgency shown by the leader enthuses team members getting into the mode.
- The best managers remain economical, practical, ethical and in harmony with the company's objectives.

Managers have to build a rapport between manufacturing and marketing teams as follows:

- With the best of manpower, machines, money can you succeed?
- What about marketing?
- We make colas—sell thirst quenchers
- We make cosmetics—sell hope of looking lovely
- We make utility—sell lifestyle

Managers wanting to win the race need to look at the following:

- Customer has limited money unlimited wants
- There are competitive products too
- Give better benefits and most important tell it to the customer
- Know customers buying behaviour, his cultural background, finance and emotional soft points

Managers must consider customer as the king as given below:

- Respect him, by listening to him, his complaints, suggestions
- He is ruthlessly loyal only to his own self
- Go by the Maslows hierarchy of needs
- Physical, safety, social acceptance, respect and self actualistion
- Ask him

Managers must understand the customer as given below:

- Bored with existing products
- Looking for novelty, thrill of experience of purchase
- Benefits surpassing existing and competitive products
- Customer's belief in your benefit story
- Who says so?

Managers must know how to organise sales story for customer appeal as given below:

- Appeal to emotions
- Product benefits
- Persuasion
- Never oversell
- Create or use proper ambience
- Language of the customer

Omnipresent Market

- Markets stand yet keep changing but not for you.
- You are for the markets—dovetail your objectives, products, terms of business to suit the market. Market is not for you as competitors are prominently making their presence felt.

New Customers, New Products

- Managers have to look for future needs—foresee the unknown
- Imaginative selling—real wants of customers
- Know your company, products, business, competition
- Understand customer and prospects
- Redefine your objectives when required
- Price promotion placement—creative thinking

Top Management and Marketing

- Brainstorming creativity in planning
- Marketing outlook and focus
- Never neglect objections, obstacles, complaints from customers/prospects
- Learning from the customers
- We are all customers

Work Alcoholics

- Get workers to enjoy work through empowerment, invitation to innovate, when mistakes cease to be suicidal, workers' self-respect is of paramount importance.
- Group work to team work, where all members work towards the same goal, a group becomes a well jointed team.
- Meaningful joyous work.
- Organisational support.

Use Workers' Wisdom

- Unheard resources, downplayed so far
- Urge to excel in workers' motivation
- Worker's progression through quality work

- Respect individuals—bring in discipline—bring disaster through disrespect
- Square peg in square hole only
- Sharpen intrinsic intelligence through training

Workers' Development

- Team work with cooperation, coordination with a single objective
- Each task is important part of the whole
- Develop natural talent, inborn ability
- Worker decision making through empowerment, training for productivity, work satisfaction
- Workers responsibility and accountability
- Organisational size
- Productivity norms through work study
- TQM
- Discipline—causes for indiscipline, remedies—grievance removal if genuine
- Meaningful work well explained
- MBO
- Leader
- Creates an ambience conducive to efficiency, delegates tasks, monitors, motivates
- Gets respect from his followers because of his sense of justice, large heart and far sightedness
- Appreciates good work, discuss mistakes, including his own

Workers' Productivity

- Attitude towards the work, routine or challenging, achievable targets—but with a stretch
- Supportive participative leadership
- Motivation through praise, awards
- Working conditions
- Failures of workers are not considered suicidal
- Experimentation encouraged
- Company helps in growth—knowledge, position, money
- Experimentation, creativity and making decisions
- Management acceptance of workers' successful experiments, rewards
- Continuous training for multitasking

Inspirational Leadership

- Sharing of knowledge, information, making the workers part of the fraternity
- Recognition of achievements with rewards
- Giving additional responsibility
- Merit promotions
- Responsible challenging tasks in work conducive atmosphere

Unions and IR

- Workers' participation in decisions connected to their work
- Genuine concern for worker welfare—build mutual confidence
- Productivity and profits serve both the workers and the management
- Problem solving always across the table with open mind on both sides

Today's Worker

- More educated, knowledgeable
- Wants freedom of action, responsible work
- Is competitive and yet helpful towards other workers
- With encouragement is ready to meet targets in time
- With TQM is ready to improve his work, work methods through experimentation
- Innovation and manager
- What is a good innovation?
- Existing plus minor modifications?
- Extend far out-rise or at times even fall
- Freedom to followers to experiment, innovate and think out of the box
- Back successes but do not condemn failures
- Decision-making
- Most difficult decisions are the people decisions—opinion on people
- Objective or judgemental view of others, followers
- Decision skills for accuracy, objectivity, impartiality, fairness
- Decision for risk taking, legitimate, calculated
- Decision plan
- Problem-falling profits
- Sales down, expenses up, product non-acceptance, advertising ineffectual, after-sales service poor, channel members demotivated
- Data collection
- Choices, alternatives
- Analysis of the choices
- Devil's advocate
- Difference of opinion
- Concensus solutions
- Catch the culprit—the reason behind profit loss
- Obstacles with the prospective customer—the real reason
- Redefine problem
- Solution to evolve
- Decision types
- Fact finding
- Creation of facts
- Universal truths in science
- Changing business scenarios—mathematical models limited utility
- How to grasp and grab the unknown in business

- Profit maximise, cost minimise
- Practicality of decision
- Stakeholders concern
- Information, data availability
- Data analysis
- Time bound decisions
- Decisions with less than required information—using experience—gut feeling
- Decision coordination points
- All decision but no action is like a non-practising MBBS doctor
- Decision by consensus
- Feedback for the next level of decisions
- Three levels of decisions
- Decision now
- To decide or not to
- Pending the decision
- Decision time
- Timing of decision-making and action important
- Strike the iron when hot
- Judgemental decisions—proof of success only at the outcome stage
- MBO
- Boss gives orders and controls action
- Leader provides the right ambience and lets followers achieve objectives set out by him
- Self-management and control by followers—leaders select the right followers
- Profit—the bottom line
- Double bottom line—stakeholders' concern
- BE THE BEST
- Long range planning—short-term action
- Critical success factors
- Performance benchmarks
- Lean organisation—less levels of hierarchy
- Performance review—retraining if needed
- Motivation—self starting mechanism or kick start
- MBO revisited
- Long term plans, short term actions
- Training and development of leaders and followers
- Delegation of not just responsibility but of authority too
- Leadership evolution and business objectives attainment.

There are three aspects of CRM which can each be implemented in isolation from each other:

Operational—automation or support of customer processes that include a company's sales or service representative.

Collaborative—direct communication with customers that does not include a company's sales or service representative.

Analytical—analysis of customer data for a broad range of purposes.

A pioneer of CRM, Help Desk Software since 1992 SOFFRONT the mid-market CRM leader gave a whole new interface and practical solutions to the CRM by offering end-to-end CRM Software solutions spanning marketing automation and sales force automation software, customer service and helpdesk software, sales order processing software, asset and project management software, defect tracking software and more.

Latest CRM Functionalities

The latest CRM should incorporate features that extend the CRM functionality beyond sales, marketing, and customer support.

- Superior user interface
- Support for Web Services

A framework, which should support integration with popular accounting systems.

Support e-mail client integration and advanced e-mail support

Support perforce integration

Features to make the engine to support automated business rules, email support and alerts etc.

Should be WEB and WAP enabled.

Zero footprint web browser : the CRM should be web based and operate from your browser. You can access the application just as you would access a web site like amazon.com. There must not be any requirement of writing code at the client's end or any requirement to download a plug-in or an applet. Standard browser access is a must should support open technologies like http/xml which provides all the functionality.

All modules should be inherently integrated with each other. The complete breadth of CRM functions spanning sales, marketing, customer support, employee support, partner management, defect tracking and customer portal applications must be integrated by design.

The product should support database like oracle, MS SQL server and sybase. A single repository should hold all the data generated across various customer touch points.

If the modules are pre-integrated then you have the flexibility to start with what you need and activate the rest when you need them.

Should be released independent so that the customizations done at installation and over the years are preserved when you upgrade. There is no need to rework them operational.

Operational CRM provides support to "front office" business processes, including sales, marketing and service. Each interaction with a customer is generally added to a customer's contact history, and staff can retrieve information from the database when necessary.

One of the main benefits of this contact history is that customers can interact with different people or different contact *channels* in a company over time without having to describe the history of their interaction each time.

Consequently, many call centers use some kind of CRM software to support their call center agents.

Operational CRM process customer data for a variety of purposes:

- Managing campaigns
- Enterprise Marketing Automation
- Sales Force Automation
- Collaborative

Collaborative CRM covers the direct interaction with customers, for a variety of different purposes, including feedback and issue-reporting. Interaction can be through a variety of channels, such as web pages, e-mail, automated phone (Automated Voice Response–AVR) or SMS.

The objectives of collaborative CRM can be broad, including cost reduction and service improvements.

Analytical

Analytical CRM analyzes customer data for a variety of purposes:

- Design and execution of targeted marketing campaigns to optimise marketing effectiveness
- Design and execution of specific customer campaigns, including customer acquisition, cross-selling, up-selling, retention
- Analysis of customer behaviour to aid product and service decision-making (e.g., pricing, new product development etc.)
- Management decisions, e.g., financial forecasting and customer profitability analysis
- Prediction of the probability of customer defection (churn analysis).
- Analytical CRM generally makes heavy use of predictive analytics strategy

Several commercial CRM software packages are available which vary in their approach to CRM. However, CRM is not just a technology, but rather a comprehensive approach to an organization's philosophy in dealing with its customers. This includes policies and processes, front-of-house customer service, employee training, marketing, systems and information management. Hence, it is important that any CRM implementation considerations stretch beyond technology, towards the broader organizational requirements.

The objectives of a CRM strategy must consider a company's specific situation and its customer's needs and expectations.

Technology Considerations

The technology requirements of a CRM strategy can be complex and far reaching.

The basic building blocks:

- A database to store customer information. This can be a CRM specific database or an enterprise data warehouse.
- Operational CRM requires customer agent support software.
- Collaborative CRM requires customer interaction systems, e.g., an interactive website, automated phone systems etc.

- Analytical CRM requires statistical analysis software as well as software that manages any specific marketing campaigns.
- Each of these can be implemented in a basic manner or in a high end complex installation.
- Key functionalities.

A typical CRM system is sub-divided into three basic sub-modules:

- Marketing
- Sales
- Service
- Sales Force Automation
- Sales Management, Sales Forecasting, Pipeline Management, Mobile Sales, Sales Commissions Mgmt
- Sales Order Processing
- Order Lifecycle Management Quotation and Invoicing Inventory Management Shipping & RMA
- Marketing Automation
- Marketing Management, Email Campaigning, Direct Mail Campaigning, Telemarketing, Marketing Analytics, Transpromotional documents (enriching transaction documents with marketing content).
- Issue/Project Management
- Defect Management, Test case Management, Product Release Mgmt, Time & Cost Tracking Project Management, Customer Help Desk
- Customer Support, Multi Channel Contact Center, Mobile Support, Customer Portal, Customer Self Service, Customer Survey, SLA Management
- Partner Management
- CRM Portal, Partner Lead Distribution, Partner Self Service, Partner Order processing,
- Helpdesk Software
- Employee Helpdesk, Multi Channel Contact Center, Mobile Support, Asset Management, Employee Portal Employee, Self Service Employee Survey
- Integration
- Object API Web Services, Back office integration

Several functionalities are:

- Service Order Management
- Service Contract Management
- Planned Services Management
- Warranty Management
- Installed Base (Equipment) Management
- Resource Planning and Scheduling
- Knowledge Management (FAQs, How to guides)
- Call Centre Support
- Resource Planning and Workforce Management
- Channels of communication

It is also important to mention here that a CRM system is capable of executing all the three sub-modules via multiple communication channels. These channels can be:

- Direct
- Online (Internet)
- Call Center (via Phone/FAX/Email etc.)
- All the three CRM Sub-modules (Marketing, Sales and Service) can be executed across these communication channels. Based on these criteria, CRM offerings can be further subdivided into following:

Communication channel/CRM module	Direct	Internet	Call centre
Marketing	Online marketing	Web marketing	Tele marketing
Sales	Online sales	Web shop	Tele sales
Service	Online service	Customer self-service portal	Tele service

Successes

While there are numerous reports of "failed" implementations of various types of CRM projects, these are often the result of unrealistic high expectations and exaggerated claims by CRM vendors.

Privacy and Data Security

The data gathered as part of CRM must consider customer privacy and data security. Customers want the assurance that their data is not shared with third parties without their consent and not accessed illegally by third parties.

Customers also want their data used by companies to provide a benefit for them. For instance, an increase in unsolicited telemarketing calls is generally resented by customers while a small number of relevant offers is generally appreciated by customers.

Market Structure

Given below is a list of top CRM software vendors in 2005 with figures in millions of United States Dollars published in a Gartner study.

Vendor	Global revenue (US$)
SAP	1,475
Siebel	966
Oracle	368
SOFFRONT	NA
Salesforce.com	281
Amdocs	276
Others	2,333
Total	5,698

CHAPTER
2

Marketing Simplified – At a Glance

CUSTOMER ORIENTATION

A market or customer-focused organization determines what its potential customers desire, and then builds the product or service to suit the desire. Marketing theory and practice is justified in thinking that customers use a product or service because they have a need, or because it provides a perceived benefit.

Three major factors of marketing are prospecting for new customers, adding new customers and then retention and expansion of relationships with existing customers. Once a marketer has converted the prospective buyer into a customer, process of management of marketing takes over. The process for management motivates the marketer to build a relationship, nurturing the linkage and adding on to the list of benefits that sold the buyer in the first place, and improving the product/service continuously to protect the business from competitive thrusts.

For a marketing plan to be successful, the wants and desires of the customers and prospects must be taken into account. Trying to convince a market segment to buy something they don't want is extremely risky, expensive and seldom successful. Marketers depend on marketing research, both formal and informal, to determine what consumers want and what they are willing to pay for it. Marketers hope that this process will give them a Sustainable Competitive Advantage. Marketing management is the practical application of this process.

Marketing Functions

The activities of the marketing function are headed by a Vice President or Director of Marketing. A growing number of organizations, especially large US companies, have a Chief Marketing Officer position, reporting to the Chief Executive Officer. In India there are Marketing Managers and VP Marketing depending on the size of the company.

These heads of marketing need to act to achieve the goals and objectives as espoused in the American Marketing Association (AMA) definition of marketing that states, "Marketing is the process of planning and executing the conception, pricing, promotion, and distribution of ideas, goods, and services to create exchanges that satisfy individual and organizational objectives".

Marketing methods have developed with the help of many of the social sciences, particularly psychology, sociology, and economics. Anthropology is also a small, but growing, influence. Market research plays the role of moulding these activities. Through advertising, it is also related to many of the creative arts. Marketing is a wide and heavily interconnected subject with extensive citations. It is also an area of activity known for re-inventing itself and its vocabulary according to the times and the culture.

Plans for Marketing

How an organization competes with its competitors in the marketplace is determined by Strategic Marketing. In particular, it aims at obtainig Sustainable Competitive Advantage relative to its competitors.

The action part of the marketing function is Operational Marketing meant to attract and keep customers and to maximize the value derived for them, as well as to satisfy the customer with prompt services and meeting the customer's expectations. Operational Marketing includes the 4 Ps of the marketing mix, their development, usage.

Marketing includes the promotion of products, especially advertising and branding. The term has a wider meaning which recognises that marketing is customer centred. Products are often developed to meet the desires of groups of customers or even, in some cases, for specific customers. Marketing can be segregated into four general sets of activities. They are the four Ps as given below:

Product: The product aspects of marketing deal with the specifications of the goods or services, and how it relates to the end-user's needs and wants. The scope of a product generally includes supporting elements such as warranties, guarantees, and support like after-sales service. Products bought and sold are given below:

- Consumer durables
- FMCG
- Industrial Capital Goods
- Industrial Consumables
- Industrial Raw Materials and Components
- Services
- R&D Outputs
- M R Outputs
- Real Estates
- Organisations
- Ideas

Pricing: This refers to the process of setting a price for a product, including discounts. The price need not be monetary. It can simply be what is exchanged for the product or services, e.g. time, energy, psychology, attention or a service.

Promotion: This includes advertising, sales promotion, publicity, public relations and personal selling, and refers to the various methods of promoting the product, brand, or company.

Placement or distribution refers to how the product gets to the customer; for example, point of sale placement or retailing. This fourth P has also sometimes been called place, referring to the channel by which a product or services is sold, online or retail, which geographic region or industry, to which segment—young adults, families, business people.

These four Ps are often referred to as the marketing mix, which marketers use to develop a marketing plan. The four Ps model is most useful when marketing low value consumer products. Industrial products, services, high value consumer products require adjustments to this model. Services marketing must account for the unique nature of services. Industrial or B2B marketing must account for the long term contractual agreements that are typical in supply chain transactions. Relationship marketing attempts to do this by looking at marketing from a long term relationship perspective rather than individual transactions.

Services Marketing

In addition to the standard four Ps Product, Pricing, Promotion and Place, Service Marketing calls upon an extra three Ps, totaling seven and known together as the extended marketing mix. These are given below:

People/Staff: Persons coming into contact with customers have an impact on overall customer satisfaction or delight. People are part of a supporting service to a product or involved in a total service, and are particularly important because, in the customer's eyes, they are the service providing company and generally inseparable from the total service. Therefore, they must be appropriately trained, motivated and the right type of person with requisite skills and attitude. It is the people like the sales persons, the serive providers who literally personify the company in customer's mind and any wrong behaviour or even frivolous misadvanture can lead to "marketing catastrophy" with total loss of the customer and his recommendations to other customers.

Process: The process of providing the sevice and the behaviour of service providers can be crucial to customer satisfaction and lead to repurchases of the product.

Physical delivery: Unlike a product, a service is intangible and cannot be experienced before it is delivered. This, therefore, means that potential customers could have imaginary risks when deciding whether to use a service. To reduce the feeling of risk and improving the chance for success, it is often vital to offer potential customers the chance to see what a service would be like. This is done by providing physical evidence, such as case studies, testimonials or demonstrations.

Marketing Around Modified 4Ps

The original 4Ps concept idea was developed to help marketers manage the four most important aspects of marketing. With the Internet and the Web, marketers need to adopt a broader perspective on these elements. The new 4Ps are Personalisation, Participation, Peer-to-Peer and Predictive Modeling.

Personalization: Customization of products and services through the use of the Internet. Early examples include Dell on-line and Amazon.com, but this concept is further extended with emerging social media and advanced algorithms. Emerging technologies will continue to push this idea forward.

Participation: This helps customer to participate in what the brand should stand for; what should be the product directions and even which advertisements to run. This concept is laying the foundation for disruptive change through democratisation of information.

Peer-to-Peer: This refers to customer networks and communities where advocacy happens. The historical problem with marketing is that it is "interruptive" in nature, trying to impose a brand on the customer. This is most apparent in TV advertising. These passive customer bases will ultimately be replaced by the active customer communities. Brand establishment happens within those conversations. P2P is now being referred to as Social Computing and will likely to be the most disruptive/ expressive force in the future of marketing.

Predictive modeling: This refers to predictive plan base, such as neural network, that are being successfully applied in marketing problems.

Product can be identified as given below:

- Number of product lines in a range
- Number of product items in a product line

Product design is based on the following:

- Design and development of product ideas
- Selection of and sifting through product ideas
- Design and testing of product concept
- Analysis of profitability of product concept
- Design and testing of physical product

Packaging and trademarks need to be carefully adopted as given below:

- Designed for target market
- Pleasing to the eye
- Suitable to product
- In line with retailers' requirements, shelf space and ease of display
- Promotes brand image of the product and the company
- Distinguishable from competitors' products
- Strong, convenient, well-designed
- Makes significant difference in service and supply of product

Packaging Plans

- Specialty packaging as per the elegance and the character of the product
- Packaging for double-use, after the product has been taken out of the package like cans for sugar
- Combination packaging two or more products packaged in the same container

- Kaleidoscopic packaging, packaging changes continually to reflect a series or particular theme
- Cost effective packaging for immediate consumption, to be thrown away after use
- Packaging for resale, packed, into appropriate quantities, for the retailer or wholesaler

Trademark and its Importance

- Differentiates one company's goods from those of another
- Works as advertisement for quality
- Protects both consumers and manufacturers
- Used in displays and advertising campaigns
- Used to market new products

A good trademark can do the following for the product:

- Confirms products' advantages
- In simple language, easily identifiable with the product
- Easily pronounced and remembered
- Distinct from names of other products
- Easily added to an existing range
- Easily registered for legal protection

Price

Price refers to the amount of money exchanged for a product. This value is determined by utility to the consumer in terms of money and/or sacrifice that he is prepared to give for it. Price can be considered as a function of competitive pricing, cost to make the product, brand equity and its place in the PLC.

Objectives of correct pricing include the following:

- Definite sales volume
- Achieve profit
- Larger market share
- Maintain market share
- Fight competition
- Advantages of mass production
- Satisfactory return on capital

Price-plans are determined by the following:

- Production and distribution costs are the first areas to be considered
- Substitute goods available help in determining the appropriate price
- Normal trade practices gives an idea of trade discounts that help build the price
- Fixed prices—sometimes the government decides the pricing formulas
- Reaction of distributors must be taken into account as they are fully aware of what price the market can bear
- Reaction of consumers must be taken into consideration as it helps in fighting price competition

- Nature of demand helps in determining the price
- Elastic
- Inelastic
- Form of market helps in firming up the price
- Perfect competition
- Monopolistic competition
- Monopoly
- Oligopoly

Pricing Techniques

- Market share to be captured
- Price strategy – penetration or skimming
- Estimate demand
- Evaluate competitors' reactions

Distribution Channels

- Manufacturer to consumer – direct marketing
- Manufacturer to wholesaler to retailer to consumer
- Manufacturer to agent to retailer to consumer
- Manufacturer to agent to wholesaler to retailer to consumer
- Manufacturer to agent to customer manufacturers

Direct Selling Methods

- Manufacturer wants to demonstrate goods.
- Wholesalers, retailers and agents not actively selling.
- Manufacturer unable to convince wholesalers or retailers to stock product.
- High profit margin added to goods by wholesalers and retailers.
- Middlemen unable to transport.

Indirect Selling Methods

- Manufacturer does not have the financial resources to distribute goods.
- Distribution channels already established and are having strong links with the customers
- Manufacturer has no knowledge of efficient distribution.
- Manufacturer wishes to use capital for further production.
- Too many consumers in a large area; difficult to reach.
- Manufacturer does not have a wide assortment of goods to enable efficient marketing.

Wholesalers Operations

- Bear risk of selling goods to retailer or consumer
- Storage space
- Decrease transport costs

- Grant credit to retailers
- Able to sell for the manufacturers
- Give advice to manufacturers
- Break down products into smaller quantities
- Bypassing wholesalers
- Limited storage facilities
- Retailers' preferences
- Wholesaler cannot promote products successfully
- Development of wholesalers' own brands
- Desire for closer market contact
- Position of power
- Cost of wholesalers' services
- Price stabilisation
- Need for rapid distribution

Bypassing Wholesalers Ways

- Sales offices or branches
- Mail orders
- Direct sales to retailers
- Travelling agents
- Direct Orders

Agents Operations

- Commission agents work for anyone who needs their services. They do not acquire ownership of goods but receive commission.
- Selling agents act on an extended contractual basis, selling all the products of the manufacturer. They have full authority regarding price and terms of sale.
- Buying agents buy goods on behalf of producers and retailers. They have an expert knowledge of the purchasing function.
- Brokers specialize in the sale of one specific product. They receive a brokerage.
- Factory representatives represent more than one manufacturer. They operate within a specific area and sell related lines of goods but have limited authority regarding price and sales terms.

Marketing Communications

Marketing communications segregates the strategies involved with marketing messages into categories based on the goals of each message. There are distinct stages in making strangers to customers that govern the communication medium that should be used.

Advertising Defined

- Paid form of public presentation and expressive promotion of ideas
- Aimed at masses, preferably from the target market segment

- Manufacturer may determine what goes into the advertisement
- Pervasive and impersonal medium

Successful advertising helps in the following ways:

- Task of the salesman made easier
- Forces manufacturer to live up to conveyed image
- Protects and warns customers against false claims and inferior products
- Enables manufacturer to mass-produce product
- Continuous reminder
- Uninterrupted production
- Increases goodwill
- Raises standards of living or perceptions thereof
- Prices decrease with increased popularity
- Educates manufacturer and wholesaler about competitors' offerings as well as shortcomings in their own.

Objectives of Advertising

- Maintain demand for well-known goods
- Introduce new and unknown goods
- Increase demand for well-known goods

Requirements of a Good Advertisement

- Attract attention, be eye catching
- Create awareness
- Stimulate interest
- Create a desire
- Bring about action

Steps in an Advertising Campaign

- Market research
- Setting out aims
- Creativity
- Budgeting
- Choice of media
- Choice of actors
- Design and wording
- Coordination
- Test results

Personal Sales

Oral presentation given by a salesman who approaches individuals or a group of potential customers:

- Live, interactive relationship
- Personal interest
- Attention and response

Sales Promotion

Short-term incentives to encourage buying of products:
- Instant appeal
- Anxiety to sell

Publicity

- Stimulation of demand through press release giving a favourable report to a product
- Higher degree of credibility
- Effectively news
- Boosts enterprise's image

Customer Focus

Many companies today have a customer focus or customer orientation in their planning and activity. This implies that the company focuses its activities and products on consumer demands. Generally, there are three ways of doing this:
- The customer-driven approach
- The sense of identifying market changes
- Product innovation approach

In the consumer-driven approach, consumer wants are the drivers of all strategic marketing decisions. No strategy is pursued until it passes the test of consumer research. Every aspect of a market offering, including the nature of the product itself, is driven by the needs of potential consumers. The starting point is always the consumer. The rationale for this approach is that there is no point spending R&D funds developing products that people will not buy. History attests to many products that were commercial failures in spite of being technological breakthroughs.

A formal approach to this customer—focused marketing is known as Solution, Information, Value, Access. This system is basically the four Ps renamed and reworded to provide a customer focus.

The model provides a demand/customer centric version alternative to the well-known 4Ps supply side model—product, price, place, promotion of marketing management.

Product needs to provide solutions to customer problems or give him benefits and satisfaction on usage and delight.

Promotion leads to information, creation of interest in the customers

Price is the perceived value of the product in the customers mindset

Place deals with the making of the product easily available to the customer

Besides the company needs to understand the following to match up with the 4 Ps-

Solution: How appropriate is the solution to the customers' problem/need?

Information: Does the customer know about the solution, and if so how, who from, do they know enough to let them make a buying decision?

Value: Does the customer know the value of the transaction, what it will cost, what are the benefits, what might they have to sacrifice, what will be their reward?

Access: Where can the customer find the solution? How easily/locally/remotely can they buy it and take delivery?

Product Focus

In a product innovation approach, the company pursues product innovation, then tries to develop a market for the product. Product innovation drives the process and marketing research is conducted primarily to ensure that a profitable market segment exists for the innovation. The rationale is that customers may not know what options will be available to them in the future so we should not expect them to tell us what they will buy in the future. However, marketers can aggressively over-pursue product innovation and try to overcapitalize on a niche. When pursuing a product innovation approach, marketers must ensure that they have a varied and multi-tiered approach to product innovation. It is claimed that if Thomas Edison depended on marketing research he would have produced larger candles rather than inventing light bulbs. Many firms, such as research and development focused companies, successfully focus on product innovation (such as Nintendo who constantly change the way video games are played). Many purists doubt whether this is really a form of marketing orientation at all, because of the ex post status of consumer research. Some even question whether it is marketing.

An emerging area of study and practice concerns internal marketing, or how employees are trained and managed to deliver the brand in a way that positively impacts the acquisition and retention of customers (employer branding).

Diffusion of innovations research explores how and why people adopt new products, services and ideas.

A relatively new form of marketing uses the Internet and is called internet marketing or more generally e-marketing, affiliate marketing, desktop advertising or online marketing. It typically tries to perfect the segmentation strategy used in traditional marketing. It targets its audience more precisely, and is sometimes called personalized marketing or one-to-one marketing.

With consumers' eroding attention span and willingness to give time to advertising messages, marketers are turning to forms of permission marketing such as, branded content, custom media and reality marketing.

The use of "follow the leader" behavior in marketing.

The basic idea is that people will buy more of products that are seen to be popular, and several feedback mechanisms to get product popularity information to consumers are mentioned, including smart-card technology and the use of Radio Frequency Identification Tag Technology.

Marketing on the Mat

Some aspects of marketing, especially promotion, are the subject of criticism. It is especially problematic in classical economic theory, which is based on the assumption that supply and demand are independent. However, product promotion is an attempt coming from the supply side to influence demand. In this way producer market power is attained as measured by profits that would not be realized under a free market. Then the argument follows that non-free markets are imperfect and lead to production and consumption of suboptimal amounts of the product.

Critics acknowledge that marketing has legitimate uses in connecting goods and services to the consumers who want them. Critics also point out that marketing techniques have been used to achieve morally dubious ends by businesses, governments and criminals. Critics see a systemic social evil inherent in marketing. Marketing is accused of creating ruthless exploitation of both consumers and workers by treating people as commodities whose purpose is to consume.

Most marketers believe that marketing techniques themselves are amoral. While it is ethically neutral, it can be used for negative purposes, such as selling unhealthy food to obese people.

Core marketing elements such as segmentation, targeting and positioning are still relevant in the modern world. However, they are complex topics that need a high level of effort, intelligent thinking as well as resources to be implemented successfully. A definitive statement cannot be made whether the conventional marketing concept is applicable in today's environment. Its relevance is very much situational and depends on many factors such as the product, the segment, time, location, political and economic conditions and the inner workings of a company.

There can be a positive statement about marketing, that marketing is full of deployment of personal charm and has enjoyed more than its fair share of conquests and the increasing academic attention that is being devoted to marketing and consumption-related phenomena by non-business disciplines such as sociology, anthropology and history; far from being the second-hand rose of the scholarship, marketing is now something of a "art of grace" leader.

On the other hand, one can decry marketing by saying that marketing has to decide whether to expose its intellectual irrelevance. This apparent love-hate relationship is proof in itself that even a skeptic finds it difficult to deny the contribution that marketing has made and can make to customer satisfaction and economic value. It has contributed to both customers' and suppliers' quality of life by selecting profitable customer satisfaction as its sole objective. The marketing concept, together with other business disciplines, helped the UK to make the transition from a 19th-century manufacturing economy to a modern model of success in the service industry, creating an economic growth period never seen before in the United Kingdom marketing has helped create value through customised products, no-questions-asked refund policies, comfortable cars, environmental attention, shopkeepers' smile, and guaranteed delivery dates. Even some government departments address the public not as 'the Queen's subjects' or 'the applicants' any more but as 'customers.' Of course all of the above is done for economic or political gain, for better or worse. Despite all this achievement, to dismiss marketing as a failure is unfair.

Marketing also helps companies avoid unnecessary R&D, operational and sales costs by helping to develop products because customers want them, not for the sake of innovation. Another success is the now commonly implemented value-pricing principle, whereby a product or service is sold for the price the customer is willing to pay, not on a cost-plus basis. They segment their markets, relate their products and services to them, define their value proposition and serve their customers accordingly. Examples are General Electric, HSBC, Price Waterhouse Coopers, Smiths Aerospace, BAE Systems, BOC Edwards, Weir Group and the BT Group to name but a few. A brief visit to their websites can make this point clear.

It can be suggested that more dynamism is required in marketing. This refers mainly to promotion, which is only one of the leading elements in the marketing thought today. The truth is that marketing today leads the way in segmentation, innovation, pricing, product management, distribution, and last but not the least, promotion.

With its contribution and its potential, promotion leads in marketing successes and is doing great justice to the marketing profession as well as to academic thought. Today, more than ever to we need objectivity, strength, quantification, models, relationships, paradigm shifts towards higher promotional inputs and some application of science as well to further induce the creative element in marketing and promotion.

CHAPTER 3

Locating New Customers

Marketers have to keep locating new customers. This exercise can be termed prospecting. In prospecting the sales person has to identify and qualify new customers as this is one of the most important ways of creatively getting new business. The next step is to set up an objective for calls on the customers as well as on prospects. The salesperson must know how to gather essential information about the prospect before making call plans. Next the call tactics need to be formulated.

The salesperson needs to have the right attitude before the call and this attitude can be developed. The salesperson should ensure that he gets the prospect interested in his preposition quickly enough. It is always useful to verify the efficacy of the call plans.

The salesperson must be fully aware of the features of the product or the service he has to sell. He must be able to distinguish between the features and the derived benefits from the features of the product. This will help him in putting together an effective presentation while maintaining the prospect's interest and believability in the presentation. Most prospects will offer objections to change in their buying patterns (as they are perhaps buying from competition). The salesperson must be able to distinguish between valid and superficial objections. The most important plan of sales calls is the way calls should be closed with the prospect's purchase orders in hand.

Finally, salespersons need to know how to arrange a post call analysis to learn the gains of the plans as well as its shortcomings.

Prospecting for Customers

Prospecting can be divided into four parts, the advantages of having a skilled salesperson in the technique of prospecting, learning the methods and sources for identifying and locating the worthwhile prospects, qualifying the prospects—by understanding the more desirable prospects from the less desirable ones, the relationship between prospecting and creative selling.

Every salesperson has to find new customer—the prospects. Customers are the existing buyers while prospects are likely buyers. Prospects can be considered potential buyers of the company's products. Prospecting can be defined as "identifying and qualifying potential customers or prospects" salespersons need to learn the prospecting of potential customers to enable them to replace lost customers due to organisational changes, relocation, competitive activities. A skilled salesperson will be able to prioritise calls on prospects more likely to become customers, making the sales calls more productive. Such salesperson will be able to broad base his customer list and increase the total number of his customers. He will reduce the number of unproductive calls in the process.

Prospect Identification

In several product groups it is easy to identify the prospects, like the cotton supplier will know the textile mills as his prospects, the airlines would identify the travel agents as the prospects. However, for products with a large number of possible customers like insurance, office supplies it is more difficult to locate the prospects. In such cases companies develop ingenious techniques for identifying the prospects. One insurance company's sales manual has a list of 140 different sources of prospects of life insurance. Published data, lists, telephone directories are good source of potential customers. Today's telemarketers use these lists for calling on the prospects to know their interest in the product being sold. Salespersons use referrals extensively for locating prospects. Company's existing customers are known to recommend another possible buyer to the salesperson. This can happen on the buyer's own volition or on salesperson's request. At times even prospects can give referrals of other prospects and the salesperson can use the endless chain of prospecting potential customers. Besides, influential business leaders, community leaders can become source of prospecting for customers. These influential persons are found at the centrestage of power. Even bankers, lawyers, educators can be used as such sources.

One major area that brings about prospects is the enquiries, (that could have been generated because of companies advertising efforts or sales promotion) that the company receives from prospects. These enquiries are passed on to the salespersons as business leads.

Salespersons should always be on the alert for locating new customers—the companies prospects. It is a good idea to develop a data bank that is kept updated for the prospects by adding the prospects from all the possible sources.

Once the salesperson has got the name of the prospect his task starts. The salesperson must find out in the prospects organisation the right person who should be met for business. Ideally the entire purchase decision hierarchy should be understood along with other particulars like phone, address, e-mail address. A study confirms that 60% of sales calls are made on wrong persons and are therefore ineffective. Sales calls are expensive as a lot of time is spent on planning and executing the calls. It is necessary that the time and effort are wisely invested. Salespersons should therefore, start with making calls on the best prospects, those whose chances of getting converted into customers are the best.

Qualifying the Customer

Qualifying helps the salesperson in selecting the best prospects on whom to call. The following three questions are used for qualifying the prospects:

- Does the prospect meet with the company's policies?
- Does the product fulfil a need of the prospect?
- What is the current and future value of the prospect to the company?

In the case of company policy the salesperson should understand the prospects' requirements on the following terms of business and the company's standards on the same:

- Pricing and discounts
- Credit as a sales tool
- Cash discounts
- Delivery needs
- Order size
- Servicing requirements

Prospects with odd or abnormal requirements that the company cannot comply with is not a good prospect as against the prospect who requires only the standard terms of business. Such prospects are likely to offer long term business association to the company. The other, even more important question is, do company's product and service, including delivery periods fill the prospects needs? Prospects with urgent needs that can be met by the company have the best chance of becoming company's customers. However, in majority of cases the prospects do not see any need for the company's products in immediate future or even in the distant future. At such times it is the job of the salesperson to find out a way in which the company's product can satisfy some need of the prospect. It must be understood clearly that even if the prospect does not see any need of the company's product but the salesperson does see a need then the prospect is worth working on. A company modernising its plant will have need of a bigger, more powerful air-conditioning system even if the company does not realise at the moment. It would be prudent for the salesperson to introduce his company's latest energy saving powerful air-conditioning system when the buyer is in the right frame of mind to listen.

A napkin salesperson read in a magazine that one industrial laboratory had many delicate instruments that needed soft lint free cloth to wipe off dust from the instruments. While the purchase person of the laboratory may never have thought of buying napkins for the purpose, the alert salesperson saw the need and now that and similar several other laboratories are using the napkins.

Therefore, the salesperson should not get worried even if the prospect shows no interest in the product, and try to locate even hidden needs of which even the prospect is not aware.

The next level is to find out the present and future value of the prospect to the company. It stands to reason that the best efforts should be made on prospects with the greatest value to the company. The prospects capacity is one yardstick for measuring the value. The biggest buyer gets to be the best prospect. Big value frequent orders from the prospect make him most valuable. However, even a small buyer with future growth possibilities can never be ignored. Besides, the prospect's reputation is a major factor in considering its value. A small buyer who is a community leader and much respected should be rated high on value even against the bigger volume buyers who may be regarded poor in the business circles.

Summarising, the good prospect can be defined as the one that meets the business policy and terms of business of the company, has a definite need of the company's products and has a high present or future value for the company, or if the prospect enjoys leadership position in the industry or in the community.

So far a variety of techniques of prospecting have been studied. It is obvious that the prospecting techniques will differ greatly among the salespersons depending on the kind of selling job they are performing, the product. Prospecting for customers requires creative ability on the part of the salesperson. Salespersons' creativity is perhaps the only limiting factor for developing prospecting plans for future customers. At the same time the creative salesperson can determine newer ways of product usage by the potential customers.

Detailed Call Planning

Salespersons need to learn in detail the various aspects of call planning before a call is made on a customer or a prospect. Sales calls are costly and time consuming both for the salesperson and the buyer, it is essential that the calls are planned in advance and thoroughly. Some salespersons feel that playing by the ear will take them through a successful sales call. However, experience shows that such calls usually end in disaster. Planning needs to be first perceived in the mind only. Planning process takes the salesperson through what will be done in future well in advance. The sales calls are important assignments and the risk of lack of preparedness must be avoided at all cost. A successful call could generate business worth millions of rupees and the reverse is equally true. Call planning needs to be done in the following three steps:

- Establish the call objective
- Gather the essential information
- Select appropriate strategies or tactics

Establishing the Call Objectives

The call objective is what the salesperson hopes to achieve when he meets the customer or the prospect face-to-face. The objective must be set before the call is made. Finally, the objective that any salesperson has is to obtain an order from the customer or the prospect. The objective may quantify the order value for the call. However, more often than not, it takes several calls before an order can be obtained. Therefore, each call may have a different objective, while the major objective of obtaining the order is always at the back of the salesperson's mind. The immediate objective could be to find out changes in buying patterns with the change of purchase team of the customer. Other objective is to persuade the customer or prospect to see a product demonstration. One objective could be to obtain permission to supply samples for trial purposes. There can be a variety of objectives of sales calls and the calls can be considered fruitful if the objective for the call has been met. In any case since the final objective is getting the order, the other minor objectives should bring the main objective a little closer to the company. The objectives of preliminary calls should be used like the steps of an escalator that lead to the final destination, the order. The number of steps, or calls leading to the order would depend on the type of selling as also it will vary from customer-to-customer. Setting up objectives help the salesperson in keeping calls on track of achieving the main objective. For example, if the salesperson wants to introduce a new type of denim cloth to the manufacturer of ready-made garments, the following route can be taken:

- First objective—to get the agreement of the buyer about need of the denim
- Second objective—demonstrate the new denim to key individuals
- Convince the buyer that the price and other terms of business are right and get the order.

As can be seen, the intermediate objectives were in line with the major objective of getting the order. The objectives must follow a sequence in ascending order like an escalator, as it will help the salesperson in getting the order rather quickly.

Gathering the Essential Information

Once the objective has been defined the next step is gathering essential information about the customer or the prospect. During the prospecting stage the salesperson has obtained some information. However, the more information he has the better chances of his success from the sales calls. While information gathering is time consuming it is important to collect the essential information.

The salesperson has to determine what constitutes the essential information on the prospect. It is the objective of the call that defines the information need of the salesperson. It is useful to prepare a check-list of information needs in order to avoid overlooking any necessary information item. Given below is a dedicated checklist, which should be altered by the salesperson to suit individual requirements.

Business Information Check-List

- Name
- Address
- Telephone numbers, Fax
- Annual sales volume in rupees and units
- Ownership
- Management philosophy
- Organisational structure
- Key decision-makers

- Reputation
- Competition details
- Credit rating
- Number of employees
- Current problems faced by the company
- Products/services sold
- Markets targeted—segments
- Key customers
- Plans and policies on purchasing
- Budget policy
- Frequency of purchase
- Seasonal factors
- Key suppliers
- Attitude towards price, quality, product innovations
- Raw material used
- Components made/bought
- Manufacturing process
- Administrative process
- Machine and equipment used
- Schedule of maintenance
- Volume potential for sales by the salesperson in rupees and in numbers
- Previous experience with the salesperson's company
- Salesperson's competition

The check-list of personal information:

- Name with correct spelling and pronunciation
- Address
- Age with date of birth
- Position-title, responsibility, authority, line of communication, basis of evaluation by superiors
- Length of time with the company
- Business background
- Education
- Business or professional affiliations
- Social affiliations
- Marital status, family background and number of children
- Other interests—outside of the job
- Personal aspirations
- Personal peculiarities
- Best time to visit

While several of the items listed may not be considered essential it is a good idea to go through the check-list to ensure nothing of vital importance is left out.

The salesperson need to know the sources from where they can gather the information. Information on existing customers is usually available with the salesperson's company. Besides, customers or prospects who give the business leads are another source of information. Trade partners, the channel members, trade publications. Business calls should be used to gain information that help in adding onto the already available information. Prospects annual reports, balance sheets reveal important details on their financial standing, plans and new product launches. Prospects literature, advertisements offer information that can be of use to the salesperson. The salesperson should use all possible means to get the information and keep it updated all the time.

Strategies and Tactics

Salespersons must plan their strategies for the sales calls to attain their call objectives. The calls normally follow the following pattern:

- Approach
- Presentation
- Objections
- Closing the call

Due to the importance of sales calls, call planning must become an essential part of the salesperson's activities and it should become a work habit with the salesperson. Planning being a mental activity, should be carried out at a place where there are no distractions. Salesperson should concentrate on the three elements of call planning, establishing the objective, gathering the essential information and selecting the appropriate tactics. The planning can be done mentally. However, it is recommended that for important call the plan must be written down. Given below is a standard form for planning sales calls.

Call Planner

- Company
- Address
- Phone, fax
- Name of the customer/ prospect
- Call objective
- Essential information on the company-on the individual
- Tactics to use
- Approach
- Presentation
- Objections
- Closing

It should be assumed that the customer is a busy person and when he gives an appointment for a sales call, it is important that the salesman makes the best use of the time given, and hence the need for careful planning for each such call.

Planning sales calls should be done using the following steps:

Study the customer's file; remember the name (with correct pronunciation), designation, level and authority of the person to be met. Review of any complaint from the customer, whether it has been attended to, satisfactorily so far or not. Is there any pending matter from the last call, which must be resolved before the call is made, or else the salesman may not be even welcome at the customer's premises? For example, if the salesman had promised replacement of defective product and it has not taken place so far, the sales call would end up in bitter criticism from the customer and undue justification from the salesman. No concrete result can come from such a situation.

Plan the sales call objectives, both major and minor ones. It is better to write them down at least in first few calls.

Carry the following in the briefcase to be used at the customers place.

- Visiting cards
- Customer's file
- Product literature, especially of new products being introduced
- Testimonials from other customers
- Firms letterheads
- Price lists
- Terms of business
- Pen, pencils, erasers, carbon paper, stapler with staples
- Product's benefits for the customer along with benefits offered by competition (make sure your benefits always outscore the competitive benefits) the benefits should be written in sequence of their priority for the customer and it may be wise to alter the sequence for different levels of customers' hierarchy.

The salesman should be smartly dressed and not gaudily and well groomed. In most cases it is essential to take prior appointment from the customer. It is useful to reach customer's office a few minutes early (while waiting the salesman can compose himself, revise the file papers, plan his opening sentences, use the toilet to feel fresh, comb his hair.)

In case of meeting a new customer, or one who has been mostly buying from competition dialogue plan, which has been found useful as at several steps the salesman is likely to find objections to his benefit story is given below. Of course the salesman must keep his wits about him to modify it as the sales call progresses.

The main objective of sales calls is getting the purchase order from the customer. Salesmen usually plan a canned talk to persuade the customer to place the order on the salesman's firm. However, the salesman mostly, encounters resistance from the buyer due to the following reasons, one or all:

- The buyer is friendly to the competitor's salesperson
- Competitive product gives better value for money in the eyes of the buyer
- Competition provides better after-sales service as per the buyer

- The users in the customer's side do not want a change, to avoid problems of duplicated inventories and confusion from unskilled/ illiterate workers about a new product
- The competition is providing some unspecified incentive, overtly or covertly to the buyer

Following are the steps needed in guiding the buyer in deciding in favour of placing the order on the firm. It is called the Decision Triangle (when more than one buying decision person is involved then the triangle could take the shape of Decision Pyramid).

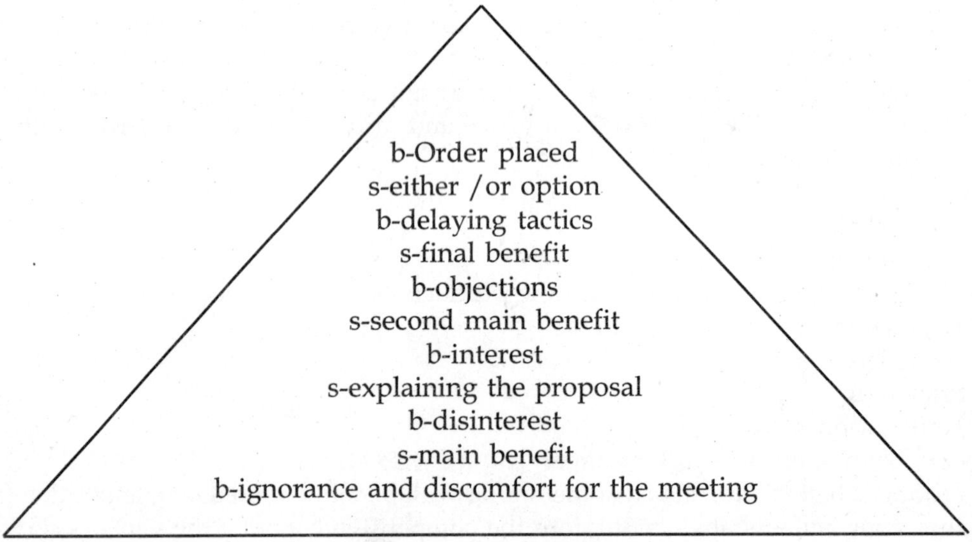

b-buyer, s-salesman

As can be seen in the beginning of the interview the salesman is at a disadvantage as the customer is ignorant of his proposal. At this juncture it is best to give the most important benefit, which would attract the attention of the buyer. If the benefit could be translated into savings in rupees, it will click well with the CEOs, Finance Managers; time saving will go well with production managers. Even after the main benefit, the salesman need not feel complacent as the competitive strengths are still working to defuse their effort. At this stage the salesman must explain the proposal and if the buyer wants he can call other members of decision-making team to join him. It will save time for both seller and the buyer. Otherwise, similar dialogue will have to be carried out with other members separately. After some interest is generated the salesman would do well to seize the opportunity by adding the other benefits till the buyer reaches the stage of purchase decision. At times there is a last hurdle, which is basically a delaying tactics on the part of the buyer, like I have to consult my father (who may not be even involved in the business at all). This can be surmounted by offering an option to the buyer, "would you want us to provide the transit insurance or you would cover it yourself?" if the customer says, "we will take the insurance cover ourselves," your deal is finalized. Once the salesman gets the purchase order, he must make sure to thank the buyer and leave his office without delay. It has been known that if the salesman stays long enough he may lose the order, "could you just give me that order back for a minute I want it to be checked once more by our auditors" you hand over the order and can wish it good by as the next day the competitors salesman would walk in, get the benefit of your sales talk which has brought the buyer in to buying mood, and he will walk away with your order.

In case there is buying committee to take decisions the salesman can act as a liaison man by getting the following to meet and put across the benefit story as per the mindset and need of the member of the committee, thus the decision triangle becomes decision pyramid:

- Firm's CEO with buyer's CEO—this could perhaps be the last meeting unless of course the two CEOs know each other well.
- Technical manager/R&D manager with the buyer's R&D manager
- Systems manager with buyer's Production manager
- Logistics manager with buyer's Materials manager
- Finance manager with buyer's Finance manager

These meetings could be on one-to-one basis or altogether.

Presentation Ready

When the salesperson comes face to face with the customer, the first few minutes make the vital impact on whatever happens afterwards. The success presentation of would largely depend on the frame of mind of the customer or the prospect. Following possibilities would prove the point:

- The prospect has been extremely busy and is meeting the salesperson just out of courtesy.
- The prospects company is passing through a minor crisis situation
- The prospect has to rush out to meet some VIP
- The prospect has to meet a deadline and he is already late

The salesperson needs to keep a positive outlook in all such times and he can gradually convert the negative frame of mind into positive approach of the prospect. The salesperson should ensure that prospect does not consider himself obligated under some duress into meeting him. The prospect should be ready and willing to meet and this happens when the salesperson is ready to help, and remains positive during the meeting. The sincerity and helpful nature are the prerequisites of success in the meeting. A negative behaviour from the salesperson would surely evoke similar response from the prospect. At times the history of earlier calls comes as a barrier of positive outlook of the salesperson and brings in a feeling of inadequacy. Conversely a successful earlier call could make the salesperson over-confident and aggressive. Salesperson's own business results can seriously affect his behaviour during the meeting. The maturity of the salesperson is in throwing off or ignoring these factors that tend to influence his behaviour.

The salesperson has to take each call as a fresh experience. The vital matter is of attitude the salesperson must have, and that should be positive and helpful towards the prospect. The attitude will help the salesperson in getting the prospect into transitional mode where the buyer's mind is gently moved from whatever he had been doing prior to the salesperson's meeting to an enthusiastic willingness to hear the presentation. The salesperson needs to build a good rapport with the prospect. Rapport is defined as a "harmonious relationship". The rapport can be built by even small things like knowing the title, and the correct pronunciation of his name. Small talk, like talk about his hobbies, sports or other non-business subjects in which the prospect is genuinely interested will contribute to the rapport building exercise. However, the small talk bit must be kept small since the prospect would not want to waste his valuable time. The salesperson should also make the best usage of the meeting time. Once the rapport has been established the salesperson has to bridge the gap between the social conversation and the specific business of the call. A variety of techniques are used for bridging the gap as in below:

- At times a question is asked for the purpose. "If I can show you how to reduce maintenance cost by 5%, would it be interest to you? "is such a question.
- The other method could be of offering assistance, "I would like to check your air-conditioning system for the coming summer. Of course there will be no charge"
- Announcing a significant fact can be used to bridge the gap like," you will be happy to learn that since last December the electricity supply company is saving rupees fifty lacs
- Each year with the use of computerised billing system supplied by us
- Sometimes the product like a miniature cell phone needs to be shown for bridging the gap

The salesperson should always avoid such trite questions," how is business" or "how do things look". Such questions are likely to get a negative response leading to the entire presentation becoming negative from the prospect viewpoint. The other failed technique is, "I was in the neighbourhood and thought I would drop in". Summarising after the rapport has been built the salesperson needs to have a technique of bridging the gap between the social conversation and serious business talk.

Call Plan Verification

Call planning involves the three steps, establishing the objective, gathering essential information and selecting the right tactics. The salesperson believes that his objectives are attainable, information sufficient and tactics appropriate. However, it is a good idea to verify the plan if the opportunity for doing so presents itself. The verification becomes easy if the prospect is given to talk fully and openly. Salesperson needs to ask a well worded question after the gap has been bridged between the small talk and serious business talk leading to the presentation. Questions like, "your new plant installation plan?" Or "your maintenance plan for the machinery" – would let the prospect hold the fort and he would enjoy talking about his ideas. The salesperson could ask, "which part of the machinery is difficult to maintain?" or "which is the most time consuming manual operation that you want to transfer to a computer?" The purpose of these questions is to have the prospect talk about his needs. The talks should be carried on till the call plan has been verified by the salesperson. The questions should be broad based to allow a general response. The salesperson should keep showing his interest by interjecting with, "this is interesting, tell me more". Attentive listening will help the salesperson in his verification process of the call plan. If the salesperson feels he can modify the plan as he goes along. He can decide if the original objective is still attainable or should he modify it to an extent. He would also realise if he has sufficient essential information or he should let the prospect keep talking. He can also understand if his tactics will work or do they need to be altered too. Can he use the tactics in handling the objections and in closing the presentation? The verification is the last step before the salesperson begins the presentation. As he is verifying his information base, the salesperson should help the prospect in redefining his needs from being generic to the needs of salesperson products through persuasive communication.

Sales Presentation

The salesperson has by now understood that unless he has a defined objective, he has obtained the essential information and planned the right tactics he should not even attempt the call on the prospect. The start of the call is when the salesperson, through his persuasive communication gets the prospect change his generic needs to specific needs of the salesperson's products. Let us discuss the persuasive communication in some detail.

The salesperson's products have some inherent unique qualities that can be defined as product features. Features need not be restricted to product physical qualities alone. They could well be part of company policy, product availability, and related service. Countrywide advertising campaign would be part of company marketing policy. When the salesperson helps the distributor in managing the inventory the service offered is unique and personal. Each company has to provide proper training to its salesperson in understanding its product's unique qualities including the service and the marketing policy. Salespersons must keep themselves abreast on these counts.

The salesperson must understand that the customers buy a product only for the benefits it offers to them. Benefits can be defined as the satisfaction the product provides to the buyers. The prospects are going to buy a product only if it provides the needed benefit to them. Youngsters do not buy motor cycles; they buy the thrill they provide on high speeds. Women do not buy cosmetics; they buy the benefit of becoming alluring by using the same. However, different people are looking for different types of benefits from a product.

The salesperson therefore needs to list down the benefits different persons are looking from their product. Such a list needs to be continuously updated for each group of customers as the customer group keeps changing; market segment keeps changing with time. In early 1960s the transistor radio was the craze with the elite of the society and today they would feel ashamed if found near a transistor set. The benefits could include reduced cost of labour, reduced maintenance cost, better quality control and increased worker safety. For retail traders the benefits could be better protection from competitive actions, increased stock turnover, higher margins, less customer returns and complaints.

A description of the product features would appear like a technical manual only. Likewise if the salesperson talks only about the benefits it would sound like parrot repeating what he has been taught. Persuasive communication should combine the two, with salesperson talking about the benefits along with the features from where the benefits are derived. Automatic transmission is a feature of some cars while convenience is the benefit to the car driver. Hence, if the salesperson tells the customer that with automatic transmission of our cars, you would find driving convenient and pleasurable, he is tying a feature with a benefit. For excelling in this type of communication the salesperson should prepare a Feature-Benefit worksheet, as given below:

Feature benefit worksheet for–product–customer

Feature 1	Benefit 1	Benefit 2	Benefit 3	Benefit 4
Feature 2	Benefit 1	Benefit 2	Benefit 3	Benefit 4
Feature 3	Benefit 1	Benefit 2	Benefit 3	Benefit 4
Feature 4	Benefit 1	Benefit 2	Benefit 3	Benefit 4

Maslow's Hierarchy of needs gives a clear definition of different types of human needs and the salesperson would do well in relating the benefits to the needs, like physiological needs, need for safety, social acceptance need, need for recognition and respect and finally need for self actualisation, when the customer has attained the heights he had planned to achieve. It is assumed in the above worksheet that each feature will have multiple benefits.

Given below is a Feature Benefit Worksheet for a car:

Features	Benefits
Big seats	Comfort and lifestyle
Leg room, head clearance	Comfort and lifestyle
Large Boot	Family luxury car
Power steering	Lifestyle
Plush finish	Self actualised owner
Country wide service facility	Peace of mind-comfort
Easy payment plan	Economical
Exchange facility	Easy on budget, economical
Test drive possible	Reconfirmation of quality, lifestyle
Service pickup and delivery	Comfort
50 years experience	Peace of mind, lifestyle

Before the salesperson starts his presentation, he should have developed the feature benefit worksheet. The features should be first listed and then the benefits added on to the worksheet. In case of a car, the benefits can be listed as given below:

- Comfort
- Economy
- Prestige enhancing lifestyle

- Convenience
- Safety

The salesperson should develop the benefit story using the possible benefits and writing down a paragraph for each benefit that will help him during the presentation, as given below:

Benefit Paragraph

Comfort

It is a comfortable car. The body is welded. The ride is so smooth you can pour tea or coffee from the jug and it will not spill. The large seats will take a well fed family of six and the leg room ensures comfortable seating for the long legged teenagers.

The large boot is much bigger than several cars with big boots. You can really load it up without damage to your luggage or to the car.

It is a comfortable car for you, your family and your luggage.

Economy

The car costs less to run. The engine is newly designed for maximum efficiency. It is made out of aluminium to save weight. As a result you get up to 20 kilometres per litre. It is a real miser with petrol.

You can see the engine is uncluttered. It results in time saving for quick adjustments.

The body is welded, which means no rattle repairs. Its rustproof too, it will stand up to all weather.

The aluminium silencer will last twice as long as the ordinary one. The finish stays shiny so you save on waxing the car.

If you have a car to trade in, we will give a fair trade–in allowance, through our used car department.

You just cannot beat the economy of this model.

Prestige Enhancer-Lifestyle Product

It is a modern car. The new engine-101 horsepower will let you climb hills as though they were not there. Cruising speed in this model will leave you with plenty to spare for passing on motor ways. You will not find a welded body like this even in the best imports of sports cars and the design and the gleaming finish makes it unusually attractive. Of course you get power steering, power breaks and automatic transmission to give the ride you will enjoy.

Convenience

The car makes driving easier and its uncluttered engine makes maintenance simpler too. It is, as can be seen 184 ″ long and can be parked in places smaller than ever before for other cars. The car provides spare space in the garage.

The boot will easily hold enough luggage for the long trips planned in the new car. The finish is a cinch to keep glistening clean; only a cold water wash does it quickly.

For ease of driving, parking and safety the car has power steering, power brakes and automatic transmission.

For periodic maintenance checkups and adjustments, there is complete modern service department at your disposal. If you like you can call me and will personally make arrangements for your service appointments. Should you need servicing in out of town locations in the country we have provided with a list of our numerous authorised service stations in the country along with a route maps so that you can never miss them. We have an easy payment plan so that you can keep your savings in the bank. I would like to take you out on a test drive to show you how easy the car is to drive, first hand.

Safety

It is a solid car. These are real doors and the engine is placed up front for balance and greater control. You see the engine is V form and it gives a lower bonnet for battery visibility. Te welded body gives you a substantial and strong car that takes all kinds of road punishments. Seat belts in rear seats are big safety plus I the car. You can rely on us to stand by the car. I have been selling cars for this dealer for the last fifteen years and hope to be here for another fifteen.

As can be seen from the benefit paragraphs that all the benefits from different features on comfort have been listed at one place. Similarly, the other list of benefits is used to form sentences in the proper sequence for highlighting the benefits. Once the benefit story has been developed the next step is to find techniques for maintaining interest of the prospect.

Maintaining Interest

Salesperson's presentations are in many ways like telling a story. An interesting story is easy to listen while the same is not true for a boring story. Therefore, the next element of persuasive communication is maintaining the interest of the prospect. There are a number of techniques of maintaining the prospects interest as given below.

Customising or Individualising the Benefits

This means that the salesperson directs everything he says towards the needs of the prospect. This is important because each prospect wants to know how the product will satisfy his specific needs. Such individualisation of benefits will ensure that prospect's interest is maintained. It must be understood that two prospects buying identical product may be motivated by different benefits. Car buyers may have different motivations as one may buy a car for its economy and the other for its convenience. Individualising the needs and benefits means selecting those benefits that would satisfy the need of a particular prospect. Hence, the salesperson would have to scan the benefit paragraphs that are ideally suited to the prospects requirements. In other words the salesperson must develop a storehouse of all possible features/ benefit stories to be able to build instant rapport and continued interest in the presentation by the prospect. The right selection of the benefit paragraph could mean success of the presentation and in obtaining the objective of the call.

Using Descriptive Language

The other method of maintaining the prospect's interest is using descriptive language. For example, the car salesperson while using the comfort paragraph, does not just say that the car ride will be smooth, he says, "the ride will be so smooth that you can pour coffee" the vivid language helps in maintaining the prospect's interest. In the economy paragraph, the salesperson says "the car is real miser on petrol" he is using the descriptive language to hold interest of the prospect. A good salesperson is ready with descriptive language that he has developed with practice and he uses it to good advantage to keep the interest of the prospect.

Participation

The salesperson can keep the interest of the prospect alive if he, instead of relating his benefit story even when the prospect is getting bored with it. Participation means getting him involved in the act. This can be done in the following ways.

Ask the prospect a question, which will ensure his active participation in the presentation. The salesperson can ask, "Do you recall the trouble you had during your last trip in your car?"

Have the prospect do some calculating or figuring out, which would involve him in the presentation. The prospect can be asked to calculate the kilometres per litre the car will give by giving him some documented figures.

For communicating persuasively the salesperson has to ensure that the prospect remains interested in the presentation, which he can do by individualising the benefits for prospect's needs, keep his language descriptive, and ensure prospect's participation.

Believability

The fifth element of persuasive communication is its believability. Unless the prospect believes in the salesperson the call can never be successful. One basic technique used by salesperson for ensuring the believability factor with the prospect is the use of testimonials. Testimonials are stories of satisfied customers that are most helpful for new products or when you are calling on a prospect. A testimonial issued by a reputed and respected company or person in the same field, helps in convincing the prospect of the desirability of the product. Salespersons with thorough knowledge of product features and the benefits sought by the prospect can also make a believable presentation. His knowledge should be so extensive and exhaustive that he is able to politely answer all the questions asked by the prospect and give his benefit story convincingly. In the event the salesperson does not know the answer to a question it is best to admit it and confirm that in a day or two he will give the answer, instead of bluffing his way. Any wrong statement made is going to have a snowballing effect and the chances are that the prospect will soon become disillusioned with the salesperson and his presentation. The third technique for creating believability in the prospect results from the demeanour of the salesperson. It is easier to believe a sincere person. The salesperson should try to take the role of a personal counsellor to the prospect. He needs to under claim and over achieve the key points of his presentation. This way he will achieve the believability factor from the prospect.

Summarising there are three methods of achieving believability of the prospect, use of testimonials, having a thorough knowledge of product features and benefits and the salesperson's sincerity towards the prospect.

Demonstration

At times words are just not enough for achieving though call objective as the words appeal only to the prospect's sense of hearing. The other four senses are therefore neglected. We come to the sixth element of persuasive communication—demonstration. Demonstration means appealing to prospect's other sense to make the verbal presentation more persuasive. Demonstration in selling is basic. It is better for the buyer to enjoy chocolate slab rather than someone telling him how good it tastes. The housewife would rather feel the sari fabric than have a TV commercial describe how it feels.

Selling to the channel member, the retailer, if the salesperson does not describe the new advertising campaign but actually shows him the print copy.

A computer buyer would like to have hands on experience on the new model rather than only descriptive eulogy on the same. Buyers of air-conditioning plant would be happy to visit an existing installation of the salespersons company and see for themselves the efficacy of the plant.

Salesperson has to decide what needs to be demonstrated and what need not be demonstrated. This requires a careful study of the benefit paragraphs. Statements that can be strengthened through an appeal to the other four senses should be carefully considered. Demonstrations make the features and benefits more believable. With some originality, zest and excitement can be added with the demonstration making the presentation more interesting.

Sellers of stainless steel products offer a key chain to the buyer as a proof of its rust proofing feature to increase the believability of the presentation.

Pictures of beautifully constructed villas can add the believability factor for the real estate salesperson.

With the huge dispersion of TV network in the country demonstration has become easy. Functions of an air compressor, farm equipment, dumpers, can be easily demonstrated on TV. In rural markets advertising vans help in demonstrating the products with the use of audio-visual equipment.

Demonstration that can involve the prospect's active participation will help in maintaining his interest. You must have noticed the detergent advertisements where the group of housewives are asked to join in the actual process of using the detergent. It is a good idea to indirectly demonstrate the service facilities the company has, by showing their pictures and a map where dotted locations of the facilities have been marked.

Demonstrations make features and benefits more understandable and believable. If they are original they make presentation more interesting. If the demonstration requires the use of physical materials like, OHP, LCD projector, charts the salesperson must ensure that the materials and the equipment are in good working order and that the salesperson has personally used it several times. If the salesperson was to fumble through the demonstration the prospect will lose confidence. Therefore, all the equipment must be thoroughly checked before each call. Smooth demonstration would increase the believability of the presentation.

Planning presentations for specific calls

Salesperson should list down the key elements of the presentation, the product features, benefits to stress, the technique of maintaining interest and achieving believability. Appeals to the other four senses that the salesperson plans to use must also be noted. The features and the benefits must be individualised for the prospect on each call. The demonstration planned must also be tailor-made for each prospect. The laptop computer salesperson gave a hands on demonstration to the users of the prospect's company, talked about the economies in usage with the prospect's Finance Director and gave the benefit story highlighting the latest features to the CEO. A good presentation converts the need to desire through persuasive communication. Individualised demonstration makes the presentation more effective.

Handling objections

As the salesperson makes his presentation towards achieving his call objectives, the prospect is likely to make statements detrimental to the achievement of objectives. These statements can be defined as objections. The salesperson must realise that these are normal parts of every sales call and should not be discouraged by them. In fact they may reveal new information that will help you to adjust your tactics. Realistically, therefore, objections should be considered not deterrents in achievement of objectives but they may serve to help you in readjusting your sales tactics.

The following five steps need to be considered for handling objections.

The first step is listening to the prospect. The salesperson must train himself in the art of listening carefully to the objections raised by the prospects. Salespersons have a tendency to talk rather than to listen. A quiet and patient listener may find the prospect himself talking out of the objection. The prospect must be encouraged to speak uninterruptedly and the salesperson may get to know some additional information that he reveals, which could be of help to the salesperson. The prospect's manner of expressing the objection may confirm his personal negative feelings. The salesperson should not just listen to the words being spoken but also note the manner in which they are expressed. This way he will understand if the prospect has negative feelings as well as he may get some new information.

The second step is classifying the objections. Objections can be classified as valid or invalid. Let us consider the invalid objections. An objection is considered invalid when there is a concealed reason for it. Actually the prospect covers up how he feels by saying something else and hence should not be taken literally. A reluctance to make purchase decision could be the concealed or underlying reason behind the stated invalid objection.

If the prospect says," I cannot afford it just now, see me in a month" there may be an invalid objection as the prospect cannot say he is unable to decide at the present time. The other concealed reason for an invalid objection could be an aversion to change on the part of the prospect. "Regarding your product I will have to talk to my partner′ the prospect may be concealing his reason for buying your product since he has been buying from his present supplier for the past seven years. A prospect may raise an invalid objection if the salesperson has said something or done something to antagonise him. Hard selling on the part of salesperson may offend some prospect. A flippant or derogatory made unwittingly by one salesperson on some favourite project of the prospect could antagonise the prospect.

An invalid objection is only a subtle front for a concealed, underlying reason for the prospect's objection. As the invalid objections are now understood, let us study the valid objections. A valid objection can be taken literally, as the prospect means exactly what he says. For example, if the prospect does not understand a technical point made by the salesperson he may raise a valid objection. " the new product is made of 16 gauge steel rather than 18 gauge" if the prospect does not know that the lower the gauge the thicker the steel, he may say, "I do not want something that is flimsy in construction". A valid objection may also be raised if the salesperson fails to stress the feature or the benefit of primary interest to the prospect. In case the buyer is especially interested in the construction of the product and the salesperson keeps emphasising on low price, he is stressing the wrong benefit.

Valid objections occur most frequently during the presentation.

Handling Objections Details

After the first part is over, that of listening and understanding valid and invalid objection, the next step is disarming. As you meet an objection you are faced with a disagreement. It is best to show consideration for the other person's viewpoint as follows:

- One popular and effective method is, "yes but" method and it is meant to show consideration to the other person's point of view.
- Other way of showing consideration is "that is an interesting observation".
- Or "I am glad you brought it up"
- And yet again, "yes I know how you feel, but"

As you show consideration for the prospect's viewpoint, you are in fact avoiding confrontation and arguments. Disarming prevents objections from developing into arguments between the prospect and the salesperson.

Once the salesperson has understood the techniques of listening, classifying and disarming it is time to understand the subject of answering the prospect's objections. Let us take the invalid objections first. For invalid objections the salespersons can use a number of answers like giving a token answer. For example, if the prospect says, "I am too busy right now" the salesperson can say disarmingly, "yes sir, everybody is busy these days but let me tell you...."

The other way of handling invalid objection is to ignore it completely by pausing and then continuing. The salesperson can divert the prospect's attention away from the objection by bringing up some other interesting fact instead of handling the invalid objection directly. If the classification of the objection as invalid is correct it will not recur. If the prospect says, "business is terrible", disarmingly the salesperson can reply, "things are pretty tough, but a few moments ago we agreed that our new machine would...."

While answering valid objections it was agreed that they need to be taken on their face value. One other technique is, "denial" that may be used to answer valid objections. The best time to use denial is when the objections are based in misunderstanding or misinterpretation of the salesperson's facts. Suppose the prospect says, "I am not interested in the sweaters as they are made of reconditioned wool" knowing that the label clearly shows that the product is 100% virgin wool, disarming the salesperson can say, "yes sir, I am glad you brought it up; the quality of wool is most important, but all our sweaters are made of 100% virgin wool. Let me show you how we clearly mark the fact on our label."

Another example is, when the prospect says, "I am not buying now, times are too uncertain" the answer given disarmingly can be, "yes sir, but, among the certainties is a steady rise in cost of living and prices generally. You should protect yourself to a reasonable degree."

Next, the valid objections can be handled using the yield technique. It is used most frequently to overcome objections based on an existing advantage offered by the competition. The success of yield technique depends on the salesperson's ability to offset the existing benefit offered by the competition. For example, if a doctor says, "your capsules are larger than those supplied by your competitor." The salesperson's response should be, "yes doctor, our capsule is larger but, it is especially designed for ease of swallowing."

In case you are uncertain if the objection is valid or not, the best way out is to ask, "why?" The 'why' question will give the salesperson the necessary information to decide whether to classify the objection as valid or as invalid. For example, if the prospect says, "I want to look into some other offers". The salesperson can say, disarmingly, "yes, but why would you want to look into other deals now?" the answer should help the salesperson determine if the objection is valid or not.

So far the discussion on answering objections has been on, listening, classifying, disarming and yielding. The last manner of answering the objections is that of continuing the presentation. After answering the prospect's objection, you should continue with the presentation. Otherwise, the prospect will feel he has to raise another objection. The direction of the presentation will depend on what the salesperson has learned from the objection. Suppose the prospect revealed a particular concern about his company's service, the salesperson should stress on those special features of his company's service that were left out in the answers to the objection.

Summarising, the salesperson well versed with the storehouse of benefit paragraphs will be able to give his presentation in response to the reactions of the prospect. The salesperson must continue his presentation as he reinforces the answers to the objection. It will prevent the objection from recurring later in the call.

Price Objection

After understanding the five ways of dealing with valid objections, let us consider a special case of valid objection, the price objection. The price objection is being handled separately because it is the one that plagues the salesperson most and is most difficult to handle. The price objections are of two types, "I cannot afford it" or, "I can get it for less."

The first type of price objection, "I cannot afford it" can be said as, "your price is too high", or "I cannot spend that much" or yet another, "I am looking for a cheaper product."

The salesperson's response in such cases can be, staring with denial, "yes sir, money is important, but, in the long run your savings will far outweigh this additional expenditure."

Normally the price objection is raised when the prospect knows that he can get the same product for a lesser price. If the salesperson knows his product has as higher price than the competitive product it is best to use the yield technique. Disarmingly the salesperson can say, "Yes our price is Rs.150 and competitive price is Rs. 125, but, the difference of Rs. 25 eliminated by the one year free service contract we are offering that the competitor does not. You will agree that one year fee service is definitely more than Rs. 25. It is best to talk about the small difference and justify it rather than talk about the main price amount."

Call Closing

Call closing can be defined as a direct attempt on the part of the salesperson to attain the objective of the call. Let us, therefore discuss the techniques the salesperson can use to obtain his call objective. At this point you may be wondering if the salesperson knows his objective, makes a good approach, gives an effective presentation, and handles objections skilfully, it should be sufficient to attain the call objectives. The problem arises because most persons are reluctant to take decisions especially if they involve spending money. Salesperson's good approach, effective presentation, skilful handling of objections normally moves the prospect to the verge of agreement with the objective. However, the reluctance may still remain. Closing techniques are, therefore, direct attempts by the salesperson to nudge the fully persuaded prospect to make a favourable decision.

The first closing technique can be called assumptive. The assumptive technique is used when the salesperson senses that the buyer is almost at the point of making a decision in favour of the objective and has met with little resistance. When the salesperson is using the assumptive technique he does nothing more than act as though a favourable decision has been made with respect to the call objective. A machine tool salesperson, whose call objective was to arrange for the buyer to visit nearby plant in order to see the machine in operation, uses the assumptive technique. Sensing the favourable decision, he says, "let me use your phone to tell them we will be over there this afternoon" the salesperson has assumed that the favourable decision has been taken.

Another closing technique is of giving choice to the prospect. The technique is used when the salesperson senses that the buyer is close to agreement with his call objective but there still remains some resistance. The choice technique is a direct way of asking the prospect to make a favourable decision. In using the technique the salesperson gives the prospect a choice between two buying alternatives. The prospect does not have to select between order or no order, he has a choice between something and another thing. A shirt salesperson saying, "Would you buy the green shirt" leaves the option of saying no and walking out. Once the salesperson knows that the prospect is nearly ready to decide in favour of his objective, he could say, "which one should I pack, the green or the light blue one?" the moment the prospect says the blue one, you have achieved your objective. In B-to-B sales, the question that can be asked just before the final decision could be, "you would like us to arrange for transit insurance or would you like to organise it?"

In another situation where installation and commissioning of a plant is involved, the salesperson can nudge the prospect into decision by saying, "should I send my installation team next week or would you prefer earlier."

Suppose the salesperson is selling room air-conditioners and for nudging the prospect into action says, "so it is the two ton one you will buy" he may get an answer, "NO", after sensing that the decision is near in his favour he should say, "1.5 ton or 2 ton, which is the one", and the chances are he will get the order for one of them.

The choice technique should be used when the salesperson has sensed that the decision in his favour is almost reached to help the prospect feel happier as he gets the last word and psychologically mastery over the salesperson. Anyway, you have achieved the call objective.

The third closing technique is the summary technique. This technique is used in conjunction with the choice technique after several features and benefits have been emphasised. The salesperson should summarise using those features and benefits that have stimulated the greatest desire in prospect's mind. In this technique the salesperson uses the summary as he reviews the features and benefits putting them in a capsule form. Your interest in economy and convenience will be fully realised by our low rate contract, our quality maintenance service and our low cost spare parts. The summary technique is best used along with the choice technique.

The fourth closing technique is named the Special Feature Technique. The features of a product have been defined earlier as unique qualities of the product. Sometimes, one of the features of the product may be used as closing technique to bring about favourable decision. If a product is in limited supply, it becomes its special feature. "These imported hoses do not come for the next six months. Shall I book hundred for you." Prospects take favourable decision because they do not want to lose out on anything.

The favourable feature technique should be used only when the salesperson is sure of his facts and should be used with utmost care. Dishonest or short-sighted approach is absolutely not recommended.

Timing

As the salesperson learns about the closing techniques where a nudge is required to gain the call objective, it is a good idea to learn how to sense the right time when the prospect has been persuaded enough and his desire to buy has reached the peak. The timing gives the salesperson the clue when to use the closing technique. If the salesperson delays too long before using the closing technique, the prospect may make a favourable decision on his own. This may be all right except too much time has gone into the presentation. If the closing technique is used prematurely he may cause an objection to be raised. When the prospect is not fully convinced he needs a nudge to help him take a favourable decision. Therefore, proper timing will help the salesperson to attain his call objective quickly as well as to avoid objections. Prospects indicate through various means that their interest and desire are at a peak and they are ready for a favourable decision. The salesperson must be alert to the cues or the signs that tell that the right time to use the closing technique has come.

Sometimes the cues are obvious like the prospect asking, how soon can he get the samples? The salesperson should know that this is the right time to use the closing technique. The salesperson should reply, "In two days, shall I deliver it to you or have them mailed?" The salesperson is using the choice technique of call closing.

Another example of obvious clue is when the prospect says, "Can the survey be done after working hours?" The salesperson's reply should be, "certainly, I will have our engineer in at 5 pm tomorrow," once the clues are seen the salesperson should move quickly to close the call.

However, the clues normally are not so obvious. The salesperson should be alert to recognise the subtle clues like a smile of agreement or a nod other mention of a specific feature or benefit. Understanding the subtle clue the salesperson should use the losing technique. Prospect may start examining the sales aid and start some figure work, examine his stock he is on the verge of a favourable decision and the time is ripe for using the closing technique.

Summarising, the salesperson should be alert to understand the obvious and also the subtle clues given by the prospect and that is the time for the use of closing technique.

Departure

The next step of the call is the departure and there are a few rules for an effective departure. At the end of the call, either the salesperson has attained his objective or he has not achieved it, in either case he must make an effective departure.

In case the objective has been achieved the salesperson should reassure the prospect that he has made a wise decision. Most people want such a reassurance. "Your decision to renew your service contract with us was an intelligent one that will mean continuous economies for your organization," once the reassurance has been given it is best to leave quickly. Lingering on is not business like. Thank for the order and leave quickly is a golden rule. If a good rapport has been built a referral can be obtained before leaving.

However, if the objective has not been achieved remember the minor objective that keeps the door open and at least achieve it. The minor objectives should all be in line with the major call objectives, like, "when do you think it would be appropriate for me to contact you again". Or "we are organising a seminar/an exhibition and I would like to personally invite you for the same." As he gains the minor objective his feeling of disappointment will vanish and he will be ready for the next call in a positive frame of mind. The minor objective may ultimately lead the salesperson in achieving the major objective sooner than the salesperson can imagine. It is difficult to realise that the customer would get disillusioned with his existing supplier and that would be the time he will think of you if you have left a good favourable impression on him.

The salesperson should appreciate that while the main objective has not been attained, the minor objective has been achieved, as well as more information has been gathered about the prospect's company as well as about the prospect himself, that will be useful in future calls.

Post-Call Analysis

After completing the call it is necessary to analyse the call just completed. The analysis starts with comparing the result of the call with the established call objective. The comparison will help the salesperson plan his next call on this prospect. If the objective of the call has been achieved the salesperson can consider the manner in which to plan the next call to escalate the prospect up towards some long range goal. If the objective was not attained the salesperson should critically review to determine the cause of failure, starting from the formulation of the call objective, was it too ambitious, too broad or, perhaps too specific. The salesperson should take a look at the essential information gathered before making the call. Were there gaps in the information, and how serious were they?

Next he should analyse the tactics used. Were the techniques used either in approach, presentation, handling of objections or closing inadequate? Were they the cause of his failure to attain the objective of the call?

Summarising the salesperson should review the three steps the salesperson had taken in planning the call as follows:

- Establish the call objective
- Gather the essential information
- Select appropriate tactics

Only after such a critical review should the salesperson plan his next call on the same prospect.

Post-call analysis serves a primary purpose of providing a sound basis for planning the next call on the prospect. Post-call analysis can serve a secondary, broader purpose of helping the salesperson in his personal development. In other words, post-call analysis should point out some of the strengths and weaknesses in the salesperson's overall performance which should go beyond this one call. The salesperson must accept the primary responsibility for the call failure and use the post-call analysis for improving his call planning. For example, did the post-call review reveal a growing deficiency in some aspects of product knowledge, or weakness in a special skill such as group presentation? Did the call analysis, instead prove the existence of some new strengths in handling people or in thinking creatively?

Summarising, post-call analysis and personal development go hand in hand. The salesperson who uses each call experience for the purpose of personal improvement will move more rapidly toward a higher level of effective sales performance.

Defining Sales Obstacles

Following are the major obstacles that a salesperson faces during making a sale:

Habit—the customer is in the habit of using competitive product or service and finds it difficult to change.

Fear—the customer fears the unknown and has unwarranted feeling of impending trouble of risk or of loss that confuses his thinking and causes him to evade opportunities that help him to maximise his capabilities.

Price—the customer fails to see the benefits that outweigh their money value.

Complaint—the customer voices or feels dissatisfaction on the company's product or service.

Detail—the customer believes that the trouble that he has to take in buying the product is not worth the effort.

Lack of information—sales progress gets impeded when the salesperson has not informed the customer either due to his own lack of knowledge on the same or when the customer lacks the technical skills to understand the sales talk. At times the customer could be lacking in imagination to visualise the benefits of the product or even when the salesperson's expressions are unclear and confusing.

Competition—the customer believes that the competitive benefits would be more suited to him.

It must be understood that at times companies face competition from dissimilar things like a housewife may choose a new cooking range over a new washing machine.

Friendship-competition—the customer likes or respects competitive sales or other personnel or when the customer or the prospect believes that the competitive product will produce equal or greater amount of benefits to him.

Difficult personality—the prospect lacks emotional control and allows the difference of opinion to degenerate or he indulges in temper, rudeness or other unwarranted behaviour that retards progress towards sales.

Time—customer feels that the company's product does not merit the time to be spent on its purchase, or if the sales call is made too late and yet any further postponement would cause failure of the talks or if the delivery requirements of the customer are urgent and cannot be met.

Release—the prospect wants a release from further discussion of the subject.

Divided release—the prospect wants release as he sincerely or insincerely says he has to discuss the matter with someone not present.

Negative mood or manner—salesperson's talk is creating through his frame of mind, manner of speaking and acting unfavourable reaction in the prospect's mind causing dislike and lack of respect.

Poor judgement—when the salesperson does not care for the following:

- Prevailing conditions
- Comparing and separating right ways of doing things from wrong ways

- Planning the sales call—when to call, what to say and what to do
- Deciding how to use the product benefits in the talk from the customers' viewpoint.
- Noting the effect on the customer on what is said or done.
- Keeping control of emotions
- Using knowledge of human nature and practical selling methods secured through study, analysis and experience.

Countering the Obstacles

Benefit—describe any good result the customer will get from putting a good quality of the product to use.

Good quality—describe clearly the inherent trait or characteristic of the product or proposition or specific parts that make it possible to produce benefits when put to use.

Poor quality—clearly but tactfully describe traits and characteristics of an alternative product (competitive), that make it produces losses when put to use.

Loss—describe the losses poor quality will bring ever so subtly.

Proposition—inform the prospect the salesperson's name, company's name, brand, price, terms of business, delivery time.

Prestige—clearly describe the reputation and achievements of his company, its personnel, its products, services, and the customers, endorsers who lend their support.

Personal Prestige—inform the prospect of the salesperson's accomplishments, experience and good reputation that creates a feeling of respect and confidence in the prospect.

Pride—inform the prospect of the respect he enjoys with the salesperson by stating his achievements, his company's accomplishments, or by asking his advice on some matter that he can comment on.

Assurance—use any combination of words to qualify the above stated counters with tactful directness or that has power to calm or reassure the prospect.

Story—give an account of an event that indirectly informs the prospect of reasons, emotions or both that help him in deciding in the salesperson's favour.

Good turn—salesperson should perform or offer to perform any good turn that has power to build liking and respect and which places the prospect under no obligation.

Contact—classify the business or personal friendship between the salesperson and the prospect and mention friends, hobbies, other outside activities that establish common interests.

Explanation—make the meaning of technical terms used by classifying words and use similes, demonstrations, charts, presentations, photographs to clarify details of an operation.

Mood and manner—salesperson's frame of mind, manner of speaking and actions should help create liking and respect for him in the prospect's mind.

Question—salesperson should ask questions indirectly as autosuggestion to reconfirm the sales story has become effective. The question could also be to elicit information in the form of investigation question.

Progress signal—The salesperson should look out for signals from prospect in the form of comment or action to confirm that the salesperson has fully answered Prospect Viewpoint Questions adequately to keep things moving.

Good judgement—classifies mindset operation where the ways of doing and saying things is done by Multiple Analysis for producing maximum benefits.

Command—any command used directly or with other counters that effectively produce desired result from the prospect.

First Benefit—is the first result produced when a good quality is put to use.

Major Interest Benefit—expresses a result that is one of the prospect's objectives.

Favourable condition—is when the prospect's industry, company, group, or personal life from where he draws benefits or will benefit in future, and that is brought to his attention to prepare him to visualise that he has an opportunity to benefit still further through the salesperson's proposition. The favourable conditions also appeals to pride elements and gives him still greater power to help him see and appreciate his opportunity.

Unfavourable Conditions—any situation that creates losses for the prospect, for which the prospect, the salesperson or his company are not responsible and which brought to his attention discretely would help him see the need for the benefits of the salesperson's proposition.

Spar—salesperson can use Spar as a special action for mood and manner, assurance, and question, to meet the obstacles in a serene and considerate manner so that the objector's mind is reopened to reason.

21st Century Challenge

With the multitude of competitive companies, national, international and multinational in the fray, the salespersons are facing probably the greatest challenge ever encountered by any salesperson before. They are required to call on to the full, all their personal resources to meet the challenge. Some salespersons with years of experience have acquired a name for themselves in the market. Now they are required to compete with highly respected and internationally known brands by retaining the existing business and adding new channel members to cater to some hitherto virtually unknown markets.

The challenge is great and yet there are ways and means of countering it and coming out a winner. The salesperson with fortified skills, and with coordinated advertising campaigns is amply confident of meeting the challenges.

Challenges always bring opportunities and by effectively meeting the new competitive environment, the salesperson can develop self-pride as the salespersons grow in stature in the eyes of the management, channel members and the customers. The main objectives of learning about the twenty-first century challenges are the following:

- To empower the salespersons to meet the challenges with new skills, as their job becomes more rewarding and satisfying with new ideas and methods for achieving profitable results that will give you pride
- To improve the confidence level of the channel members in the company as the salespersons with skills and ability would provide help the channel members in solving difficult problems.

- To help the salespersons in effectively meeting the competition and with success their stature and value in the eyes of the company and the customers will increase. Salespersons should develop better personal resources for achieving the kind of sales and profits that will enhance their prestige and importance in their company and with the channel members.

Analysing present knowledge plans the students should attempt to understand the following:

- Describe what they consider the basic goals or objectives of a salesperson's job.
- Describe the Critical Success Factors for any company from the customer's, channel member's and the company's viewpoint
- Describe the type of relationship they should have with the channel members in the present highly competitive age.
- Pick up a well known product and list down all possible benefits that would accrue to the customer by its use.
- Describe what is considered important for fighting competition.

Understanding people and dealing with them effectively.

Given below is Sales Analysis Chart:

As effective sellers the entire approach to sales has to be customer oriented. Hence the first analysis is from the customer or the prospect's viewpoint as follows:

- Attention—do I like and respect the salesperson?
- Interest—what can his proposition do for me?
- Desire—can he support his claim?
- Decision—is it the best thing to do now?
- Sale or action—I will buy or act.

Given below are the emotion movers that persuade the buyer into favourable action.

- Mood and manner
- Personal prestige
- Good turn
- Contact
- Assurance
- Question
- Command

Reason Movers

- Benefit
- Good quality
- Poor quality (negative for competition)
- Loss
- Proposition
- Prestige

- Explanation
- Story
- Good judgement

The sale calls face the following obstacles:
- Habit
- Fear
- Price
- Complaint
- Detail
- Lack of information
- Competition
- Friendship competition
- Difficult personality
- Time
- Release
- Divided release
- Negative mood and manner
- Poor judgement

As is noticed there are favourable and unfavourable conditions when the salesperson has to use or perceive the following:
- Use test question
- Perceive signal

Obstacles can be handled by using spar or practice or solution efforts.
- Scene one

A benefit mover describes clearly good results that a prospect will get from putting to use a good quality.

Material benefits examples:
- Save thirty thousand rupees
- Reduce switching costs by 10%
- Bring in more customers at lunch time
- Enable you to finish your work in half the time
- Improve the strength of the foundation

Physical benefits—examples:
- Make you more comfortable
- Save you that heavy lifting
- Prevent foot, leg, back pain
- You can work in a more upright position
- Keep the dust out of your nose lungs

Mental benefits – examples:

- You get more satisfaction out of your work
- It will take a load out of your mind
- Dealing with the company will be pleasant
- The children will be perfectly safe
- It may please the big boss

The benefit movers are have certain powers and some limitations too as given below.

Powers

The benefit movers enable the salesperson to predict for his prospect listener, the interesting and desirable results of doing what he has proposed. It appeals to the listener's basic motive for taking action in favour of the company. It answers the Prospects Viewpoint Question, " What good will your plan do?" and therefore noblest salesperson to talk from the prospect's viewpoint and best interest.

Limitations

The benefit movers lack the power to support itself. It cannot answer the Prospect Viewpoint Question, "Can you support your claim" and therefore, unsupported, cannot give the prospect reason to believe benefit predictions or claims.

Scene 2

Good quality movers examples

A good quality mover describes the inherent trait or characteristic of a proposition or a specific part that makes it possible to produce benefits when put to use.

Good quality in products

- Fine workmanship
- Improved design
- Mounted on live rubber
- Top grain cowhide
- Spring steel coils
- Three ply construction

Good quality in service

- Our servicemen are well trained and experienced
- Company is sound in finance
- We have carefully planned direct mail campaign
- We take hourly meter readings
- We apply heat evenly
- Our methodology is well tested in the field
- It is the practical way

Good quality in persons

- Honest and steady
- Skilled and experienced
- Intelligent
- Alert and enterprising
- Good natured
- Full of common sense
- Tactful
- Physically strong

Powers and Limitations of the Good Quality Mover

Powers

The good quality mover enables salesperson to tell his prospect what makes possible the beneficial results of using the product he is offering. It has power to support the benefit claim and get them believed.

Limitations

The Good Quality Mover lacks the power to create interest and desire since it cannot describe the basic reason for buying, which is to obtain the benefit.

Analysing a talk for its movers

The student need to identify the benefit or the good quality mover as the analysis is made.

Example 1

A bank equipment salesperson sees in a bank that the bus carrying bank money was being bumped against the walls, scratching and marring the walls. He got an idea and he expressed himself as follows in his talk with the bank personnel.

Salesperson—you could easily protect your walls and decorations by placing a continuous rubber bumper at the bottom of each bus. That would eliminate the scratches and the accidents the buses make and save a lot of repair and maintenance costs.

Prospect—what are the bumpers like?

The talk has started revolving around the salesperson's objective.

Example 2

An engineer wants his prospect to appreciate the benefits that can be gained by the use of a automatic oil pump.

Engineer—machine shutdowns will be reduced to a minimum because this positive gear oil pump will automatically keep every bearing coated with oil.

Example 3

Salesperson-you always wanted to guard your workers' health, I have just the practical way to protect their lungs. Got the time to hear about it?

Prospect—I will make time. What is it?

Benefits are possible because of the good qualities of the product.

Example 4

The shirt will be comfortable and long wearing because it is carefully tailored using terry silk material. It stays fresh, resists soiling all day long.

Analysing product for sale movers

Salesperson needs to understand the sequencing of his thought process as he builds the benefit, good quality mover's story. The analysis studies different kinds of reasons, as given below:

Product—Chest of drawers—extension arms

Benefits	Good Quality
File drawer can be rolled in and out of the cabinet rapidly with least effort Saves operators energy Reduce errors due to fatigue Gets the desired correspondence quicker Time and expense saved	Sturdy, steel extension arms using giant size ball bearings

Analysis of a proposition having both product and service parts

Market Analysis	Benefits	Good Qualities
Copy writing	First benefit-make a study of problems for which advertising is required Write the copy then perfect it Create copy that will get read Bring inquiries	Trained and skilled copy writers, directed by experience and able supervisors
Art work Printing Papers		

Analysing a faulty situation for correction-machine operation.

The correct plan		The situation	
Benefits	Right way	Wrong way	Losses
4. Keeps wrists for touching the bar 5. Machine will space perfectly	3. By holding wrists in arched position	Machine operator's wrists sag slightly at times	Cuffs and wrists touch space bars that causes machine to space at wrong time.

Correction Talk

Salesperson – (in a pleasant manner) the easy way to make the machine space perfectly is by holding the wrists higher than usual. That keeps cuffs and wrists from even the lightest touch of the space bar. You get perfect results.

4-column situation and correction analysis.

- Wrong actions
- Kitchen utensils stored where they cause the cook to take extra steps, not justified
- Lawn mowing done in a shaggy way
- Child strews things in a room which looks dirty

Select a situation and analyses using the analysis sequence.

Write short talk on correction of the situation, using the presentation sequence stating only the benefits which the right way of doing things will provide.

The thinking sequence starts with the wrong way and related losses and next come the right way and the benefits.

However, the presentation sequence starts by presenting the benefits of the right way. The salesperson can mention the wrong and the losses only after pointing out the right way benefits.

Examples of Poor Quality and Loss Movers

Poor quality movers clearly but tactfully describe the inherent traits and characteristics of a proposition, a situation or alternative product and plans that make it probable that it will produce looses when put to use. It is recommended for highlighting the competitive products.

Loss mover clearly but tactfully describes an undesirable result of putting poor quality product to use.

Examples

Steel corners of the truck carrying money will mar metal work and plaster walls that will cause considerable repair expense.

Engineers have found that reinforcement of steel bars less tan 0.25 inch thick are too light and will fail to support even a slight overload

Untested methods might prove unworkable

Men lacking in experience can cause roads accidents

Power and Limitations of Poor Quality and Loss Movers

Powers

Help listeners to make wise choice when used after the Benefit and Good Quality Movers.

Limitations

When used alone, they often sound threatening, one-sided and arouse opposition.

Conclusion

Benefit and good quality movers are compared with poor quality and loss movers to help prospect reach the right decision.

Salesperson – in cold climate Kota stone will stand up well because its square edges will hold mortar better during summer when the snow would melt. Slate has slanting thin edges which often fail to hold mortar when snow is melting and the sun is hot. Kota stone is cheaper to remain and hold appearance longer I would recommend it.

(Students should analyse the sentence by segregating the benefits, good quality, loss and bad quality).

The material salesperson should arrange the 4-column analysis of sale movers as given below:

Kota stone Good qualities	Kota stone Benefits	Slate Poor quality	Slate Losses
Kota stone has thick, strong slabs, with square edges	Will hold mortar well in freezing and melting weather. Retain looks and appearance for years and is cheaper to maintain	Slate has razor edge thin slanting edges	Mortar will split away from edges during melting season, requiring expensive repairs

Multiple Analysis of Products

The analysis covers the benefits and losses of different products, including competitive products as it helps in making a comparative study on the product having more benefits and less losses in comparison to the competitive product.

Kota stone

Benefits	Qualities	Losses
Holds mortar well under cool conditions or hot weather. Retain good appearance for years at low upkeep cost. Save on extra labour cost in a few years	Large sawn slabs having square edges one inch thick	More labour required to handle and to set. Costs about Rs. 10000 more in labour to install

Slate

Benefits	Qualities	Losses
Provides delicate beauty in pattern and colour Easier and faster to handle and save about Rs. 10,000 on labour of installing	Has a variety of colours and scallop edged shapes. Edges thin and sharp	Mortar splits away from edges during snow melting season, beauty is marred, repair expense estimate at Rs. 5000 annually for over a ten year period

Analysis can be made in such a manner that only the benefits are highlighted as the losses are listed down by underplaying them. This gives the salesperson better idea on how to manage prospect's questions on competitive product. The best course ultimately is to lay stress on his own product's good qualities and benefits that accrue through its use rather than decry competition where the chances of going wrong with incorrect statements are present.

Multiple Analysis of a Situation

The salesperson should make an effort to find the true interests of competitors with most benefits and fewest losses will be found.

Galvanised Conduit

Benefits	Problem	Losses
Initial cost less to consumer, it will help the dealer procure the order and a quick sure profit will be made by the dealer	Can the galvanised conduit be sold for use where acid fumes are present	Acid will get through the conduit. Corrosion, stoppages will occur. Dealer's reputation will be damaged
Benefits	**Problem**	**Losses**
Consumer will find it will stand acid for years. Will save more than its cost by avoiding a single breakdown More profit for the dealer Effort to sell the right product will get respect of the buyers	2. Will there be stress on the buyer to buy zinc conduit with sealed surface?	3. Purchase will cost 40% more 4. Buyer may place order on someone else as his opposition may increase

In order to understand the above stated analyses the following dialogue gives real life situations that will take the students as close to corporate world as possible.

Reasoning Process in a Multi-Comparison Form

Salesperson—(approaches his dealer, greets him pleasantly, shows appreciation for a new vehicle the dealer has purchased. Takes care of routine business and says calmly)- I talked to my office and was told you and one of your contractors were working on a major wiring job with the Singh Corporation (pauses, waits for reply).

Dealer (says sadly)—yes, Ramesh, you know, the contractor is and he tells me that a young assistant to the Works Manager is deaf to everything but low price.

Salesperson (slowly and thoughtfully) I see, well, he can make sure, quick profit that way.

Dealer—I guess that the young fellow is really tough. He is trying for a shrewd bargain. Just a wise guy.

Salesperson—yes, I see, how much does the company need protection? How corrosive is the acid?

Dealer—plenty. That is what worries me.

Salesperson—I can see how you feel, but as a guess, how soon the corrosion might develop into power failures and production stoppages, if these stocks are used?

Dealer—well, it will take some time, may be months. But a price-chiseller usually gets what he pays for. And some contractors go for low bids and quote these stocks

Salesperson—it is a tough situation. I see that. There is a big profit if zinc conduits are used for all of us. But what will happen if the stocks are used when wire failure starts? Will this young fellow convince his boss that the contractor and us are to be blamed and we will get a black eye with the local business.

Dealer—it could hurt the contractor. But people ought to know that a dealer only fills a contractor's orders.

Salesperson—they should know that. Do you think it would put the contractor in right with the customers Works Manager if he went to him and helped him to see the years of protection he will get by using zinc conduits?

Dealer—well-maybe. Making a big issue of protecting each days production might even make a big change in the young fellow's thinking and make it unnecessary to go up. But as you know these contractors often make low bids and do not fight for zinc conduits enough. But if he had your kind of backing he would feel strong. So how about going to the customer with him? I think I can fix a meeting just now.

Salesperson—it is a deal. I will try to make the young fellow or his boss see how much more good the zinc conduit will do. Make sure that the contractor understands that in or lose we insist on zinc conduits.

Dealer—right boss (picks the phone).

Prospects Basic Needs and Desires

Most people have certain common basic needs and desires as given below:

Security—people need protection from loss of what they have protection to health, income, skills, mental powers, their company assets that are connected to their security and survival and of others whose welfare they have at heart.

Progress—people want to improve their personal and their team or group conditions, want to learn more, to do things better, besides they want the following:

- To earn more
- To live better
- To give better things and opportunities to their families
- To do work that increases in importance and responsibility
- To help their company so that in turn they get more opportunities

Respect—people want the respect of customers, peers, employees, bosses, families and neighbours.

Satisfaction and Enjoyment from Work and Life—people want a sense of achievement, peace of mind, happy associations, a sense of belonging, a feeling that their work is important and beneficial, besides they want the happiness of doing more than just for money.

Responsibilities and Objectives of the Prospects Job

Once the salesperson appreciates and understands the type of responsibilities, the prospects have he would be in a better position to tailor-made his sales presentation. A few of the responsibilities and job objectives are given below as examples:

President	Production Manager	Materials Manager
Keep company financially sound for survival, security and development	Keep production levels high, costs low enough to beat competition	Keep company adequately supplied and able to operate efficiently
Long-term planning	Constantly improve production facilities	Avoid wastage of company funds
Build skilled competent management team for profitable successful operation	Constantly improve people skills, knowledge	Constantly improve the knowledge, skills, performance and morale of department personnel.
Build company's brand equity	Improve health standards, reduce accident rate	Keep company's prestige high with sellers and secure helpful ideas and coopertion from them
Encourage and guide morale building human relations	Maintain and improve human relations. Keep morale high and be respected	Get along with company's other departments, hold respect of their people and get department's helpful service fully understood and used
Get along with others and be respected	Get along with others both vertically and horizontally, while getting the things right	Get satisfaction and pleasure out of work
Get satisfaction and pleasure out of work	Get satisfaction and pleasure out of work	

Given below is similar statement for the supervisors and the workers.

Supervisors	Workers
Get along with management and the workers	Be respected as a person by management and fellow workers
Get work done on schedule	Feel that the work done is important to the company and the customer
Help maintain and improve quality	

Keep costs low enough to compete and serve customer's best interest
Successfully interpret workers problems and attitudes to management
Successfully interpret company problems and policies to workers
Hold respect of workers and others in supervision and management
Handle complaints effectively and diplomatically and avoid possible grievances
Be successful in persuading others to accept and cooperate with proposed ideas, plans
Get satisfaction, pleasure and reward out of work and life

Steady work and good pay
Good bosses
Chance to get ahead
Good working conditions
Job satisfaction, peace of mind and happiness

Salespersons having learnt the value of customer analysis needs to fit the benefits to prospect's job objectives as given below:

Example 1

The salesperson is talking to a road building contractor whose company security often depends upon making a profit in closely bid jobs. Hence, that becomes his job objective and a major interest area.

Salesperson (for road grader is talking to road contractor whom he knows well) – to help our road contractor customers make a profit, our company makes a constant study of problems. The study goes right back to our designers. Take a tough problem of making a profit on closely bid jobs. One thing done, to help cut costs, to equip the controls of our new road grader with an improved hydraulic dumper. It eases pressure surges and eliminates the shock of starting and stopping the cutting blade. An operator can now place the blade faster and make more accurate cuts and yet do 20% more work per hour.

Example 2

The salesperson talks to the supervisor of the above stated road contracting company. He has learnt that this prospect has had trouble in keeping good operators because of many rural road jobs.

Road grader salesperson – to help keep good persons on the job when they are long way from home, our designers have equipped the controls of the new model with improved hydraulic dumper. It eases pressure surges and eliminates shocks of starting and stopping the blade. With less effort, the operator can place the blade faster, make more accurate cuts, and do 20 per cent more work. The workmen love the machine and they actually stay on the job longer.

The talk continues—
Fit the Movers to Prospects Job Objectives
The table given below summarises the way it is done.

Part	Benefits	Good Qualities
Damper	Eases pressure surges Cutting blade starting stopping shocks eliminated Blade placement by operator faster Cut more accurate 20 per cent more work with less effort Cut operating costs Make a profit on closely bid jobs	New model controls have an improved hydraulic damper

Bridge of Understanding

The first benefit expresses the first helpful thing a good quality will do for any user.

A Major Interest Benefit expresses a final result that is one of the prospect's objectives.

Operating cost cut	Up to 20% more work with less effort	Keep the depth of cut more accurate	Operator can place blade faster	Shock of starting and stopping cutting eliminated	Eases pressure surges
Bridge of understanding Major interest benefit Make a profit on closely bid jobs Road Grader				Good quality New model controls have an improved hydraulic damper	

Mood and Manner Mover

A person's frame of mind and manner of speaking and acting that help to create liking and respect is a Mood and Manner Mover.

When a listener/prospect sees a salesperson exhibit such Mood and Manner as the following, his emotions are favourably influenced.

- Consideration and respect
- Business-like intent
- Friendliness
- Enthusiasm
- Confidence
- Tactfulness
- Emotional control
- Patience

Besides the above, when a listener / prospect sees a salesperson exhibit such moods and manners as follows his emotions are favourably influenced.

- Earnestness
- Seriousness
- Due concern
- Sympathy
- Thoughtfulness
- Alertness
- Self-respect
- Resolution

The inviting appearance of a shop, displays, product, brochure, person on the counter, that create a favourable impression and helps to create liking and respect are also classified under Mood and Manner Movers.

Negative Mood and Manner

On the other hand there are Negative Mood and Manner that work as obstacles as given below:

A salesperson's frame of mind and manner of speaking and acting that impresses a listener/prospect unfavourably and that creates dislike and lack of respect form Negative Mood and Manner Obstacle.

When a salesperson shows the following to the prospect through looks and actions his (prospects) emotions are affected unfavourably.

- Selfishness
- Arrogance
- Impatience
- Slyness
- Overconfidence
- Brittle temper
- Insincerity
- Superiority
- Dislike

When a prospect sees a salesperson whose looks and actions indicate the following the prospect's emotions are affected unfavourably.

When the appearance of a shop, display, brochure is uninviting and creates an atmosphere that puts the prospect in a negative mood the Negative Mood and Manner is active.

Is Negative Mood and Manner an Obstacle?

Do the Negative Moods and Manners, shown in these examples, place a negative influence over all that is said and therefore weaken or ruin their reasoning power?

Example 1

Supervisor—do you want to stay out of trouble with the inspectors? If so, watch these edges better. You are getting careless.

Example 2

Salesperson—listen, pack the glass right hereafter that is the only way to save us from this kind of trouble.

Emotion moves used to present reason movers.

Example 1

An assurance mover is any combination used to present other movers with tactful directness, or that has power to calm or reassure the prospect.

The Question Mover

A question used by the salesperson to present other movers indirectly is a suggestion question.

A command mover is any command used by itself or in conjunction with some other movers that effectively produce a desired action from the prospect.

A story mover is an account of an occurrence that indirectly informs the prospect of reason movers, emotion movers or both.

An assurance mover, presents benefit ideas positively.

Example

Machinery Salesperson-yes, Mr. Gupta, your men will have even more protection than they have now.

The question mover, used to present benefits respectfully and open the door to more positive tactics.

Example

Salesperson to experienced retailer—what would you think of this idea for getting faster turnover on storage cabinets? (shows window display plans)

Retailer Prospect—why do you have household items rather than office items in two of these cabinets?

Salesperson—I think it will catch the eye of many of the women who pass the shop and bring some of them in to buy cabinets or some other items.

(Talk continues)

The common mover, used to present reason movers.

Example

Salesperson (to retailer)—take the lower profit, faster turnover plan!

The story mover, used to present reason movers indirectly.

Example

Salesperson—over in Kolkata last week I saw how Hindustan Motors is making their big reduction in rejects. First of all, they are practically eliminating paint fading by. . . (story continues).

Food for Thought

It is interesting to understand that conclusions made are the product of a person's own mind and they become the basis on which he plans and acts. See how well you agree with the following:

- The basic motive in taking any action is to benefit. A prospect can become interested only when he sees benefits available
- A prospect is a person or group that can be benefited to a desirable degree and who has the money or credit or is able to take the action proposed
- Effective planning of a sale begins with the finding of benefits that will be of interest to each prospect, benefits for himself and others whose interest he has at heart
- The Benefit Mover has the power to create interest by answering the Prospect-Viewpoint question, "What good will your plan do?"
- The Benefit, Good Quality, Poor Quality and Loss Movers have power to develop interest into desire to take action since they answer the Prospect-Viewpoint question, "Can you support your (benefit) claim?"

Three forms in which the prospects reason, when they make it clear that their purpose is to benefit are as given below:

- The Benefit and God Quality Form
- The Comparison Form
- The Conclusion Form

Any form of reasoning can be in Assurance style, Question style, Command or Story style, or in a mixture of these styles. The Assurance and Command styles are direct, the Question and Story styles are indirect.

Styles of presenting Reason Movers appeal mainly to the emotions and have power to open the listening mind to the reception of speaker's reasoning.

The Mood and Manner Mover is an essential part of all presentation styles. It is the Emotion Mover that goes to work first in creating "liking and respect" and in answering the Prospect-viewpoint question, "Do I like and respect you".

Tact is practiced by avoiding the expression of Negative Impulse Judgements.

The recognition of Forms of Reasoning and Styles of Presenting Reason Movers will provide a guide for practicing to-the-point reasoning of Reason Movers. Such practise provides a background to present ideas effectively without conscious effort.

It is not expected that facing his prospect the salesperson will pause and say to himself, "Now I will use the Conclusion Form and present my ideas in Assurance Style" anymore than he will pause and think, "Now I will use a noun, a verb and an adverb."

PERSONAL PRESTIGE MOVER

A Personal Prestige Mover clearly describes the good reputation or achievement of the salesperson's company, its personnel, its products, its services or customers, endorsers who lend prestige. It provides the prospect with evidence that benefit claims can be believed.

Example 1

Purchase Manager to the Purchase Committee—the most experienced and reliable person in the paper business is Raghav Gupta.

Example 2

Prospect-on phone—Mr. Mathur told me of the clerical time and expense you have saved him. I would be happy if you come over to see me.

The examples show that good reputation built previously is active. In the next example the speaker tries to build his prestige.

Example 1

Salesperson—during the two years I was at the factory, a problem in electronic controls crept up and we could solve it in no time.

Example 2

Manager to worker—sure, I know this machine, Verma. I operated it for four years.

Personal prestige can be built by action.

Example

Salesperson dismantles part of the machine he is selling and then puts it together.

Limitation

The power of the Personal Prestige Mover gets weak if the listener gets the impression that the speaker is trying to brag or is talking mainly to build his own confidence.

Appeal to Pride Mover

An Appeal to Pride Mover confirms the salesperson's respect for the prospect by stating the achievements of the prospect, his company or by asking for advice.

Example 1

Salesperson to his dealer—as I came in I heard some persons saying some nice things about the excellent job done on your display windows. You are making quite a success with you, is it not?

Example 2

Salesperson to another non-competitive salesperson—we are working on the colour scheme of our carton. Since you have done pioneering job in this area we would welcome any advice you would kindly give.

Example 3

Salesperson—our engineers thought that a reduction in maintenance costs would be one of the main things an engineer of your special experience would demand.

Example 4

Service Engineer—the engineers in our head office will understand how you feel. They know you have always been fair-minded; so I am sure I can have this corrected in a day or two.

Example 5

Service Manager—our Delhi Manager wrote to me about how well you planned the increase in sales of your engines in North India.

Example 6

Salesperson—I really like the hardwood shop floors, they look nice and are long lasting.

Misuse of Compliments

Example 1

Salesperson—you have a really well appointed office. It looks great.

The prospect has heard such a remark often over the past six years and further, he knows his office is nice but nothing unusual. On the day of the compliment it was rather dirty.

Example 2

Salesperson—you have made one of the best displays in the windows that I have seen. However, the way the special products are displayed really look shabby from the street.

If you soft paddle your criticism with a compliment the listener will always expect criticism whenever you offer a compliment.

Example 3

Salesperson of bank equipment to bank teller—you sure can count money fast.

Teller—I ought to, I have been doing it for twenty years.

A prospect may not get any pleasure or satisfaction from a compliment on a task he performs as routine. On the other hand, a compliment put in a Question Style like, 'in counting these brand new notes how do you keep a few from sticking together?' can appeal to Pride Power.

Good Turn Mover

A Good Turn Mover is a favour or free service performed or offered by the salesperson that has the power to build liking and respect and that places the prospect under no obligation.

Example 1

Salesperson—you can have my copy of the Planning Commission's Report on the Five Year Plan.

Example 2

Salesperson to the prospect—your supplier is in Rampur, is it not. I am going there tomorrow on business. Suppose I drop in at the supplier's place and see if I speed up things a little.

Example 3

Salesperson to prospect—I just heard you are planning to go to Jaipur next monday. I too have plans of going there by car. You are most welcome to come with me and I will drop you in Jaipur wherever you want.

Example 4

Salesperson for retail prospect—I have time on hand, if you want I can count the stock just arrived for you.

Example 5

An experienced engineer solved his prospect's problem unconnected to his own business. In this way he did a good turn and later, the prospect said to another person in his company, "that fellow really knows his business" (Personal prestige is earned through doing a good turn).

Contact Mover

A Contact Mover is defined as classifying the business or personal friendship developed between a salesperson and a customer or the mention of common friends, hobbies, and other outside interest activities that help establish common interests.

When a prospect likes and treats a salesperson with more consideration because he is impressed by his Mood and Manner a contact has begun. When a prospect is favourably impressed on finding that the salesperson is having a common friend or a person he respects, a degree of contact is formed. When a prospect and the salesperson love to talk about a practice the same hobby a contact is active. The strongest type of contact comes about when the customer appreciates the benefits that the salesperson has enabled him to enjoy.

Examples of Contact Mover in Action

Example 1

Salesperson—I am Ramesh from Colgate company. Your friend Mr Kapil suggested I drop in and introduce myself.

Prospect—oh yes, Kapil phoned me about you.

Example 2

Salesperson—I may have a solution to your leaks problem. Can I call you tomorrow, I want half an hour of your time.

Prospect—how about nine thirty?

Common Uses of the Command, Question and Assurance Movers

The student must understand that the Command, Question and Assurance Movers are not used only to present Reason Movers. The following examples:

Example 1

Command Mover—command used for routine directions.

Salesperson to associate—look at the second paragraph son.

Example 2

Command used to calm the customer.

Salesperson on phone—do not worry I will do your job.

Mrs. Raj—it will do the cleaning easily.

Example 1

Question Mover used to elicit needed information.

Salesperson—at your Rampur plant how many barrels of oil you use daily?

Example 1

Assurance Mover used to calm

Salesperson—I know how you feel. I understand, you can rely on the delivery date

Assurance used to calm help prepare the prospect to listen to reason

Assurance mover used to instil trust and confidence and to help prepare prospect to open his mind to reason.

Example

Salesperson—there are four models Mr. Roy. All are built differently. The one that will do your work best is model 3 (follow with the Benefit Mover).

The first two assurances used in the example have power to build confidence in the prospect and they therefore help prepare him to open his mind to the reception of benefit ideas.

The purpose of emotion movers is to place the listener in a mood that will open his psyche to reason. The effective use of emotion movers, which is so much part of effective personality, is made possible by sales analysis. Such analysis often enables a salesperson to make specific improvements in his use of emotion movers. The foundation of instinctive or conscious utilisation of such movers is the conviction that the listener can be benefited to a degree that will outweigh the cost.

Getting the Sales Talks Started

Example 1

Salesperson—I am Ramesh of Shiv Papers and since I am new to the area I came in to introduce myself.

Prospect—glad you did. Have a chair.

Salesperson—thank you. For the past five years I have worked out of Jaipur. By the way before I left Mr. Gopal said to say hello for him.

Prospect—Gopal? I saw him at the Mumbai convention last month. Good man.

Salesperson—yes that he is. During the past three years he has taught me a lot about producing low cost frozen food boxes.

Secretary—sorry for interrupting Mr. Verma is here to see you.

Prospect—all right. Ask him to come in.

Salesperson—rising, thanks for letting me call on you without appointment. I am glad to have met you.

Prospect—yes, call me up in a week or so. I want to hear about the low cost boxes experience.

Example 2

Salesperson is making a repeat call on a customer who has been benefited a lot from the salesperson's company in the past. Personal prestige and contact are therefore established, plus a reasonable degree of liking and respect. On his last call he created interest in a plan he proposed, was stopped by a problem and now he starts in a friendly and pleasant manner.

Salesperson—how are you Mr. Verma?

Prospect—fine. Thanks. Have a seat. I will be right back. (Leaves and comes back shortly) been to movies lately?

Salesperson—have not had a chance. I was called back to the Head Office. And while I was there I think we found the solution to your colour draining problem.

Prospect—is that so?

Salesperson— (continues his story)

Example 3-Inquiry

Prospect—(enters the office and asks) is your salesperson named Sinha in?

Salesperson—(who is in) how do you do sir?

Prospect—my name is P.K. Agarwal of the Planet Publishing House. I have seen your desk top publishing unit with BB and company in working status. I thought I would come in and see the new model 55 you advertise.

Salesperson—good. Come with me Mr. Agarwal and I will show you the model. It is in the demonstration room down the hall. (PAUSE) I appreciate your coming to see us and I am glad I happened to be here too. (PAUSE)—Do you have a problem something like what they had at the BB?

Prospect—no, we send out about ten thousand notices per month and they are printed as you can see. Raja of BB Company thinks your process might save us considerable money and I want to find that out.

Salesperson-(decides that the sale has MOVED into Desire zone for him and as he demonstrates the model he will carry on for rupees savings as his Major-Interest Benefit says)- I think we will find that Mr. Raja is right.

Types of Calls and Objectives of the Calls

The completely creative call exists when the prospect has no intention of buying and when motion has to be created from the start.

Various objectives of the completely creative call are given below:

- To get acquainted, build personal prestige, make a contact and secure essential information for future use.
- To get permission to make a survey or a demonstration or to get the prospect to try or test a product.
- To start and move the sale to interest, desire or decision.

Partly Created Sales

The Inquiry—when the prospect has been moved to interest or desire to buy by means of advertising, satisfied customers, articles in magazines, and make an inquiry, one type of partly created sales exist.

Objectives in dealing with an inquiry—to build liking and respect for self, to find out how far the sale has progressed, to pick the sale up at whatever point it has reached and move it forward as far as possible by use of Emotion and Reason Movers.

The Favourable-Attention Call—when on his first call the salesperson finds that his company or product or plan is already known and respected to the extent that favourable attention is easily secured, or when someone has built personal prestige for him or when a user has created interest for him.

The problem for the salesperson is to capitalise upon the help secured and to use Emotion and Reason Movers to develop the sale further.

The Follow-up Call exists when the salesperson has gained attention on a previous call or created interest and develop it into desire to buy.

The objective is to maintain favourable attention by means of Emotion Movers and to move the sale forward by use of Emotion and Reason Movers.

The service call exists when the purpose of the visit is to give service or find out if service is needed or to clear up misunderstandings or errors.

The main purpose of these classifications of the types of calls is to make it clear that wherever progress has already been made, it is not necessary to start back from the beginning but to use movers to take it from there and carry on from the progress point that exists.

Prestige Movers

When the good reputation of a company, its personnel, product or service or its customers and endorsers provides the prospect with evidence that benefit claim can be believed, the prestige mover is active.

Examples of Prestige Movers in Action

User Prestige

The Delhi plant of Smart ACs has been using the system for the past ten years.

The Parliament house, the President's house and the PMs house have all been renovated by our company.

Jayant Enterprises have been using our accounting software for the last six years.

Company and Personnel Prestige

- The new monitoring software is one of the greatest achievements of our research laboratories.
- Each one of our GMs has received national commendation for their efforts.
- Our company has been the pioneer in seamless tubing, a fact that makes us proud.
- We are responsible of at least 70% of production of artificial rubber in the country.
- We are the largest and oldest company in the business and also the most respected one.
- We hold the record of 100% zero defect production.

Product or Service Prestige

- More of these painting machines are employed in the automobile industry than any other.
- It was the first cooker in the market and has remained the market leader ever since.
- The TV manufacturers of the country have taken our standards as their norms.
- Yes, this road paving machine is used in every state of the country.

Prestige of Process, Plan, Idea, Policy

- The plan has been approved by the Government recognised Railway Reconstruction Authority.
- The formula has worked in managing the mines in Bihar.
- Our MD has approved of the idea to merge the two production units.
- Problems in the use of the Prestige Mover.

Example A

Systems salesperson (after introducing himself, and having been invited to have a chair, thanks the prospect and says easily).

From your recent magazine article I learnt of your interest in reducing the cost of operating records as well as machines. Since a practical and economically operated system for inventory control record has been developed by our company I hope you would like to see it. I have come with an invitation for you to visit our factory to give you a demonstration. Could you give me about ten minutes now.

Prospect—let us hear it.

Example B

Systems salesperson (after introducing himself and having been invited to have a seat, thanks the prospect and says proudly).

My company is the oldest and largest in the field. We serve the Brass Group of Companies. As an example of the advantage there is, in dealing with us, here is the inventory control system we produce for that group.

The Story Mover

A Story Mover is an account of an occurrence that indirectly informs the prospect of the Reason Movers, Emotion Movers or both.

Example 1

A salesperson whose products are industrial motors had, three weeks before, been told by a customer that cutting operating costs was his major problem. Now he returns and on his follow-up call, is told by a secretary that the prospect is about to leave for a trip through one of the company plants. Here is how he uses emotion and benefit movers to answer the first two prospect-view questions and thereafter uses the story to provide evidence that his claim can be believed.

Salesperson—how are you Mr. Singh.

Prospect—very good, thanks.

Salesperson—do you remember that last month you had told me cost cutting was a major problem.

Prospect—it still is. I am about to leave for the plant and that is one thing on my mind.

Salesperson—good. I think I have an idea that can save them about 20% on finishing bases.

Prospect—is that so? What is it?

Salesperson—by using a 10 hp motor instead of a smaller one and by using carbide cutters a smooth finish can be made with one fast cut. The reason I am sure of this is that I have seen it done at the Banguluru plant of HMT. As they stated, chips fall like graveldeep and smooth cuts are made and their cost reduction has come to more than 25%.

Prospect—but what about the chatter?

Salesperson—I am glad you thought of that. They control it by. . . (talk continues).

Example 2

Salesperson—(to customer who has just taken delivery of 10 drums of transformer oil)—I dropped in to thank you for your lube oil order and to make sure you have received intact. Your stores manager tells me that he is planning to move it into the closed store area this afternoon which is a good news this will ensure that the oil is protected from moisture and hold its dielectric strength. The reason I am concerned is that two years ago a customer in Mumbai insisted upon taking delivery of 50 drums of the same oil, while they did not have storage room for the same. When I checked it had not been stored yet but they promised to get it under cover. However, it stayed outside through out the monsoon. When they wanted to use it they found that its dielectric strength was affected so much by the moisture that it had to be condemned and they lost the entire investment.

The stories are given in some detail to show the various reason movers they contain. Examples of some stories that have been used:

- Story that contains appeal to Pride, Personal Prestige, Contact Movers. Used to build liking and respect.
- Story that presents benefit and other movers indirectly. Used to answer prospect's viewpoint questions.
- Story of a company achievement in developing products, services or plans that increased benefits to users. Used to support benefit claims.
- Stories telling endorsements won from doctors, scientists, associations used to support benefit claims.
- Story that presents poor quality and loss movers indirectly, following the direct use of benefit and good quality movers.

Research

Some examples of the use of prestige movers to research the need of company's products.

Example 1

Salesperson—I heard about your big increase in sales in Gujarat, your dealers must be full of praise of your products and their lasting quality.

Prospect—we are proud of our record there, and all through the area for that matter.

Salesperson—the reason I came today to see you was on the problem of increasing the life of your cutting tools. . .

Example 2

Salesperson—the last time I had called on you I was told about how you started out small and built this big business empire. The most interesting thing was how you made all the rich people of the town your customers.

It made me think that with such a fine trade, you are in a special positing to make a nice profit on high quality storage cabinets.

Favourable Condition

A favourable condition is a situation in a prospect's industry, company, group or personal life that he is already benefiting or will benefit and that, when brought to his attention helps prepare him to see he has an opportunity to benefit still further through the salesperson's proposition.

When the efforts of the prospect or his company have created the favourable condition it has appeal to pride elements and still greater power to help him see and appreciate his opportunity.

Appeal to Pride on Favourable Conditions

Example 1

Salesperson to distributor—you have built a fine team of salespersons, Ram. You can trust them to solve problems for your prospects and customers on your regular line. Hence, it seems to me you are set to make some nice extra profit by taking on small motors (talk continues).

Example 2

Research Officer to Management—the survey shows that the area has grown steadily for the last twenty years. It gives indication of continuous growth. Its per capita income is above the country's average. Its farms are highly productive and its manufacture diversified. While details are ready to be given, the general view is that it is a safe, profitable location for a storage depot.

Example 3

Salesperson—how large is the payroll estimated for your new plant?

Prospect—around Rs. 100 lacs.

Salesperson—so much! Well you must be bringing some top mechanical engineers too?

Prospect—yes, several, in fact.

Salesperson—what an opportunity for a housing complex, like this for instance (shows some layouts of such complexes his company has built in the past).

Unfavourable Conditions

An unfavourable condition is any situation creating losses for the prospect, for which the prospect, the salesperson or their companies are not responsible, and which brought to the attention of the prospect, tactfully will help him see his need for the benefits of the salesperson's proposition.

Part of the talk illustrating use of unfavourable conditions.

Sales Engineer—as long as the coal is loaded in open cars in monsoon time, it will be full of moisture. When this coal is pulverised it packs like putty and causes sparkles in the furnace, that quickly lowers the efficiency of the furnace.

The one way to solve the problem of getting full efficiency from such fuel is, of course, to have a pulverize equipped with a properly designed hot plate.

Salesperson now shows illustrations and tells how the hot plate in his product dries coal and makes it as efficient as coal from the mine in proper condition.

The difference between unfavourable conditions and poor quality and loss movers.

The usefulness of separating poor quality and loss movers from unfavourable conditions for the prospect is that it reminds that unfavourable condition idea can usually be mentioned before benefits without arousing resentment while poor quality and loss movers are effective when used after benefit and good quality movers.

Example 1

Use of unfavourable conditions.

Salesperson—is the monsoon giving your bus drivers the same schedule -troubles I hear so much about?

Prospect—it sure is. We are having our troubles.

Salesperson—to help solve the schedule problems our engineers are doing a lot of careful research on wheel bearing protection.

Last winter, for example BEST in Mumbai made tests which, their records show make it possible to practically eliminate bearing failures (develops the story).

Example 2

Use of poor quality and loss mover.

Salesperson—I know you are having a lot of wheel bearing failures, due to the grease you are using and;

Prospect—where did you get the idea we are having a lot of failures? (relations can get strained).

Unfavourable and favourable conditions used to prepare prospect to appreciate his need and opportunity to benefit.

Example 1

Salesperson—(has built personal prestige and contact)—how is the new raise in shipping rates going to affect your Kerala market?

Prospect—well, the southern competition will have the advantage in price. That is the picture.

Salesperson—what about this idea? With the dealers, there, getting such good prices and demand for your product, could you hold up your sales and profits if I could get you a big supply of rare raw materials at old prices?

Prospect—how big a supply are you thinking of?

Proposition Mover

The name of the company and its salesperson, the product, service or plan and the price, terms of business, delivery are classified as the proposition movers.

Example 1

The Capital Cabinet Manufacturing Company will furnish two models of cabinets at Rs. 35,000 each for Delhi. The payment terms are 30 days from despatch and shipment will be made within six weeks of receipt of the order.

Example 2

These direct mail folders will cost Rs. 25 each for a minimum order of 10,000 numbers.

Example 3

The Singh Corporation offers this annual maintenance contract for your air-conditioners.

Example 4

I am Mitra from the Krone Crane Company.

Forms of closing the sale.

The benefit sum-up and close (Assurance form).

Salesperson—to sum up, Mr. Roy, this cable will give you complete protection from breakdown. Your workmen will be protected from accidents due to the cutting of the cover. You will always be glad you chose it.

The benefit sum up and close (Question form)

Salesperson—now, are there any questions I can answer about protection from breakdowns, or protection from accidents or time saving? Would you want it all sent to this mining area?

The Split-Decision Form of Close

- How would you want it to be sent, by truck or by train?
- Which colour would you prefer, white or blue?
- Would you prefer a May delivery better than June?

The Question Form of Close

- What is your idea on your quantity requirement?
- How soon would you want it installed?

The Assurance Form of Close

- You will do well to take this offer Mr. Gupta
- Ramesh, I will order fast if I were you.

The Command Form of Close

- Order the purchase now, do not delay
- Do what is recommended Mr. Seth

Combination Closes

- Do that Ram. You will be glad you did.
- You will need it for monsoon will you not? If so, order should be placed now.

The Explanation Mover

Works used to make clear the meaning of a technical term or details of an operation, are explanation movers. Demonstrations, photographs, blue-prints, when used to make details clear are too known as Explanation Movers.

Example 1

The system should work well for us. The schedule is well planned. In this area the metres are ready on Tuesday. The billing machine operators prepare the bills on Thursday and they are sent to the customers on Friday.

Example 2

It will reduce the amount of power required because it works on sound gravity principle shown here.

Example 3

Salesperson—(about a poisonous matter sold as powder) you will find the material safe to handle and easy to measure as it is compressed into uniform tablets, looking like mini moth balls.

Example 4

Salesperson—you place the sheets of paper on paper on the transfer surface like this and pull the lever. . .

Example 5

To get perfect results you place the paper sheets accurately on the transfer plate like this. . . Next you pull down the lever like this, slowly and evenly.

Example 6

This is the delicious pure custard we advertised in *India Today*. Please taste it.

The usefulness of a technical equipment is made easy and clear by demonstration and trial run.

Progress Signals and the Progress Test Questions

Progress signals are comments and actions of a prospect that indicate that prospect viewpoint questions have been or are being answered adequately enough to keep them moving.

A question asked by the salesperson to test the progress being made in a talk is a Progress Test Question.

Example 1

Salesperson—your workers will be fully protected from shock-accidents since the tough tellurium cover has been placed on the cable. It will protect the men even if they hit it with a pick axe.

Prospect—will it not cut?

Salesperson—it not only does not cut that way, it stays whole even if one of your switch engines accidentally runs over it. Does it surprise you?

Prospect—well it is a welcome surprise.

Salesperson—over at the Mayurbhanj mines the workers have not only been protected from such accidents, but there has not been a production breakdown, due to cable cutting in two years.

Example 2

Salesperson—how does that look to you Mr. Prospect?

Example 3

Salesperson—have I made that clear to you Mr. Prospect?

Prospect—yes I understand

Salesperson—(continues his talk)

Example 4

Salesperson—would it be safe to say that the time of at least two workers could be saved?

Prospect—well, I would say so.

Salesperson—in that case the system would pay for itself in just one year as its total cost is.

Example 5

Salesperson—(after covering certain benefit and several important Good Quality Movers)—that is sound construction, is it not Mr. Jai?

Prospect—good. Well thought out.

Types of Progress Signals

- Prospect listens carefully.
- Prospect nods and says "very interesting".

- Prospect says, "I understand. That is clear.
- Prospect asks, "sounds good but I do not quite see how the oil can do that? (wants more information on Good Quality).

Test Question Types

(Sometimes they can be combined with other movers)

- Is that clear Mr. Ghosh?
- Did I make it clear why the noise gets reduced by anchoring the motor like this?
- Is the saving desirable?
- Are you happy with the safety part of the investment?

Timely Placement of the Test Question

Success of the test question depends on keeping it in line with the prospect's viewpoint question being answered and by not asking the question that goes beyond the information given to the prospect.

Examples

Salesperson—is there a problem of that type in your industry?

Salesperson selling financial deals regarding security features of an investment—that is the most important thing for you, is it not?

Salesperson—have we offered a satisfactory solution to your quality improvement problem?

Prospect—yes I think you have.

Salesperson—good. The next problem then is, can operating costs be reduced to a decent level. . . (talks carry on).

Limitations of the Test Question

The listener cannot answer in a manner that indicates progress if the question relates to something on which he has not yet been educated.

The question that lies back into a difference of opinion in a way that is embarrassing to the prospect is a non-use of the test. For example, "do you see how wrong you have been?"

Obstacle Descriptors

Habit

The habit obstacle is active when a person has been performed a task in a particular way for a long time and just by the force of habit would not like to change even if there is a much better way of performing the task. Such people become immune to change of ideas and create a strong resistance to the progress of sale.

Fear

The fear obstacle operates when a person has an justified fear of impending problems, of risk and consequent loss that overtakes his rational thinking. It causes him to bypass the opportunity and keep performing below his potential with the help of new ideas.

Price

The price obstacle is active when the prospect does not realise the benefits offered would outweigh their money value.

Complaint

The complaint obstacle is active when the prospect shows his dissatisfaction through words or actions.

Detail

The detail obstacle operates when the prospect is of the opinion that the proposed plan is not worth the effort it will require to obtain and put it to use.

Lack of Information

The lack of information obstacle is operating when the progress of sales gets hampered when the salesperson has not yet fully informed the prospect or he lacks the information. At times the prospect may not have the technical knowledge to understand the proposal. Prospect may not be able to get the full significance of the benefits that will be enjoyed. It can also happen if the salesperson's talk is unclear or confusing to the prospect.

Competition

The competition obstacle is active when the prospect compares the benefits or good qualities of the plan with another competitive plan and believes the latter offers better benefits than the proposed plan.

(At times competition can be in dissimilar things like microwave oven and washing machine).

Friendship

The friendship competition obstacle works when a competitive salesperson or his company's personnel has the liking and respect of the prospect and when the prospect believes that competitive product would produce similar or even better benefits.

Difficult Personality

The difficult personality obstacle is active when a prospect lacks emotional control when he allows a difference of opinion to deteriorate into a personal attack or when he bursts out in anger, in rudeness, in deceit or other uncalled for behaviour which retards the progress.

Time

The time obstacle is active when the prospect thinks that the product or the plan under consideration is not worth the time it will need or it is late for making any changes. On the positive side the time obstacle can be used to convey to the prospect that any delay in decision will endanger success.

Release

The release obstacle is operative when the prospect wants to be released from further consideration of the plan.

The Divided Release

The divided release obstacle is active when the prospect sincerely or insincerely seeks to end the interview by saying that he will take up the matter with a person not present.

Negative Mood and Manner

The negative mood and manner obstacle is active when a salesperson's frame of mind and manner of speaking and acting impresses the prospect unfavourably and creates dislike and lack of confidence.

Poor Judgement

The poor judgement obstacle is created by the salesperson's lack of consideration in looking at the ground realities, in separating the right ways of doing things from wrong, in planning the sales call, in deciding how to use the benefit story from the prospect's viewpoint. At times the salesperson can show disregard for the prospects reactions as the talks progress. The worst happens when the salesperson loses control of his emotions and forgets his knowledge of human nature and the practical selling techniques of study, analysis, planning and experience.

Examples of Obstacles

Prospect—your proposal is likely to upset our work. We would not be interested.

Prospect—it is too much money. There is no point in talking about it.

Financier—if we have to choose between air compressor you offer and the new furniture; one thing is sure our budget cannot stand both.

Prospect—if you had called even a week ago we would have been glad to have you in on the deal.

Prospect—we would need to keep our office force working overtime for weeks to install such a system.

Prospect—frankly we buy all our supplies from X-Tone Company. Swami of that company is very well liked around here.

Prospect—how do you people expect to be believed with your kind of delivery performance?

The Spar

The spar is a special use of emotion movers, frequently mood and manners, assurance and question, to meet obstacles in a calming and considerate manner so the objector's mind is reopened to reason. Conditions are also used as spar at times.

The Spar in Action

Example 1

Prospect—what are you trying to get away with? This new machine looks hard to operate to me.

Salesperson—it does? Well, I guess it would look that way to anybody—yet you will be running it like feather touch only as an expert in just two hours. I mean it.

Prospect—right, that suits me!

Example 2

Lady Prospect—do not try to talk me into that. My husband would become mad if I bought the sofa of that colour.

Salesperson—he would? Well I can understand that—would this colour please him?

Example 3

Prospect—Ram, we have been using riveted joints in our castings for years and our customers have been perfectly satisfied.

Salesperson—that is right Sir. It was the cost cutting angle I have been thinking of. . . (continues).

Note—the Spar may take just a second or two or it might be quite long.

How the movers in the Spar have been expressed?

- Assurance
- I know how you feel
- I understand
- That is how it struck me at first
- I am glad you told me
- Question
- Is that so?
- It has?
- You did?
- Mood and manner
- Calmly

- Sincerely
- Earnestly
- Politely
- Sympathetically
- Surprised

Meeting the Obstacles

Obstacle

Prospect—why do we have to keep records for twenty years. Our work is quite satisfactory. Is it not?

Example 1-The Spar

We know your work has been satisfactory. You have been doing great job. The idea now is to make your job more satisfactory to you, to lighten your rush hour burden. And with the modern visible record system, you will find it easy to keep posting up to the minute.

Example 2-The Dominating Method

Calm down. Listen to me. This is being done for your own good, to make it easier for you to keep your work and you better appreciate it.

Check List for Situations

Does the company have a need for my proposition? Can the money be secured? Have I got a prospect?

Are things being done, used or planned by this company that are causing or will cause loss?

Are the laws, economic environment, operating conditions or acts of others causing unfavourable conditions that create a need for my product, service or plan?

Do favourable conditions exist that provide the prospect with an opportunity to benefit through my proposition?

What major benefits can I use to answer the second prospect-viewpoint question and create interest?

How can I best expand and support my major benefit claims?—shall I rely on benefit, good quality, prestige and story movers or poor quality and loss movers essential to understanding and appreciation of the benefits?

Of all the possible obstacles which are the most likely to be active?

How can I use major benefits to avoid or weaken such obstacles? Am I prepared to Spar effectively and make a good and sound solution/effort if obstacles are voiced?

What company official should I see? What do I know about him? Is personal prestige or contact active? How can I use emotion movers to build or maintain liking and respect? What style shall I use to present my major benefit?

After studying the situation can I say that I have faith in my plan? Do I feel that I can help the prospect reach worthwhile objectives and do I look forward to seeing him?

If satisfactory answers to all the above questions cannot be found before the sales call, tactful use of the investigative question will be needed during the call.

Prospect's Situation

Started day-night medical shop

24-hour operation by medical shop in the heart of the city centre.

Yes

Do you gain late and early hours business.

Yes

City laws permit 24-hour operation by medical shops.

Extra sales and profits

Earlier there was fear, lack of information and the force of habit inhibiting the prospect

Extra profit outweighs extra expenses

Sales talk outline

24-hour operation

Night service also friendly earnest and sincere

Business build plans to be worked out

Build friendship

Good operation, good staff, better service to customers

Good location

Extra sales, extra profits over extra expense

Night person hiring who can take care of details—send direct mail, post records in the computer, keep the shop clean

Prospect—worth a trial, certainly!

Note benefit of the night person doing detailing work proved to be desirable to the prospect.

Sales expense budget-marketing manager has the following expense categories in his department.

Salaries—these are normally standard and not subject to change except once a year when increments and promotions are announced.

Travelling expense—to keep a watch on travelling expense, the firm should plan structured tours of the salesmen wherever possible. Exigencies can be taken care of on ad hoc basis.

Research expense—can be kept under control by keeping the research files updated by doing small surveys and also using secondary research when available.

Communications—telephone, fax, letters—judicious use of the facilities would help reduce costs.

Office rentals—these are fixed expenses and not much can be done unless some drastic steps are required like closing down some of the offices, when the firm may have decided to divest from some product.

Stationery expense—this is another hidden expense which if controlled can bring noticeable results.

Goods transport/logistics/depots/firms own shops—the chapter on logistics covers the expense control possible in the area.

Commission to channel members—the commission to channel members depends mostly on competitive factors and the strengths of the members. Dealers are for ever complaining of the bigger discount offered by the competition, which in fact could possibly be only a method of getting bigger discounts from the firm.

Advertising and promotion—use of advertising and promotion in these days of severe competition is absolutely essential for keeping the market share. To make these tools effective, pre-testing should be undertaken in all cases. At times, publicity, which is free, not paid for can help build the firms image and sales much more than paid advertising as there is an aura of truth attached to publicity due to its editorial nature.

Yearly expense budget is made and reviewed on a quarterly basis to ensure that the people in the department are well within the allocated budget. Any deviations are also monitored, accounted for and justified. Corrective action where needed is taken.

Firm's profitability comes from the gross profit reduced by expenses. To increase profit, attempts are made to increase gross profit by increasing sales and by reducing expenses. Marketing manager must keep a close watch on the sales expenses; else even with increase in sales there would be lower profits. In most firms due to competition based profit squeeze, attempts are made on a continuous basis to keep expenses under control and budgeting is a method of achieving the same.

Sales Cost Control: As the costs of marketing comes from each of the salesman, the budget can be subdivided into budget for each sales territory and the manager can keep proper control while approving the expense vouchers of the salesmen. Any deviation from the budget must have prior approval of the manager.

Reporting and Control System: In today's world of e-mail and Internet, it is easy for the salesmen to post even daily reports to the manager. However, structured reporting helps as it becomes universal and not people specific. Besides travel itinerary, the salesman should send the following reports to the manager on a time bound basis to enable the manager take corrective steps where needed and to provide the desired timely assistance to the salesman.

Sales forecast and actual orders received, dispatches made on a customer-wise product-wise basis as per the suggested format given below:

Customer_ (Dealer) or Direct-customer________________________ Period 2002-2003

Product	Sales objective	Orders received	Orders dispatched	Shortfall in orders/dispatches
PCs	250	210	205	40/45
Modems	120	120	110	0/10
Printers	60	35	30	25/30
UPS	100	80	60	20/40

Besides, a consolidated territory picture can be sent on the same basis. Another report, which is important, is the age analysis of outstanding dues in each territory. And salesmen's plan on a time bound manner of liquidating the same, as can be seen from below.

The following format can be used.

Customer	Overdue amount	15 days old	30 days old	60 days old	120 days old	>120 days old
ABC Ltd.	320,5000	20,0000	100,0000	1050000	500000	500000
XYZ Ltd.	2500000	2000000	500000	Nil	Nil	Nil

The form can be extended by one more column where the salesman can write the dates when the outstanding would be cleared.

Questions for discussion–

- What are purely the sales functions?
- What are the methods employed for selecting and retaining salesmen?
- How the tours should be planned to make them effective?
- What are methods the salesmen should use in preparing their sales calls?
- How should the marketing manager keep control of the salesmen's activities?

Business leaders have realized the importance of understanding the technological developments in the area of manufacturing technology and technology of product itself. Internationally they find opportunities emerging in a spectrum of nations that are ready to join the world market economy. The real effects of globalisation need to be seen in the context of opening of markets in hitherto closed countries, which were trying to safeguard the interests of their own industries. India was among these nations till 1991.

The other area that has emerged in recent years is the number and types of products that are available for sale. A partial list of the products is given below:

- FMCG products
- Consumer durables
- Industrial capital goods
- Industrial consumables
- Industrial raw materials and components
- Services
- Events
- Ideas
- Research outputs
- Manpower
- Property
- Places
- Information
- Ideas
- Organisations

Companies have found that unless they can build a meaningful relationship with their customers there is every possibility that the customers would go for competitive products. Companies have to build relationships not only with their customers but also with the channel members, suppliers and even financiers. These long-term relationships bind the company with these important groups of people for long-term loyalty on both sides.

Next companies need to learn the art and science of creating and managing demand for their products. Decisions on the marketing mix factors have assumed great importance with competition ever ready to look for loop holes in the companies planning process. Companies have to carefully formulate their product specifications, package design, pricing, channels of distribution, after sales service besides advertising and promotion. These need to be totally and directly in line with the customers' known and even unknown expectations. Product benefits for different customers have to identified and refined to become close to the language spoken and understood by the selected customers. Companies have to carve out market segments for this purpose. Companies' plan marketing research for knowing the real needs of the customers, the way they buy the products, from mega marts, neighbourhood shops or from virtual electronic market-place.

Companies have to find out on a continuous basis the changing environment of business and competition to remain proactive and ahead of competition. Michael Porter's five-force model is a good starting point for analysing competitive environment. Considering the competitive strength companies can ill afford to remain oriented to production, as was the case in the first half of the last century. Today, market has to be main or the only focus for the companies while planning their marketing strategies. However, companies have to keep the interests of stakeholders in their decision-making and work towards a double bottom line that includes the welfare of stakeholders besides that of shareholders alone.

Customer Value

Customer buys products for the benefits he derives from the same. These benefits are the perceived values as per the customer's notions. The perceived value can be defined as the difference between the total customer assigned value and the total customer cost for buying the product. Sellers have to understand the perceived value by the customer and if it is low then the product is in the wrong market segment or is not being properly marketed. It is said that nobody buys a product. People buy the satisfaction or the benefits the products provide to them. The seller may make tall claim about the value or product performance that will provide customer satisfaction or even customer delight. However, what really matters is the customer's belief regarding the product satisfaction levels with him. Providing customer satisfaction and customers delight has become the most important mission for the company and if the company can use it as its driving force it is bound to succeed despite tough competition.

Companies survive and thrive only if they make their customers loyal to them and add on to other customers, either from the non-buyer groupes or from among the customers presently buying from competition. The companies need to continuously innovate, research for new products for which the demand may be obvious or even dormant. Besides proper management of key areas as materials management with just in time inventory controls and training of the marketing personnel, both of the company and from the channel members would go a long way in optimized value chain management for the increased value addition for the customer. The supply line starts from suppliers of raw materials through the assembly process to the movement of finished goods to the customers' premises. Customers could be the channel members or the final users in case of B-to-B business. Companies with better supply chain management get sustainable competitive advantage, as they are able to deliver the products at the right time needed by the customers. Companies realize that it is much cheaper, (about 70%) to retain customers than to get new customers. Financial benefits like loans, training in proper usage of the product, publicizing company's social assistance programmes like, free education for village children, adopting villages for overall development and even planting trees for providing green coverage in towns. These activities create goodwill for the company amongst the citizens, who are also the company's customers.

Product and service quality plays an important role in forming customers' attitudes in favour of the products. Consistency in quality, meeting the quality standards laid down by the government for the products (especially true for medicines and food products) and usage ease are the main factors considered by the customers regarding formation of attitudes towards the product. Initially, prospective customers try to get the opinion of their elders, peers and knowledgeable people about the product. Once they buy and use it their own experience forms their attitudes towards the product. Total Quality Management (TQM) is therefore the essential ingredient in the success story as it is followed by Total Customer Management (TQM). Product quality is just one area of quality to be looked into in TQM. Others are quality of service being provided to the customer, quality of knowledge about customers, and their behaviour, buying habits. Marketing research too requires top quality work for obtaining the correct information about the product demand, customers' likes and dislikes and their buying patterns. For providing quality service companies have to train their sales team along with the sales teams of the channel members.

Salesperson, the Strategist

Salespersons are known as the eyes and ears of a company. They are the most reliable and timely source of information on market dynamics, business general and competitive environment. They are also the vital links the company has with its customers. They are the personal communicators to the customers, prospective customers and company's most effective PR persons.

Companies decide about the sales teams taking into account the sales objectives, the geographic area that needs to be covered, the distribution of sales territory amongst the team members and their compensation packets. Companies need sales persons who are committed and motivated to sell its products, who believe in its products, policies, and its culture and business philosophies. With increasing competition, new players keep trying to attract the best salespersons. Companies must keep a close vigil on the loyalty factor of the sales team. For this reason alone, companies do well to keep them happy by providing them with adequate incentives, both monetary and non-monetary like improved perks, paid holidays for good work done by them.

Sales team has the following tasks cut out for them:

- Researching for customers, knowing their buying habits, likes and dislikes
- Planning sales calls on the customers and the prospects for effective results—improving profitable sales
- Informing the customers about company's plans for product launches, pricing strategies and options.
- Personal selling—this is the most important part both for Business-to Business sales and sales to the channel members.
- Providing or organizing service to the customers for optimizing use of the products sold.
- Maintaining relationships with the customers through non-sales contacts
- Gathering market information and communicating the same to the company.

Companies organize their sales teams in the following manner:

- Dividing their sales area into territories that can be managed by a single salesperson that are easy to cover, have enough business potential not to frustrate the salesperson.
- Recruiting the sales person considering their education, experience, personal background, ability and keenness to learn the companies' way of doing business and those who are happy with their initial package.
- Training the sales persons into knowledge about company's products, sales policies, competition and the way they have to go about doing their business with on the job training (usually given by sending the recruit with experienced member of the team.), making them understand the communication plans for giving the correct benefit story to the customers about the products. Besides they need to be trained in relationship building both with external and internal customers and for being a good PR person for the company.
- Monitoring and supervising the sales team for ensuring they achieve their targets of sales, expense budgets and profitability.
- Motivating the sales persons through incentives, praise for jobs done well, for achieving targets.
- Making proper evaluation of the efforts made by the sales persons individually and in teams to encourage team efforts.

Sales results come with a clear understanding of the sale persons about the customer's behaviour patterns, buying habits, buying motivations and buying periods. Besides, they should be fully knowledgeable in the art of salesmanship, the art of persuasion where the customer is led through steps from his area of ignorance or even dislike of company's products to liking, and leading to purchase action. Later, they have to ensure proper usage of the products by the customers so that they derive the promised benefits from the products. This would lead to customer re-buy, retention and his loyalty towards the products and the firm. The decision steps used are given below:

Customer ignorant about the product	Inform about the most attractive benefit of the product to catch customer's attention
Customer becomes curious, still undecided	Give details of product specifications if required or just fresh lot of benefits
Customer says competitive product cheaper	Add benefits that overshadow the price
Customer says competitors offering free services	Counter by saying that while the product does not need any service, yet if required it would be given free of cost. Add testimonials from other satisfied customers
Customer says competitor product easily available	Offer to give most appropriate delivery time that would not add on to his inventory costs
Customer says he needs time to decide	Offer attractive some instant buy benefit
Customer places the order	Make sure of proper usage of the product by the customer, check out re-buy time

At times in the end when the customer is still dithering it is best to give him "either or option", would like to insure the transportation or should we do it?" the moment he opts for one of the two, you can get his signatures on the dotted line of the purchase order.

Sales persons need to learn the art of negotiations that involves give and take. In such cases they must be fully aware of how much they can offer to the customer without losing out on the business and ending up in losses. They have to know the thin line between good business and a losing preposition. Sales persons should become genuine friends of their customer, never giving them wrong inputs, creating positive vibes for long term business relationship.

Knowledge Base of the Customers

Companies need to know the customers now than ever before, as with knowledgeable customers, companies have to provide them with a lot of information about the product, the company. Companies are facing non-price base competition where competitors are using credit extensions, giveaways, and financial help in the management of channels. Besides market economy and globalisation of the markets has clearly dictated that unless companies are fully knowledgeable about the customers and their needs, physical, psychological and sociological, companies could find themselves out of the marketplace, in the wilderness.

Marketing Information System

MIS provides the marketing team with reliable inputs regarding the market dynamics, demand trends, consumer behaviour and impact of competitive activities in the market.

Companies could remain proactive as their MIS keeps their knowledge base updated always. MIS can be generated firstly from the company's own records like sales figures, age analysis of outstanding dues, new competition in the market, new customers gained and customers lost with reasons thereof. Besides marketing research fills in the information gaps and provides information on changing customer needs. Information on the market is gathered by the field sales force and can be termed market intelligence as it incorporates subtle deviations in competitor's planning and attitudinal changes occurring in the customer groups. These changes can happen due to new product introduction having better technology, greater advertising force of the competitors, competitive promotional plans and new distribution methods adopted by competition that suit the customers better. Companies can update their MIS regularly with the help of computer that would store and analyse the information as required by the company.

Marketing research is today an essential tool in the armoury of marketing team. In the first half of the last century, most marketing decisions were made on the company's past experience and the manager's gut feeling. In today's environment such a decision can only cause disaster for the company. Companies can have the option of getting the research done from within the company's personnel or it can get it done from outside. Research is done on scientific lines with some well-defined methods, after understanding the cost versus benefit analysis. Companies are using the research quite frequently to obviate defective decision-making for lack of information. Data analysis tools are available today that remove the incorrect data stream and lets the marketing team take more accurate decisions based on the research. Both qualitative research and quantitative research are undertaken for specific objectives for which the research has been envisaged. Therefore the first essential decision to be taken is defining the research objectives, which should be clearly worded with no ambiguity, giving both the time frame and finance allocation made towards the research. The company could be having a marketing problem like loss of market share or it may be looking for an opportunity like introduction of new product in the market or yet still it could be for making marketing plans. Initially the company can look at the secondary data that may be available as it would be invariably at a much lower cost than a full-scale primary research. Exploratory research, focus group, panel groups can be tried before statistical research is undertaken. Causal research that talks about the cause and effect can be taken up in areas like for finding out the relationship between sales increase and price reduction. Market opportunities, new product demand, and competitive strengths and demand growth patterns can be understood through the research. Sales forecasts, marketing expense planning, production, procurements and advertising expenditure can be decided on the basis of the research. Research can give the demand pattern of the total industry product plus demand for individual brands. Sales force estimates, research data, managers gut feeling can be supplemented with test marketing of the product in the desired market segment, besides advanced statistical techniques, mathematical models regression analysis would lead to accurate forecasting of demand.

Market Consumers Behaviour Patterns

Companies have to carefully understand the reasons why consumers buy their products, competitive products and they have to get the answers to the following questions:

- What products are bought in the selected market segment?
- Why these are bought?
- What price the consumers are ready to pay for the products?
- When they buy the product normally or how often it is purchased?
- Where do the consumers buy the product—the right channel for market segment?
- How do they buy—the buying decision process, influence of the family, friends, peers, celebrities and experts?

The factors that influence individual buying behaviour are the cultural milieu in which the consumers are living. Besides the societal factors like the social status, financial standing, family size and age of family members are important factors. Besides psychographics and psychological factors are important considerations that cannot be ignored. These provide the motivation levels for making purchases and help in the formation of attitude, and beliefs. Buying is a complex process, especially of expensive products, where the following pattern is likely to be followed, may be with some variations at times.

Usually there is a user who wants the product for his use.

- This person could be the initiator of the demand or it could be someone else too. For example, a teenage son may want a motorcycle and yet his demand may be placed before the head of the family, the father by his mother or elder brother.
- There are at times people who influence the buying decision who could be a neighbour with a motorcycle or it could be the grandfather who is afraid that the teenager would meet with an accident and hence should not beg given the bike.
- These are people who decide about the purchase, the deciders.

Each of the above would have individual personality traits and buying motivations and hence while dealing with them the seller must give the benefit picture of the product in such a way that it suits the listener.

Buying Decisions

Buying decisions are taken through the route given below:

- Firstly, the need is identified or a problem that needs to be solved is located.
- Next information is gathered regarding products that would satisfy the need and solve the problem.
- Then the information gathered is sifted and evaluated for finding out the best solution.
- This would lead to making the purchase.
- After the purchase is made and the product has been used the after-purchase actions take place, like repurchase, abandoning the product or finding out a new buyer for the second hand product.
- The total product cost includes the cost of the search for solutions, analysis cost, product price, maintenance costs as the sale price of the used product is deducted from the initial cost to buy and use.

Strategies for Services Marketing

With rapid growth of service industry, its leaders have accepted the importance of services marketing. Service has a product associated with it as products too have service attached to them. Restaurants sell food to eat and that is the product while service is the main part of the business. Service product is intangible and usually gets destroyed if not used. An empty airline seat can never be used again and the customer enjoys the service but they cannot take it away with them. A passenger cannot carry the plane seat with him.

The way the service is provided to the customers can provide the service provider with sustainable competitive advantage. Most 5-star hotels have documented and standardized methods of serving tea and coffee, liquor and food. Even then the scientific approach has to be carefully blended with the art of providing service. The quality of service separates different service providers.

Service industry is the one that analyses the customer's value to it. The big spender guest in a 5-star hotel gets a lot of freebees like fruit basket in his room, free entry to the hotel gym while the poor spender gets the normal facilities only. However, there cannot be any difference in the courtesy offered to the two as the hotel realizes that today's small spender can become tomorrow's big spender. Airlines have the frequent fliers benefit schemes like offer of free tickets, seat upgrades.

Service industry has not only to offer services to the customers but also ensure that the employees get trained in providing proper service to the customers. Bad service, rude behaviour will certainly put off the customer who would never come again to the provider. With the advance technological innovations like e-booking, smart cards room entry (instead of the regular keys), automatic temperature controllers, hotels still have to ensure that soft areas like personalized pleasant service is the norm rather than an exception in the hotel.

Service industry has to ensure high level of quality service, high brand equity and easy access to their business areas. Service gives them the competitive advantage and there can never be any compromise on the same. The industry must train its employees for better service productivity, to ensure that their customers leave lot of their chores to the employees to have free time for their business and pleasure. Hotels arrange for unpacking of suitcases laundry and business meetings. The 5-star hotel business centres take care of customers including their business conferences.

Product companies provide post-purchase service like the car sellers. They have to have service during the sales to convince the customers into buying their products.

An example from the Service Industry.

Customer Care in Service Industry Like Hotels

Hotels, especially the 5-Star ones keep getting VIP guests. It is therefore important for them to ensure that they go back with fond memories of their stay when they will become spokesperson for the hotel and get more business for it, besides coming over themselves again and again. Several hotels have planned their service pattern for their guests and one such plan is given below:

How to Care for the VIP Guests

Planning

If the guest is on a repeat visit the hotel computer should have information on the following:

- Favourite room or suite, its location, its outside view.
- Favourite drink, cocktail, soft drink, juice.
- Favourite food, one's on the hotel menu and also those that need to be especially prepared for the guest.

Welcome

Resident Manager should welcome the guest in the lobby. For international guests garlands, tika on the forehead and a welcome drink in the guest room are appreciated by the guests. The RM or his nominee should escort the guest to his room.

Welcome in Restaurants

Food and beverage executive or restaurant manager to escort the guest and assist in proper seating. Fresh warm or cold towel should be offered as appropriate. The food order should be taken by F&B executive and offer recommendation if asked for by the guest. As a gesture of goodwill the restaurant manager and the chef can be introduced to the guest.

Service

The section holder and captain will do the serving of food and beverage.

Captain will ensure the standard time parameters and standard phrases are followed.

Feedback: Feedback will be taken by the F&B executive. This will be done within ten minutes of serving the food.

Delivery of Order: F&B Executive has to closely co-ordinate to ensure the order is delivered at the stipulated time. In case of delay, it should be brought to the notice of the guest in advance (exact time to be informed).

Handling Complaints: Listen to the complaint fully. Do not interrupt or jump to any conclusion.

If you are authorized, take action without delay.

Refer the complaint to the F&B executive who would be able to handle it.

F&B Executive will investigate the complaint properly and make an incident report. F&B manager to be informed accordingly.

Fond Farewell: Last impression is the lasting impression.

F&B executive will escort the guest from the outlet to the lobby at the end of the meal.

Plus

Check for billing instruction with F&B executive in advance.

Staff/executives should be aware of the guest preferences.
Update the guest history by giving comment cards.
All the staff in the restaurant should recognize the VIP.

Miscommunication leads to confusion in terms of guest service. Captain/section holder is advised to make sure that guest orders are taken and executed properly. For this, each and every order is repeated for accuracy.

CHAPTER

4

Community as a Stakeholder: Prelude to CRM

The famous Dale Carnegie was invited for dinner by a ultra rich lord in London. There he started discussing several issues about literature with the lord. Soon there was an argument about a quotation, which Carnegie knew was from one of the Shakespeare's plays. The lord was adamant that it was from the Bible. When they could not come to a conclusion, the lord called a church minister to their side to get his expert opinion. On hearing the problem, the minister thought for a moment then declared that, indeed it was from the Bible. The lord beamed happily and even consoled Carnegie saying that Bible is too vast and it was just unfortunate that Carnegie did not know the Bible as well as he did.

Next day Carnegie went to the ministers house with a copy of Shakespeare's play underlining the passage in dispute the previous day. The minister did not even look at it and straightaway admitted that yes the passage was indeed from Shakespeare. He however, added that they both knew the value of their friendship with the lord and that is why he did not want to prove him wrong and lose a friend.

This was the first of many lessons Carnegie was to learn on friendship before he could write the famous book "Winning Friends and Influencing People".

Companies operating globally need to have a world vision of community service, as they are virtual world citizens. Their own task will become simplified if they extend wholehearted support to the community welfare, as they plan their business strategies. The areas of CRM and corporate social responsibility, while remaining separate entities, do overlap as both care for the ultimate customer.

Corporate's primary aim therefore needs to be the "Service to the community, the town and the country they operate in."

The entire thought process makes excellent business sense as the following aspects come to surface.

- Builds goodwill, brand equity
- Helps in getting better work persons from the community
- Gets better business from the community
- Gives the "Good Corporate Citizen" tag to the company
- Helps generate funds from institutions and public alike
- Gets the best suppliers
- Arranges customer relationships (CRM)

Team Involvement

The team players represent the community besides outsiders too. The company's vision propels both the types of team members to uphold the company's vision of superior service to the community. Community programmes like healthcare, education scholarships and local recruitments convert even the die-hard competitive buyers into enthusiastic customers for life. The team takes pride in such activities that is showcased in its commitment towards the company goals.

Rome was not built in a day, and similarly strong communities cannot be built in short time. Furthermore, building strong communities require teamwork. Solutions to complex, and often long-standing problems depend upon resources, talents and expertise. No single company or individual can supply all the answers. And yet each individual effort helps as it promotes the company's goodwill.

It is therefore necessary to focus on issues close to the hearts of the team members and their communities, as well as business interests and objectives. Creating jobs for the community, for example, good healthcare and clean environment. One should understand that these and other issues have a direct impact on the quality of life; not only of the team, but also on the communities they call home.

One should plan to see that every community where one has a presence would be a better place to live and work. The ideal way should "be active contributing members of the communities."

Around the world where one operates and to focus on issues where one can make a difference. To provide meaningful support beyond traditional financial grants and gifts. To use resources wisely so that communities, and businesses all benefit. To encourage the team to enhance their personal lives and their communities through volunteer work. To set an example of community involvement that, customers, business partners and others will want to follow community outreach begins with identifying the critical needs of your community and the resources and expertise needed to address them. Although there may be a wide variety of initiatives and organizations one can support, it is important to focus on key areas where the team can best use its resources and make the biggest impact on the community. Community relations' plan should include activities in the following areas where the team's knowledge, experience and products can do the most good.

The smooth functioning of both society and business depends upon an educated and skilled workforce. Yet, those who might benefit most from classroom and on-the-job training often face financial, family-related obstacles. Family, health and personal issues can be a major source of stress and affect job performance. In the hospitality industry, one knows first-hand that an unhappy or distracted employee cannot provide the high level of service which customers depend on. Finding solutions to problems at home benefits everyone: families, customers and communities. For example, one hotel partnered with medical professionals to sponsor a medical clinic in a remote village, another helped a local orphanage with facilities maintenance and repairs and yet another provided free food to a centre for mentally handicapped children. Partnering with an organization to address social concerns can increase your hotel's ability to make a difference and can offer valuable marketing opportunities.

CHAPTER

5

Winning the Rural Customers

India is a country where majority of population, almost 70% lives in villages. There are 6,27,000 villages in the country spread across its length and the breadth. However, the village people are poorer than the city people as the village contributes less than 50% of the total country's income. However, now the situation is gradually changing for the better.

There are 25 official languages and some four hundred dialects spoken in the country. Most world religions have their adherents here.

In the first half of the twentieth century, people were using Neem or Babul tree's twig for cleaning their teeth. Today, they are using tooth powder or toothpaste. Instead of groundnuts the children are asking for chocolate candies. Face cream or lotions have replaced Besan as a face cleanser.

Appreciating the size of the rural market, major companies, including, Hindustan Lever, P&G have made special strategies for targeting rural markets and related CRM.

Business environment in rural India is given below:

Demographic—the population has been steadily increasing in the villages, making per capita land holdings ever so small, reducing their income in the same proportion. This has resulted in migration from villages to towns either on temporary basis during off seasons for agriculture or on a more permanent basis as people come to cities looking for employment.

Social—there are women in the agriculture fields, in panchayats, child marriages are still prevalent in certain parts of the country, like Rajasthan. In certain states villagers have taken to arms and crime due to lack of employment, perhaps. Education levels differ from state to state, as Kerala boasts of highest percentage of educated persons.

Cultural—villagers celebrate festivals with a lot of gusto, especially the harvest time, religious festivals, marriages and childbirths.

Political – the green revolution was the result of the government's policy of research on agriculture. Milk cooperatives came about for the milk farmers with the pioneering efforts of the Amul organization. The government has been providing subsidies on farm inputs, tax holidays for farm profits, purchase of farm produce on a minimum price fixed by the government and has of late given a lot of concessions on agro packaging and processing industry.

Legal – government has enacted laws against child marriage and dowry. However, it would need a concerted effort from the village folk themselves before the evil can be eradicated.

Macroeconomics – a lot of effort has gone into setting up of rural banks, farm insurance schemes. Rural electrification, roads have been given priority in the government's planning process. Cottage industries and handicrafts have been given the desired impetus by the government.

Technology – today most villages of the country have the radio coverage and the TV spread is increasing by the day. Next, telephones, Internet would become ubiquitous in the villages soon. Tractors, harvesters, seeders, pesticides, fertilizers, quality seeds, scientific guidance on farming by the agriculture research institutes is enabling the farmers to get better yield from their farms.

Global – WTO has clearly defined the methods of agriculture exports from India and the government is finding it hard to counter the extra subsidies given by the affluent nations that make their produce more competitive. Our leadership is busy in countering it through diplomacy in the WTO. Some countries have patented some of Indian products, like Basmati rice, turmeric, as their own much to the country's regret.

Rural products – most products required in cities are also needed in the rural markets with a few exceptions as given below:

- FMCG products like cosmetics, food items like cooking oil, kerosene, and medicines
- Consumer durables like refrigerators, stoves, motor cycles.
- Farm products like tractors, harvesters, seeders, seeds, fertilizers, pesticides, and diesel, water supply for household use including drinking purposes and for watering the farms.
- Services like, health clinics, water supply, electricity, eateries, inns.
- Housing

Pricing in rural markets is tricky because the companies spend more on transporting the products as compared to transporting to the cities. However, the paying power in rural areas is much less. Companies can therefore plan to have low cost packaging with a bit of attractive glitter while keeping the product unchanged in most cases. The companies can work out the rural customers Mean Time Between Purchase (MTPB). They will find that the rural customer will stretch the purchase time much longer. This would be true for most FMCG products. Food items however would be needed as per household requirements.

Product distribution in rural markets takes the following route:

Products are kept for sale at the grocers' shops, diesel/kerosene dealers, and tractor repair shops. Besides, companies sell through mobile vans that cover the villages mostly on the days of their weekly markets. These vans carry advertising materials, audiovisual equipment for showing movies besides company's advertisements and the products for sale, samples like shampoo sachets for test marketing of the products.

Product promotion in rural markets is done through the vans. Besides, radio has a wide coverage as it covers the entire country geographically, is used. Additionally, television reach has increased of late and with better electricity availability it has become a good option, more especially because of its universal appeal. Pamphlets, loudspeaker announcements during weekly markets, mostly on roaming rickshaws, banner on elephants and camels are used in many areas.

Villages need schools, as the literacy levels are still poor. Technical and computer education are becoming increasingly important even in villages. There is a great need for libraries, bookstores and newspapers, magazines in local languages.

Income levels in the rural India can be described as follows:

- High in certain areas for rich land owning farmers
- Low for farmers with small lands
- Very low for farm hands and migratory farmers

Village industries, cottage and small scale, handlooms, milk farming, sheep rearing need governmental support or infusion of cooperatives in these areas. The Amul examples must be replicated in other parts of the country. The village Bania, who has been the proverbial loan shark, is fast disappearing as a tribe and yet the rural banking needs much more thrust. A number of banks have started branches in villages and yet they are affected by non-availability of collaterals for giving loans to farmers. Farm insurance would go a long way in settling this problem. Bad crops further derail the interest payments leading to bad debts that retard the progress for which the banks have been set up.

Strategic Challenge: Understanding Customers' Needs

Customers have needs, which are obvious, like the need for food, clothing, and shelter. Some of these needs are explicitly mentioned like the need of a house. However, what is real is the need of the house in a locality close to office, school and shopping plaza. Besides, the unsaid need could be of a big house.

Firms face the challenges of new competition, both local and global, new technologies as they cater to consumers in business-to-business area and individuals. In order to ascertain the product needed by the consumers, market research is undertaken, which offers information about the product, price, placement, i.e., distribution system needed and the methods of communicating to the consumers about the product, i.e., advertising and promotion, the famous 4 Ps of marketing.

In order to prepare the right 4 Ps, firms define their market segment in which the product would be best accepted. The firms try to understand the exact needs of the segment in order to be able to meet the same. In order to build loyal customers firms are trying relationship marketing, to ensure that consumers feel obligated to buy the same product again and again. Quantity discounts, free gifts are some of the means to build relationships with the consumers. Since the competition is doing exactly the same, it is the firm with better strategy, which wins. Changes from the earlier concepts of product orientation, to product orientation and later on to market orientation has helped firms in fine tuning their marketing strategies to suit the consumers from their chosen market segment. The concept of providing socially acceptable products, which do not affect the biodiversity, which are not ecologically degrading the area, is gaining ground rapidly.

Marketing Relativity through Competition

Companies do not operate in vacuum, they have to face and deal with the competitive forces operating in the market. It is therefore of paramount importance for companies to know the exact competitive situation, their moves, their strengths and weaknesses, pricing and promotion strategies, channels they use for distribution and their reaction time towards the company's strategic move like price modifications, introduction of new channels of distribution and advertising thrusts.

Competitive analysis should be made using the Michael Porter's 5-force model as it covers the entire gamut of possible competition.

Companies face competition from different sources as given below:

- Firms selling similar products in same volumes to same customers for giving satisfaction of similar nature
- Firms likely to offer alternative solutions for similar problems (the airlines meeting the fare structure of railways is a case in point)
- Firms getting their R&D operations to bring out innovative uses of existing products or developing new better products giving superior satisfaction to the buyers.

Companies must plan to have a covert intelligence network that is legal and yet provides them the competitive information. Once collected the information must be sifted and the unnecessary data should be deleted while the good data disseminated to those concerned. Companies should get the customer's perspective regarding competitive product's value to the customers, how they perceive its benefits as compared to the benefits offered by the company's products.

Companies with the largest market share are the market leaders, belonging to the star quadrant in the BCG Matrix. To stay on the top companies have to keep enlarging their market base, retain their existing customers and get some no users to become users as well as take customers from competition. This involves price reduction; besides better market management including training of selling team and promotion plans with increased advertising efforts. These activities take a sizable amount of finances reducing the profits earned by the company.

Companies that are having lesser share of the market attempt to increase the same with bigger thrust on marketing efforts. They try product innovations and differentiations, price penetrations, lower costs of manufacturing through higher scales of manufacture and experience curve along with speedier reach to the marketplace. They also get into a niche market where their product has the best acceptance. In their niche market they can communicate with the customers in a language most easily understood by them.

Competitive understanding should be achieved by comparing the market share of competitors and the status of different players in the industry. Competitive information can be gathered through market surveys, interaction with channel members and industry publication. Competitors' balance sheets too provide companies information about competition. Such information collected from different sources should then be collated, analysed and the results disseminated to the concerned persons.

Market leaders can at times become low profit entities and the second and the third level players can take the leadership position if they find it attractive enough for their products. These companies use penetrating pricing policy, attractive promotion plans, low cost production and product differentiation. However, the cost-benefit analysis must be undertaken before increasing the market share.

The companies having low market share could be making good profits compared to high share companies because they are not investing in marketing expenses to that extent. They could be claiming better-personalized service and tailor-made solutions to their customer's problems or product needs. "We are second and we strive harder for your satisfaction". These companies could cater to niche markets better as they understand their needs better.

Unique Selling Proposition

Companies do a cost benefit analysis before planning marketing communication as the advertising, promotion and personal selling would revolve around the USP. A single product benefit well advertised can capture customers' imagination and get firmly planted in their psyche. Attitudes, beliefs and purchase decisions are taken due to such mindsets. However, at times multi-benefit communication can be used to further focus the product into the psyche. Products need to be differentiated for achieving distinctive competitive advantage. The differentiation can be made in product itself, and in the following areas:

- Product features
- Service, both sales service and after sales service
- Quality, both static structure and dynamic specifications
- Consistency of quality
- Reliability of product and service
- Availability of spares and repair facility
- Customer training in proper use of the product
- Channel members personnel
- Advertising campaigns

The differentiation in any or several of these areas needs to be highlighted for the customer to take notice. Products have to be categorized as distinctive, affordable, showcasing buyers' life style as an intelligent and experienced buyer.

Companies need to plan marketing strategies all through the product life cycle, the introductory stage, early growth, late growth, maturity and finally the decline stage. In

India most products are in growing stage as the economy of the country is poised for growth with continuous increase in its GDP and GNP. However, products like VCRs have reached the decline stage with a big increase in satellite channels available on the TV. Introductory stage gives big profits for the first arrivals on the scene as with no competition skimming prices can be charged. The selling power devolves around the channel members, as they are closer to the customers than the new players. Product specifications are also in a fluid state waiting for total customer acceptance. Companies, however, need to have a cautious approach as when others see large profit margins, they too jump in the fray, creating competition. In growing stage competition increases while the selling power starts shifting to the manufacturers from the channel members because by this time the brand gets established and companies start having direct bonding with the customers with their promotional plans. In the maturity stage, price wars start, brands sell and promotions become commonplace. Some late entrants with little foothold in the market may quietly slip out of it, leaving a bigger cake for the remaining players. In declining stage several players close shop and the one's remaining can plan niche marketing and harvest the balance business. Others can hang on to the product as it might be used for bundling with other fast selling products to make offers more attractive.

CHAPTER

6

e-CRM: Customer Communications and Advertising

e-CRM

With the advent of internet corporate world has woken up to its relevance in improving service while reducing costs as well as organising better CRM. Marketing communication can be personalized to a large extent. e-CRM helps the sales team in getting a foot in the customer's door. Customer data base can be analysed to understand the buying motivation, habits and tradition. This has become the bedrock of e-CRM in today's business world. e-CRM can be defined as creativity needed in managing customer relationship. It helps in providing communication, information, data and product specifications to prospective customers on relevant areas as per their personal requirements.

e-CRM can be considered a communication channel that creates positive and special ambience in which the prospects can assimilate the product nuances in the luxury of their own place with unique experiences as virtual world gets created for them. They bring in the required cordination between physical channels and e-CRM. It is believed that with time and progression of computerisation e-CRM would further strenghten its effectiveness as an interactive tool between the prospect and the corporate. Its interactive quality helps in responding to the custoner queries instantly.

IT or information technology has added the required impetus for e-CRM as can be seen with Website that can be personalised for ease of recognition and customization of product and services. CRM, or e-CRM helps build value for the customers as it reduces the search time, saves money and customer satisfaction for the brand accepted.

There are a few areas of e-CRM as given below:

Basic services for improving website usage and response

Customised services where each customer gets treated as per his/her need

Order focus, product specification needs and secure communication are targeted with e-CRM and it becomes possible to offer value added services, such as, on line auction, training and education and self-services, with coordination with traditional channels of ommunication, such as, advertising, PR and publicity. The latest addition to e-CRM is the mobile interaction with users of mobile phones. This has become effective as it comes directly to the customer irrespective of age, location income and other demographic factors. The challenge therefore, is to find the right target audience.

While e-CRM allows customers to access company services from more and more places, since the internet access points are increasing by the day, mCRM takes this one step further and allows customers or managers to access the systems for instance from a mobile phone.

CRM packages available today include creation of customer orientation in the company, customer service, FAQs, fast track followup with prospects and customers. CRM becomes more effective when it gets integrated with other informjation systems, like real time data processing, sales, finane coordination. CRM is not totally fool proof as there are intangible benefits for the customer that cannot be quantified. Besides keeping customer data base secure against hackers remains a major challenge for e-CRM.

Advertising as Customer Communication

Advertising management today has become an important area of business, where the sellers interact with the buyers, which include practically everyone on the planet, and that is why, even lay persons are quite aware of the subject. However, for a professional businessperson, it is essential that not only the subject is learnt thoroughly but also even subtle nuances are understood so that the person becomes comfortable with it. With practice, expertise can be gained to strengthen the skills. Advertising is a fast moving, glamorous discipline and yet without proper concepts it can become quite banal.

In daily life we encounter hundreds of messages through myriads of media that at least people living in towns can never remain untouched by advertising. Fast Moving Consumer Goods, (FMCG) firms have realized the importance of even the rural market and growing demand of certain goods that they have created products, services and mass communication and advertising plans to suit the rural segment. HLL and Procter & Gamble are two firms well into rural marketing, and hence into rural advertising as well.

Advertising often grips people's minds, their psyche that they create for them and a make-belief world, like virtual world, sometimes. So, what exactly is advertising? Who wants it, for whom is it created and how? These and several such questions will be answered in this and following chapters. How the advertiser can hit the bullseye of consumer psyche every time!

Advertising Defined

Advertising texts have given a few definitions of advertising. With the thrust of media variants, i.e., several new media becoming available, the definition can now be modified.

First we take the most popular definition, which is as follows:

AMA (American Marketing Association), defines advertising as:

Any paid form of non-personal presentation and promotion of ideas, goods and services by an identified sponsor

We see, hear or read an advertisement, without perhaps realizing that somebody or some firm has paid for it. Analyzing the definition we can see that:

- Advertising is a form of communication for which payment has been made to the media, which has carried the communication. When no payment is involved then the communication is known as publicity.

- The communication is non-personal, as nobody has personally conveyed it. What we witness in retail shops when the salesman talks to us to sell a product is that he is personally communicating with us and hence by the definition it is not advertising but it is personal selling.
- The presentation is for promoting the ideas, goods and services to create awareness and assist in selling the product.
- A known person or firm does the advertising. This becomes essential to avoid wrong messages being advertised, or sometimes the message becoming useless, as the potential buyer would not know to whom to approach for buying the product, idea or service advertised if the advertiser is unknown.

Advertising can be defined as the soul of marketing in today's world of complex and severe competition, or a substitute elder brother who helps in purchase decisions.

Whatever is required to be done by the marketer to non-personally communicate to the market segment he wants to sell his product through the channel/s of communication can be defined as advertising.

It would therefore be apparent to the student of advertising that irrespective of the definition, it is: (a) the message (creativity) (b) the target segment (c) the communication and (d) the media that form the core of advertising.

Alyque Padamsee, the advertising wizard says about his Liril AD "more then the freshness which comes from its features, Liril promised 20 minutes of freedom to the Indian housewife who gets pulled in different directions the rest of the time."

Advertisement can be subdivided into four ways according to the book entitled *Advertising Excellence* by Bovee, Thill Dovel and Wood as follows:

By target audience	By geographic area	By media used	By purpose
Consumer	International	Print	Product/service marketing
Business	National	Newspaper	Commercial or non-profit
Industrial Trade	Regional	Magazines	Primary/selective demand
Professional	Local	Electronic	Direct/indirect action
Agricultural		Radio	
		TV	
		Outdoor	
		Billboards	
		Buses/trains	
		Direct mail	
		Directories	
		Other media	

Advertisement for target audience is important that the people who are likely buyers see the advertisement message. Hence, advertisers cater to different market segments with the help of separate media as also target-specific message. Advertisement for Mercedes car would not have any effect in a slum cluster; advertisement for low cost clothing material would be of no use to the wealthy elite.

Consumer advertising deals with the actual buyers and users of the market segment and therefore uses a language and a medium best seen by the target segment.

Business advertising converging on target segment has to be in magazines seen by purchase and technical persons of firms. For instance an advertisement for TV picture tubes would be best seen in magazines of TV trade.

Geographic area coverage of media assists in focusing on the target segment where the firm believes the business potential is maximum. A firm wanting to distribute its products on all India bases would have to look at national press, magazines with national circulation and readership, and national TV, including satellite and cable TV channels.

Similarly, firms wanting to do business internationally would locate the right media; satellite TV, Internet or national press of the defined countries where the firms want to do business.

Firms selling in local areas would look for city cable network, local press, and hoardings.

Defining advertising class by media is required as media like TV assures the advertiser a wide coverage due to its reach. Local press conversely can be focused on a small segment.

Advertisement is done for a purpose, like increasing product awareness in the target segment, for introducing a new product to the target audience (product launches).

Advertising and Publicity

There can be some confusion about the roles of advertising and that of publicity. It is therefore necessary to understand the differences and usage of each, which are as follows:

- Advertising is a paid form of communication while publicity comes free to the sponsor. Firm's press releases are common form of publicity.
- For advertising a known sponsor is necessary, for publicity it is not, as it can be a third party making assertions or comments, which give rise to publicity.
- In advertising the sponsor is giving and is responsible for the message, the choice of media and frequency of insertions of the advertisement, while in publicity, at times the media's own comments and editorials play their role, which lend authenticity to the message. However, only if the comments are favourable they work well, otherwise these could become counterproductive.

Similarly, personal selling differs from advertising inasmuch as personal selling requires salesman and buyer to interact while in advertising there is no such direct interaction.

Modern Definition of Advertising

Reaching the target market segment to promote firm's brands through especially selected for the segment media, using the creativity in language and expressions best understood by the segment when direct personal contact is not there. To lend authenticity, the identity of advertiser, the firm's signatures become intrinsic elements of advertising.

Hence, it can be surmised that advertising plays multi-faceted roles in business. Not only it informs the target segment of customers but persuades them to buy the product or use the service offered by the advertiser.

Since the communication is non-personal, one drawback remains, as no immediate and direct reaction or response is available or becomes known to the sponsor of the advertising, as he has to wait for the product sales to increase as a result of advertising.

How it All Began?

In ancient times people lived in villages a life of self-sufficiency. They produced from earth their food, killed animals for food, and used animal skin for clothing.

Later on, as can be visualized from the ancient rock carvings and paintings of Pompeii, Ajanta and Ellora and in the Indus valley civilization when craftsmen made special signs to keep their identity unique with their products. It can be considered advertising in its embryonic form.

In Greece, town criers were used to announce important events, happenings and Middle-ages found them as only means of advertising.

In fifteenth century with the advent of printing press, the first advertisements started appearing, the first one being an Englishman Caxton's handbill advertising his book on religion. Only from the nineteenth century regular press or newspaper advertising as we see today became popular.

The industrial revolution brought mass production and with it, need for informing wider audience about the products available, as local market could not consume the entire produce.

Later on, Radio and Television came as means of communication and marketers started using them for advertising their goods and till today they are growing as popular media. With the current age of technology no facet of human life has remained untouched. Information technology Internet cell phones and voicemail have brought about significant changes in quality and speed of communications globally. Marketers have been quick to grab these media. Besides, the thrust on "live" demonstration on TV has triggered the creative instincts making advertising highly productive and creative.

Business booms are becoming more apparent then ever. Mass production techniques are possible with Computer Aided Design (CAD), and Computer Aided Manufacturing (CAM) and Robotronics, where robots do the work of humans faster when humans can plan to build better robots.

Living in the information age both the advertisers and advertising agencies have come of age with respect to creativity using human emotions, psyche and media thrust.

Jayashree Sundar of Lintas avers, "Marketing and Brand building are evolutionary exercises. All products commence by promising USP "Unique Selling Preposition.". Over a period of time, when product parity kicks in, what endears brands to customers is their emotional attachment."

Case Study: Old Spice Cosmetics for Men

Old Spice has been a global brand of cosmetics for men. Their range includes, after-shave lotion, lather shaving cream, talcum powder, shampoos and hair cream. In India the first and most successful product launched was after-shave lotion.

In the year 1986 the market share of Old Spice products in India was as follows:

- After shave lotion 65%
- Lather shaving cream 9%
- Talcum powder 1%
- Shampoo trace
- Hair cream trace

Colfax Lab. Ltd. the manufacturers had been marketing the products in the west through Departmental Stores. They planned strategy to boost their products sale in India in 1987. They decided to reduce reliance on after shave lotion and promote other products as well, as they had found there was good market for other products too.

Shampoo—as Colfax had only one type of shampoo, whereas competitors had several types, the decided to lie low on this product.

Talcum powder—as talcum powder was purchased mostly by women, and Old Spice was a brand for men the sales were restricted.

Hence, it was decided to promote lather shaving cream along with after-shave lotion as the two products complemented each other.

A market survey gave the following figures of use of cosmetics by men:

- Shaving cream is used by 94% of men
- After shave lotion by 79%
- Hair cream by 33%

- Talcum powder by 86%
- Shampoo by 63%

Advertising Plan

Advertising budget was not enough for multi-product campaign.

After-shave lotion to be the umbrella product and from 1985 the Surfer Ad campaign was launched. The advertisement gives a masculine macho image to the product. It gave a fillip to after-shave lotion and had marginal impact on sales of other products.

Forty towns with 70% business were selected for the campaign.

TV was taken as the primary medium.

Product differentiation was through package size, with introduction of 50 ml pack with atomizer.

Objectives of the advertising plan were to increase awareness of the product in customer's minds, encourage trial usage of lather shaving cream.

Strategy was to keep the brand personality of lather shaving cream same as that of after-shave lotion, that of a masculine macho man and gradually increase focus on lather shaving cream without decreasing the importance of after-shave lotion.

Since the lather shaving cream was a superior product as compared to other shaving creams, keeping advertisements of both the products, lather shaving cream and after-shave lotion consistent, improved the brand image of both the products.

The product was targeted towards 25 plus men with income of Rs. 10,000 per month.

Research had shown that as the brand image is most important, brand character had to be clearly defined.

Old Spice man is adventurous—devil-may-care man. His activities and sports have a touch of danger. He thrives on risks and women pine for him.

Creative strategy leads to making of the polo film, horses symbolizing the macho in men, who are irresistibly attractive to the elitist women. Polo is exclusively adventurous and full of risks.

Medium had to be elitist i.e., TV which provides the following:

- Maximum excitement to brand for large target audience.
- High reach
- Quick building of sales
- Cost effective

Three spots a month were given of twenty seconds duration on national network.

Evaluation – the figures given are enough evidence of the success of the campaign:

	1986	1987	1988	1989
Volume	100	131	158	213
Value	100	134	180	277

The market share also improved as can be seen from the next table (given in percentage).

Year/%	1988	1989	1990	1991	1992
Old Spice	13.1	16.2	19.2	26.8	33.5
Palmolive	34.5	33.4	36.9	35.5	33.6
Godrej	19.5	20.2	18.7	18.6	19.3

Old Spice has remained one of the most respected brands worldwide. In 1988 lather shaving cream advertisement was among top ten advertisements in the world.*

Marketing Mix Factors

Marketing mix factors can be equated to the ingredients a chef has when he wants to cook a tasty dish. Marketing manager too has the factors, some in his control, others not, which are required to successfully and profitably market his products and/or services. Advertising is one of the factors of marketing mix.

Most marketing books talk of four Ps, i.e., Product, Price, Placement and Promotion as marketing mix factors. If we go in little detail we find the following as marketing mix factors:

- Market research, market survey and analysis.
- Product, its detailed dynamic and static specifications. (Most relevant in industrial products.) With product come brand, packaging, trademark, and label.
- Price, discounts, credit, payment terms, inclusion of taxes and duties.
- Placement, which is another word for distribution.
- Promotion, which broadly includes advertising and promotion.
- Personal selling.
- After-sales service.
- Credit and its control.
- Personnel, their training and career plan.

In the fascinating game of marketing, each of the factors is important. Achieving marketing objectives is possible through clever usage of these factors.

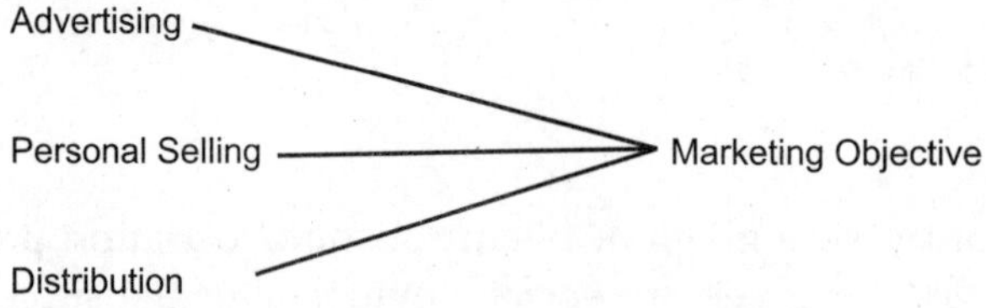

The advertising efforts can be focused and strengthened by market segments, creativity levels, and media.

It is worthwhile to understand in brief the marketing mix factors and their relation to advertising.

Market Research

The ongoing continuous market information a firm needs is best achieved by delegating the job of gaining the information to the field sales force of the firm, who are the eyes and ears of the firm. For some specific reasons, market research is obtained by outside market research agencies.

Market research can be conducted for any of the marketing mix factors.

Product development, new product launch should be done after thorough research of the demand of the product in the market segment for which the product has been planned. Except for new innovations or inventions where the prospective customer has not even a clue, most products succeed in the market if they have been launched after understanding the market needs through market research.

Selecting distribution channels, price and promotional plans and advertising can benefit from research.

Research Methods

Following are the two main methods of conducting marketing research:

Primary Research

Secondary Research

Primary research is conducted by collecting information from the actual customers/ consumers. Details would be discussed in the chapter covering advertising research. Suffice it to say that information/data is collected with the help of a questionnaire, which is filled by talking to selected customers. It requires the marketer to take a sample of customers in a particular geographic area and ask customers questions, which would evoke unbiased replies so that even with the sample of the total market segment, quite accurate results can be obtained. Greater the sample, greater accuracy! However, as contacting large number of respondents (prospective customers) would entail lot of money and time and since these could be crucial factors, large sample could be self-defeating. By the time the research findings become available to the sellers, the information could become obsolete.

Secondary research consists of data, which is already available somewhere as previously the data has been collected as primary data. Sources of such data could be found from the following:

- Firm's own records
- Press
- Trade associations
- Government publications
- Research organizations
- Trade publications
- International press, International trade organizations and associations
- UN and allied bodies

Firms keep records of their own activities and business results as well as information related to competitive activity. In the era of multi-brand retailers, information on competitive activity can be obtained from these retailers. As the firms plan advertising campaigns such information would be found of importance to them.

Marketing Information System

When, later in the book discussion on activities relating to interaction between the advertiser and the advertising agency would be taken up the importance of the information would become apparent, which is available as Marketing Information System (MIS). For example,

- For Each Dealer
- Product Sale for the Month
- Sales for the Year upto the Month
- Competitor's Sale for the Month
- Competitor's Sale for the Year upto the Month

Once the Data has been obtained the task of data analysis starts. It is the interpretation of data, which gives an insight to the real position of the firm in market.

Press, newspapers and magazines keep publishing special supplements covering one or two aspects of business. These supplements provide valuable information about the market situation for the product.

Trade associations like, ASSOCHEM CII, FICCI maintain data about industrial growth and market potential.

Government publishes a lot of industrial data through Director General Audiovisual Publicity (DAVP).

Research organizations like, ORG-MARG keep lot of data of their own research.

Each trade has its own magazine from where data can be obtained. Textile manufacturers have their own magazine and likewise, TV and radio makers have their own publications.

Similarly, international business data can be obtained from international trade bodies and the UNO and its allied agencies.

Two most important assets or possessions of any firm are the market share and the brand. Market research analysis can give a true picture of both.

Market Share

In today's competitive market, profits come from market share. Larger the share better the profits. Sometimes this may not be entirely true. In trying to gain better share, marketers tend to reduce price, give additional benefits to the customers, extra credit periods, all of which reduce profit margins. It is therefore important for firms to have a balanced view of the market share. It is sometimes dictated by production and marketing capacity of firms too.

Brand distinguishes products or product groups from those of the competition and it can become the single most important factor responsible for the firm's profits, name and at times its very existence.

Product

Products can be categorized as follows:
- Consumer Durables e.g., cars, scooters, TV sets, ACs.
- Fast Moving Consumer Goods, e.g., soaps, shampoos
- Industrial Capital Goods e.g., textile mill, sugar factory
- Industrial Consumables, e.g., electricity, water
- Industrial Raw Materials and Components, e.g., steel sheets for car manufacture
- Services, e.g., hotels, airlines, hospitals

It may be mentioned here that most products have an element of service attached to them and similarly, most services also have some product with them.

It is said that nobody buys a product. Every one buys the satisfaction the product provides to the person. Hence, one cosmetic marketer advertised that we sell hope. Hope that by using their cosmetics the person would become a beautiful individual.

What is a product? Is soap, just soap? As per advertisers apparently it is much more than a mere soap. It is a complexion improver, skin softener, germ killer, beautifier, and perhaps much more. Or sometimes soap is not even soap as in the case of Dove. Imagination and creativity are synonymous with advertising.

For industrial or consumer durables detailed specifications both static and dynamic, characterize the product. For example, a car, besides its brand would be, so long, wide, with so much seating capacity. Besides, dynamically, its horsepower, braking torque, acceleration would be important specifications, which help buyers to decide the car he wants to buy.

Take the case of chemical plant, steel mill, telephone exchange, the complex specifications could run into thousands of pages and hence advertising gets more detail oriented.

Brand

Brand is the most valued possession of a firm. Take Mercedes away from the car and what have you got? Brand gives a product its separate identity, taking it away from other run-of-the-mill products. Firms increase their market share and profits on the basis of the brand, or brand image or brand equity. It helps firms in advertising as brand image is built through advertising.

Jajshree Sundar of Lintas offers, "At the end of the day, brands are but promises packaged with emotion. The stronger the emotional bonding, the greater the probability a brand will have of accessing additional revenue streams."

Packaging

In case of fast moving consumer goods, FMCGs packaging plays a vital role. It distinguishes the product, helps in positioning it at the right market segment and package itself is used as part of advertising. Can we imagine Lux soap without its wrapper? Or, Pantene shampoo in ink bottle? The examples are merely meant to focus on the packaging.

Trademark

To avoid competition getting to use same name of similar products to reap the benefit of firms brand image, it becomes essential for firms to register the trademarks with trademark registration authority. These trademarks are useful in advertising the products and they avoid danger of competition taking advantage of using the name and getting the benefit of brand image.

Label

Again, in FMCG products, the label on the package can attract customers hence can act as advertising labels are used to give product information like its weight, formulation, dimensions.

Logo

Firms consider their logos as their personality and hence lot of creative effort goes into making of the logo. Starting from firm's letterheads to visiting cards, packing cases of products, retail outlets, and offices have logos prominently displayed for ease of identification and inbuilt attraction.

Price

Price, in case of virtually all products is the most important feature, which makes people take buying decisions. Price changes, discount offers, exchange offers, credit or installment payment terms are used for increasing market share. To make market segment aware of these, firms advertise them in right media.

We shall discuss in detail what entails the right media in relation to target market segment later on in the text. Suffice it to say that lower price does not necessarily mean better sales or higher market share, as many times, price does get associated to quality of the product. Hence resorting to price reduction could lead to reduction in business and market share as Daewoo Motors learnt to their dismay that when they reduced the price, business did not increase. In fact they must have irked their existing customers for having charged them a higher price, which even according to the sellers was not justified.

Placement

This P corresponds to the distribution system of the firm for its products. The conventional distribution consists of the following channels:

- Wholesalers
- Sole Distributors
- Area Distributors
- Retailers
- Franchisees
- Commission Agents
- Dealers
- Firms own retail outlets

Selection of distribution system depends on the size of the firm, product, area coverage planned and possible mark-ups available for the channel members. Study of distribution patterns is required in this book only from the viewpoint of advertising the channels in appropriate media. In addition, firms advertise to get the right channel members to sell their products and then plan joint advertising, which includes the channel members too.

Promotion

Promotion of products in the market is done through advertising and promotion. Since advertising is the subject of the book, let us discuss promotion.

To increase sales, capture larger market share, launch a new product, firm's resort to promoting product by offering concessions by way of incentives to buy. Buy one get one free. Buy a car, get a TV free. Buy toothpaste, toothbrush is free. These and similar promotion campaigns are introduced to attract customers to buy the product. To the marketer it really means price reduction, with the advantage that unlike a proper price reduction announced by a firm and advertised, promotional plans can be withdrawn any time. Price reductions tend to become more permanent in nature. Maruti's price reduction could be retracted only after a period of more than a year. Most promotion campaigns have words conveying to the customer that the promotion is valid till the stocks last or it can be withdrawn without giving any notice to this effect. From advertising point of view, promotions do not become effective unless they are advertised in the right media for target market segment. In times of recession there is a marked upswing in promotional plans of most firms who are not able to sell their entire produce. Hence, advertising too gets a big boost, as all promotional plans need to be advertised to enable buyers take advantage of the promotions.

Personal Selling

- In case of consumer goods, personal selling effort is 20% and advertising backup support is 80%.
- In case of industrial products personal selling is 80% and advertising support is 20%.

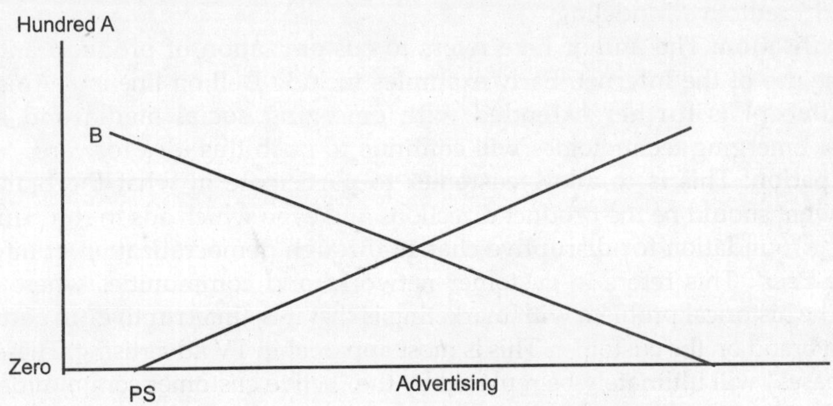

- Are the consumer goods where advertising plays a major role, yet PS (personal selling) is not totally absent?
- Are the industrial products where PS, personal selling plays a major role and advertising too has a significant value in their marketing?

After-Sales Service

Repeat purchase decisions are taken by customers on the basis of the after-sales service offered by the firms. A product, after its purchase becomes as good as the service provided by the seller. Firms do advertise about the availability of service facilities with them to reassure the customers. After-sales service is really like insurance provided by the firm and both customers and firms are happy in its non-use.

Credit and its Control

Credit is a good sales tool, as a credit buyer tends to buy more. However, firms have to keep on monitoring not only the credit worthiness of their customers but also their intentions of making timely payments. From the advertising viewpoint, since credit extensions or leasing options attract additional business they must be advertised so that the target market segment becomes aware of the facility.

Training of Sales Force

Marketing manager needs a live-wire team to achieve sales targets and people like to join such firms whose brand equity is high. As such advertisement does help firms in getting better managers. The importance of training and development, career planning cannot be over emphasized.

Marketing New 4Ps

The original 4Ps concept idea was developed to help marketers manage the four most important aspect of marketing. With the Internet marketers need to adapt a broader perspective on these elements. Idris Mootee devised a "New 4Ps" model in 2001 to supplement the traditional marketing 4Ps. They are: Personalisation, Participation, Peer-to-Peer and Predictive Modeling.

Personalisation: The author here refers to customization of products and services through the use of the Internet. Early examples include Dell on-line and Amazon.com, but this concept is further extended with emerging social media and advanced algorithms. Emerging technologies will continue to push this idea forward.

Participation: This is to allow customer to participate in what the brand should stand for; what should be the product directions and even which ads to run. This concept is laying the foundation for disruptive change through democratization of information.

Peer-to-Peer': This refers to customer networks and communities where advocacy happens. The historical problem with marketing is that it is "interruptive" in nature, trying to impose a brand on the customer. This is most apparent in TV advertising. These "passive customer bases" will ultimately be replaced by the "active customer communities". Brand engagement happens within those conversations. P2P is now being referred as social computing and will likely to be the most disruptive force in the future of marketing.

Predictive modeling: This refers to predictive algorithms, such as neural network, that are being successfully applied in marketing problems (both a regression as well as a classification problem).

Tasks for Advertising in the 21st Century

Let us discuss the tasks before advertising in the twenty-first century. New products, innovative products are being launched these days as never before. In case of new innovating products, the target segment may not even be aware of the product. Hence the first task of advertising is to bring about product awareness in the segment. The task steps are given below:

- Taking the viewer or reader from the level of

  Unawareness-to and Awareness-to:
- Knowledge about the existence of the product in the market-to
- Desire of possession of the product-to
- Conviction about its utility value and related benefits-to
- Brand preference-to
- Purchase action-to
- Product's continuous evaluation-to
- Repeat purchase decisions.

Imagine the time when cell phones had not invaded our country. The marketers had to resort to teaser advertisements to arouse curiosity among target segment, which created awareness, and as the product was launched firms got good response.

It is worthwhile to mention that a bad product cannot be sold and as a corollary should not be advertised.

Advertising Mix Factors

Advertising is one of the marketing mix factors. Let us analyze advertising mix factors. There are six sides to advertising in totality. They are given below:

- Advertiser
- Advertising Agency
- Media
- PR Consultants
- Ancillary Services
- Freelance Services

Advertisers

They can be categorized as profit making organizations and non-profit making organizations. The first category consists of the following:

Government and government bodies including public sector companies. The government advertises for purchasing through tenders, selling surpluses, recruitment through Public Service Commissions.

Manufacturers advertise when they have to sell direct to consumer like power, industrial raw materials. They advertise to buy from the market what raw material components they need to manufacture their finished products.

Service providers like travel agents, hotels, airlines, advertise to sell their services.

Importers advertise to sell their goods to the target segment.

Distributors, retailers and other members of distribution channel advertise to sell their products. Since their area of operation is limited their advertising is also confined to the geographic area they serve.

Mail order suppliers advertise so that their catalogues are purchased by their target segment, which could result in their getting orders by mail. *Burlington's* and *Reader's Digest* are examples of mail order suppliers.

The second category of advertisers are non-governmental organizations, like family planning groups, destitute children help groups, de-addiction centres.

Advertising Agency

The main role played by an advertising agency is that of communication experts, who assist the advertisers in obtaining optimized benefit for the money they spend on advertising by ensuring that the target segment gets at least an opportunity to see (OTS) the product advertisement. The advertisements given in properly selected media, which result in improved brand awareness and consequently improved sales and profits is the major task of advertising?

There are several types of advertising agencies operating in the marketplace to suit different needs of advertisers. Many times one advertiser uses one agency for one type of advertisement and a separate one for other needs. Major types of agencies are given below:

- Large full function agency
- Medium size full function agency
- Specialized technical agencies
- Hot Shops
- Agency of Records

Large full function agency comprises the following departments:

- Account servicing department
- Account planning department
- Creative department, including Art Director, Copy Writer, Visualizer, Electronic Media Coordinator
- Research Director
- Media Planner
- Budgeting and Billing
- In India HTA, Lintas, Saatchi & Saatchi, Contract are but a few examples of such agencies.

Medium size full function agency may not have research and account planning departments. Otherwise they are similar to large agencies and they graduate to large agencies as their billing and business increases.

Specialized technical agencies are agencies working for niche market i.e., financial firms, IT companies, TV companies. They normally keep experts in their area of specialization either on their role or on consultancy panel. Saubhagya and Clea are two representatives of such agencies.

Hot shops are small lean mean agencies, which operate on low overheads and do quality work by hiring experts on job basis.

AOR or Agency of Records is the agency with large business portfolio and surplus resources. Such agencies buy popular media space in bulk, use it at advantageous cost and sell it to smaller agencies in times of their need. For their investment they take 2% profit margin from the smaller agencies.

Media

From the earlier days of hand painted posters, media has come up with cable and satellite TV revolution. Joining the bandwagon is Internet and computer designing of advertisements.

Broadly media are characterized as follows:

- Press
- Electronic
- Computer, Internet
- Outdoor
- Point of purchase
- Direct Mail
- Miscellaneous

Press relates to newspapers, magazines, in various languages, targeting various segments, cultural, religious, sports, fashion, films, wildlife the list is a long one. The advertiser has to look for the right paper, magazines which are read by the target segment to ensure OTS (Opportunity to See). Many top executives have virtually no time to watch television and hence they get the news and other information from newspapers and business magazines. Marketers of products meant for this market segment should therefore use newspapers and magazines to reach the target segment effectively. Expensive cars, laptop computers, and expensive dress materials could fall in the category.

Andre Hattum, President & CEO, Pan Asia Paper Co. has the following thoughts on print media "In an internet vs. newspaper scenario we find that newspapers are still mass carriers of advertising. Internet gives one access to information but it is not as effective. In a country like India the penetration of computers is negligible. Even in the US, where Internet penetration is high, the newsprint business is doing quite well."

Electronic Media

It relates to television, radio, videocassettes. Television as a media for advertising has made the biggest impact on almost all the segments of customers. Satellite and cable TV have invaded practically all homes. Viewership of TV has increased manifold and terms like couch potato have been invented for people who are constantly viewing the TV. This fact has opened up advertising vistas for majority of the products. The advertiser has to understand the programme one segment views and then he can plan to place the advertisement during that particular programme. Similarly, FM channels of the radio have become popular in metro towns with a large teenage following. Products meant for teens can be advertised on FM with great certainty of success. Tele-marketing and Tele-shopping are making strides as the latest media. Products are sold through telephones in one case while in the other; TV is used for demonstrating the working of the product and orders are solicited.

Computer and Internet: The medium of communication of computers and the Internet are relatively new in India but they are making giant strides in advertising and marketing world.

And hence, in present-day context it is important to understand these to succeed. With on-line e-commerce, banking, and purchasing selling it is expected that people with buying power will be more hooked to computers then ever before. It is important to note that information technology is the future of communications with computers and telecommunications joining hands to provide the safest, fastest and low cost reliable communication. Advertisers need to understand the medium and take full advantage of the same.

Outdoor: Relates to hoardings, billboards, neon signs, bus panels, kiosks, balloons and the like. These are used by advertisers as reminder advertisements as well as product launch ads too.

Direct Mail: Several marketers resort to sending technical literature by post to prospective customers, including *Reader's Digest, Burlington.*

Point of Purchase Advertising: It has been updated with technological advances. Retail shops were content earlier with posters, danglers and innovative packaging. Today, multimedia has provided with interactive computer screens where the customers can get any information about the shop including availability of product, stocks prices. Many shops keep continuous TV programmes with animation, cartoons and product advertisements.

Tele shopping is becoming popular but gradually, as the Indian shopper wants to see and feel the touch of the product before buying it. Additionally, shopping expeditions become fun time outings for the family and it would be difficult to replace them by television—on screen-shops.

Tele-marketing uses the telephone line to tell the prospective customers about the services the marketer is providing and is, at times a good approach to elicit right response from the customer.

Miscellaneous Advertising Media

We have all seen big balloons in the sky carrying advertising messages, advertisements on bus panels, yellow pages, directories, rail and air tickets, even on matchboxes. We have also witnessed advertisements on camels and elephants especially designed for

village fairs. Human imagination can only limit to the extent people will locate an existing unutilized medium, discover, or invent one for the purpose.

PR Consultants

As we compare advertising with newspaper's own coverage it becomes clear that editorial coverage invariably gets better credence to advertisement, since it appears as unbiased opinion of a third party, i.e., the newspaper editor. Hence, advertisers always wish to boost their image and they find Public Relation (PR) consultants have good contacts with the press and as a PR exercise they get features written about the firm and its products making invaluable and significant contribution towards image building programme of the firm as independent views unconnected to the firm have better credibility with the prospective customer then the advertising campaign of the firm.

Public relations as function helps firms evaluate their standing, brand image and credibility in the market place. Since brand building and brand equity come through advertising and PR, it becomes imperative to integrate these at certain level.

Ancillary Services

Advertising agencies have to take the help of several ancillary service providers, as it would be too expensive to have every one on the payroll. Major services, which are hired by agencies, are:

- Independent producers of advertising short films for TV or cinema. Not even large advertising agencies keep a film making division. They all hire on contract independent specialist producers. These producers are then briefed by the agency persons regarding their client's requirements from then on, from selection of film script to location, models cameraman, lights among other film making items are arranged by the producer in consultation with the agency and the advertiser.
- Manufacturers of point of purchase advertising material, like, posters and danglers.

- Direct mail houses who take upon themselves to arrange the address data bank and the advertising material to be sent along with its frequency of dispatch.
- Manufacturers of containers, packing material and cartons who provide the advertiser with packages, which become part of advertisement.
- Printing presses, litho press, typesetters, who are required for print media advertisements.
- Electrical and electronic panel makers
- Manufacturers of working models
- Gift suppliers
- Audio-visual equipment suppliers
- Merchandisers
- Desk top publishers

Freelance service providers like, copywriters, artists, visualizers, who are hired for specific jobs by small agencies like hot shops, and at times by small advertisers themselves, who cannot afford to hire an agency.

The challenge of creating a powerful advertisement, which can change the mindset of the market segment, has assumed great importance in the twenty-first century. With advancements in technology of communication as also in product groups and constant upgradations more and more money is going to be spent in years to come on advertising. Are we as marketers and advertisers ready with the necessary tools of the job?

Advertising, as understood by now, is part of the marketing game. To better plan advertising, firms will have to reinforce their marketing plans. Selection of markets for the product, distribution network, pricing and the timing of its launch would affect and determine the type of advertisement campaign should be created and what would be the best media for the same. Therefore from marketing plans and budgets, advertising plans and budgets would evolve.

As can be seen competitors are also planning their strategy on almost similar lines. The question therefore is how do we succeed and beat the competition? The most useful method would include a continuous scan of the general and competitive environment by the firm where any delays or wrong information could lead to disastrous results. On the positive side, correct and timely information would certainly lead to market successes.

General Environment Factors

These include the following:

- Demographic
- Socio-cultural
- Political-legal
- Technological
- Macroeconomics
- Global

Demographic factors: It is important to understand the demographic pattern of the market the firm wants to do business in. It gives the customer profile by age, sex, income, family size, occupation and residential locations. Shifts of population from rural to urban areas and to metro towns could provide marketing opportunities for certain products.

Socio-cultural factors: Include increase in women in workforce, larger single parent group, larger population of senior citizens and teenagers. Product needs and motivation for these segments can create huge market potential where innovative products like pre-cooked foods, readymade garments and home help products like vacuum cleaners, washing machines are finding big market.

Political-legal factors: Must be understood by advertisers and advertising agencies as it is because of political action preceded by political will that taxation changes take place resulting in price increases or decrease which affect the purchasing power of potential buyers.

Sometimes courts of law, for public good, put hindrances in the marketplace like the court order which prevented the sale of new cars unless they abided by pollution emission norms of euro-II.

Technological factors: Can be understood as we go through the range of new products available in the marketplace. Consumer durables have been vying with each other with microprocessor based logics for faster improved performance. Advertiser/manufacturer has to market the products with the state-of-the-art technology in order to keep existing customers satisfied and for adding new customers. Cars with multipoint fuel injection systems are one such example.

Macroeconomics factors: These include state tax structure, balance of payment position with countries the firm wants to do business with, exchange rates of currencies involved and the money supply position in the market.

Global: Business environment worldwide is bound to affect the Indian business and marketers and advertisers would do well to keep a close vigil on day-to-day happenings. Indian rupee does fluctuate with dollar. Technological changes worldwide, natural disasters, political upheavals in any country cause positive or negative disturbances in other countries. And they would do well by keep a sharp eye to take pre-emptive measures and gain from the situation. This would include advertising campaigns, promotion plans and continuous upgradation of both.

Finally, the day has come when advertising faces the challenge of being answerable to the client. Agency can prepare advertising campaign with serious thought process, it could be comical, informative or mysterious; it may get some laughs or sympathy, but as long as it does not meet the advertising objectives, it falls flat on the client's pockets. Hence, the criteria of a successful campaign are its ability to move the target segment into knowing, wanting the advertised product. This accountability sifts the mediocre agencies from the genuine good ones.

Now let us state the different parts of advertising. Before making a plan for advertising campaign, agencies arrange to get market research conducted, which helps in defining detailed specifications of the product as accepted by the target market segment, in understanding consumers' reaction to the product and in analyzing the market segment. Only after a proper research can the agency plan the advertising campaign with a good degree of accuracy.

Next, planning is undertaken, which helps in crystallizing the objectives of advertising campaign, besides providing yardstick for creative and media strategy.

At this point of time decisions like the amount to be spent on the campaign, final media selection and actual date-wise schedules are formulated.

The stage for creative wing of agency gets set and the art director, copywriter, visualiser get busy along with the production people to produce the final advertisement.

Only success of the campaign can be celebrated.

Besides the general environment factors advertiser has also to learn about competitive situation. Michael Porter's 5 Force model is ideally suited for understanding competitive business environment, which is described below:

Michael Porter's 5 Force Model

Bargaining power of suppliers C	Threat of new entrants A Rivalry among existing players E Threat of substitute products B	Bargaining power of buyers D

With international players coming with latest technology Indian business is facing this real threat.

Threat of substitute products is apparent in some industries like paint. People can get wood panelling done instead of paint for their walls.

If the RM or component is critical and available with only a few suppliers they have the bargaining power. In such cases the large manufacturer who can afford to buy in bulk gets better prices and other terms like credit.

Bargaining power of buyers can be envisioned with multitudes of manufacturers of the same product with low product differential.

The rivalry amongst existing players manifests itself especially in times of recession. With MNCs spreading their business in India, small Indian firms are facing severe

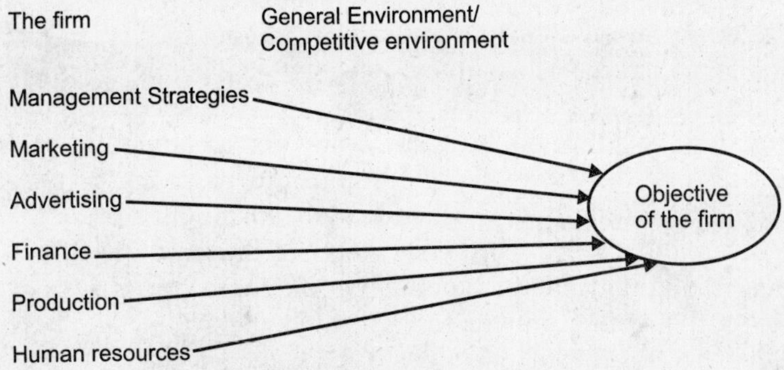

competition. In this game the customer is the main beneficiary as he gets better products at competitive prices.

Advertising is therefore part of business strategy as can be seen below:

The firm does not operate in a vacuum. It operates in a business environment, comprising both general and competitive environmental factors, which are continuously making an impact on the business. In order to achieve its objectives of improving the brand equity and its market share, the firm needs to plan its strategies. Advertising has become a major part of today's firms marketing strategy. Firms want to create demand for their products, make their customers aware of the product, and all the competing firms are doing the same. Better strategy, creativity, positioning in the market segment help the firms in winning the race. Since competition does not give any breathing space and are relentlessly bombarding the customers with innovative advertising, no firm can even think of letting up the efforts at any point of time.

21st century has brought great opportunities and yet greater challenges to the sellers and only the better prepared one's are likely to survive in the continuously increasing rat race. The opportunities are available from opening up of new markets, new media, creativity vistas and challenges from the international competition.

USE THE KNOWLEDGE GAINED

Describe the main market segment and sub-segments for the following products. Also write the type of advertising agency the advertiser should have and two media you consider suitable for the product. Take only Indian market in making your assessment.

- Ready-made gents suits costing between Rs. 7,000 to Rs. 10,000 each.
- Maruti 800 car.
- Cosmetics, including lipsticks, mascara, eye shadow and eye liner costing about Rs. 2000 per set.
- Men's shirt worth Rs. 80/-

Objectives of Advertising: As a Means of Building CRM

These days a lot of money is spent on advertising, up to even 40 per cent of the firm's turnover. It is therefore important that proper care is taken on the spending, especially in the view that most advertising pundits consider it incorrect to try gauging the efficacy of advertising. It is imperative that firms have clear goals for marketing and these can be further dovetailed to the discipline of advertising. Each firm must therefore define its advertising objectives. Given below are some of the possible objectives of advertising.

- Achieving sales targets
- Communication with the customers
- Inviting prompt direct action
- Encouraging customer to ask for information
- Giving information about obvious or hidden needs and their satisfaction
- Products success stories to reinforce product/ brand loyalty
- The benefit story, highlighting the benefits customers would derive from the product
- Customer's attitude change in favour of the product
- Reassurances, which are needed to counter direct or indirect adverse publicity of the product arranged by competition

Besides, the aims and objectives of advertising are as follows:

- Launch of a new product
- Modification in products
- Changes in price
- New packing

- Promotional plans, e.g., buy one get one free
- Distributor's and retailer's address
- Educating the customers for proper use of the product
- To retrieve lost sales, e.g., due to strike in the factory
- Reminder ads for maintaining sales
- To recruit staff
- To appoint distributors and dealers
- To invite technical staff of industrial customer to ask for literature, come to visit
- Competitive comparative advertising
- To assist retail sale
- To help salesperson get a foot in the door of industrial customers
- To attract investors through special ad campaigns
- To export/go international
- To announce financial results of the firm
- To sell direct e.g., *Reader's Digest*

Sales as Objective

Business requires continuous improvement in the bottom line. Profit remains the prime motive and to achieve a reasonable return on investment firms have to struggle as competitors are equally focused on the same subject. Advertising is a distinct aid to improving sales. Many advertising agencies believe that advertising should not be linked to increase or decrease in sales. However, the ultimate use of advertising must be to improve profitable sales.

Communication

Advertising is used as a means of communication as marketers want to provide information about their products to the target segment. Marketers also inform about new products in the pipeline, discount offers, new retail outlets and of late exchange offers.

A) The first step in business communication through advertising is of creating awareness, for product launches it becomes critical that target segment customer gets to know about the product
B) Comprehension it should result in potential customer getting to know features of the product
C) Acceptance of the product as a means of satisfying customer's needs, whether they buy it or not.
D) Belief that it is this product only which the customer needs.
E) Purchase action is the next step, as the customer has fully understood the value he/ she will derive from the product.
F) Usage and repeat buy results from satisfaction of customer and going beyond satisfaction the product delights the customer.

Thus the chain goes on, which starts with customer's awareness of the product.

Price Changes

Product prices convey to the buyers a lot more than just what they are paying for. Prices denote quality of the product besides authenticity of supply. In industrial products prices could include packing, taxes, duties and transport/insurance costs. Unless marketers make a clean statement of the prices there can be lot of room for cheating the customers. Hence, good marketers invariably announce the price changes (and what all are included in the prices like sales tax, excise duty), through advertising in the media appropriate for the segment.

Prompt Direct Action

"Buy today and get a 20% discount or the offer ends in just two days" – are the gimmicks to prompt the customer into action. These offers must be advertised for letting the segment customers know and take advantage of the offer, and make the offer a success for the seller.

Customers are Encouraged to Seek more Information

Through teaser advertisement. When Bharti Telecom introduced Airtel their cellular phone service in Delhi the city roads were carrying banners saying. "There is Some Thing New in the Air- Airtel" Several industrial product ads give only basic specifications to generate curiosity and interest which prompts the customer to ask for specification details.

Message of Need and its Satisfaction

It has become one of the most common objectives of advertising. In summer months the emphasis on thirst and cold drinks, the colas is well known and literally millions of rupees are spent on such ads. Advertising in college billboards for books pinpoints the need for books and how this can be fulfilled.

Product Success Stories

These are advertised to reinforce customer's commitment to purchasing the product. Hero Honda has been advertising the fact that their scooter is the only one to have climbed the high mountain pass of Khardungla, confirming the high quality of the product, which in turn would make the customers delighted and prospective buyers consider strongly about purchasing the scooter. Customer's brand loyalty cannot be taken for granted by any marketer. Such stories could improve the chances of having brand loyal customers.

Benefit Story

It is usually the fundamental theme of most ads. It could be promise of fairer skin (creams), better health (tonics), better mileage (fuel efficient car), the list is endless.

Researchers tell that people do not buy products; they buy the satisfaction or delight they are likely to obtain from the product. Car is not just a car; it is a comfortable means of transportation. An example of the benefit story is given below for Maruti Esteem car.

The benefit story can be made for any product as it sifts the features from the benefits, which can be gained from a product. These benefits ultimately converge on the basic needs of people as per Maslow's hierarchy of needs.

An example of a benefit story is given below:

Product-Maruti Esteem

Car features	Benefits from the feature
Sleek sedan model	Projecting high life style
Comfortable seats, leg room	Physical comfort
Big luggage boot	Family car
High power engine	High life style/youth
Power windows	Comfort
Countrywide service	Peace of mind

Now if we recall the birthday ad, where the husband is driving in his esteem with his wife and a child, he stops the car to buy some thing and the child brings out the cake from the dickey sitting in the backseat, the wife puts the happy birthday tape and they surprise the husband on his return when he hears the song and sees the cake. Then the family drives away towards the horizon. The Ad tells that Esteem is a luxury family car.

Attitude Change

When the marketer finds that the competitor is firmly entrenched in the target segment, advertising becomes more aggressive, as it is necessary to have a change of attitude in the customer group. Lot of comparative ads are used for this purpose. The customers are informed in great detail about the shortcomings of competitive products as compared to their products. However, this approach is wrought with difficulties, as it may not be possible to prove the point and then the competitor can go to the court of law and claim heavy damages.

The toothpaste ads of Colgate were too farfetched as the claims made by them were not easy to prove and hence they had to revise the ads.

Reassurance

It becomes imperative for marketers to keep their customers on their side as competition is always trying to get them to their side. Reassuring ads, which keep confirming the quality of the product, its availability at reasonable price and in products with long life cycles are a must to keep the sales going.

Product Launches

Every day a new product is being introduced in the market, sometimes with great fanfare and sometimes tamely. Medimix soap was introduced with minimum advertising. Only when its sales picked up that the makers started big AD campaign, which has raised the awareness level and hopefully would get increased market share. Whirlpool started sales of their washing machines with much advertising and is reaping the bounty of good share of the market.

Product launch provides the biggest challenge to both advertiser and the advertising agency, since the success of the product depends greatly on its launch.

It is important to learn about product's life cycle at this stage. Each product goes through its life cycle, which starts with its introduction, and then it comes to growth followed by maturity and finally terminating in decline stage.

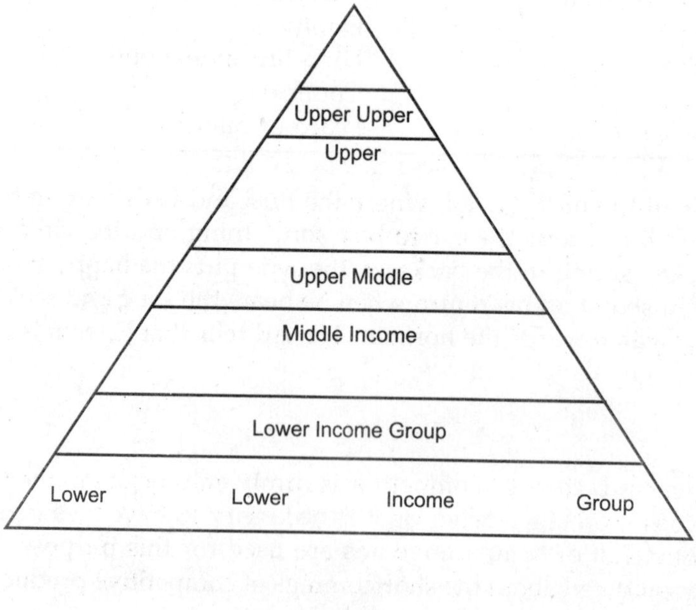

Introduction stage—when a new product is introduced in the market, as cell-phones were, in the beginning the first buyers purchase it. These people are society leaders, innovators and experimenters. Naturally, they have the financial power to back their purchases. Since the number of such buyers is small the sales graph moves slowly during this stage.

Growth stage—after the first buyers (early birds), the first followers buy the product, which wait to see the utility of the product through the experience of early birds. Since this category of buyers is larger than the first one the sales jump up and marketers must provide for increased supplies of the product in the market. (It can be assumed that in India most products are in growth stage as product demand keeps increasing due to economic policies each year a small percent of lower income group gets into the next slab of income with better purchasing power).

Income Life Cycle

- The top most part is of the elitist group with a small percent of population in it say 0.5%
- The second level is bigger than the first like 5%
- The third level could be 15%, while the fourth is 20%. The lower income group could be 25% and lower 30% of the population. Hence, any shift of even one per cent of lower to lower and lower to middle could change the demographic pattern considerably.

Product Life Cycle

Each product is born like a human being, it goes through the growth, maturity and decline stages, like a human being too, as seen in the chart below:

Introduction stage of product needs major advertising effort for product launch, which could include concept selling, product introduction, and price and distribution network and announcements for the target segment customers.

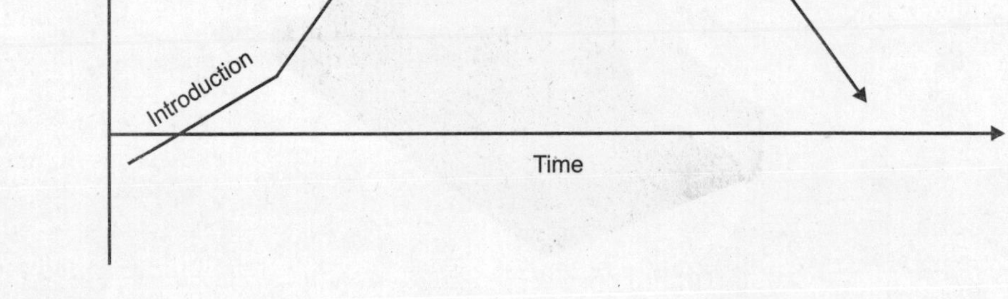

In growth stage, the early marketers have the initial advantage. They cannot relax because competition with ME TOO or even better products come in the market.

In maturity stage as the market gets stagnant, sales is almost static, only replacement purchases take place. In such situations firms have to plan their strategies, whether they want to stay in the market with heavy advertisement or divest, quit.

In decline stage with severe competition many firms do quit, as can be seen in the VCR market. If the firm decides to stay it will have to create new markets for the product.

Product modifications call for informing the prospective customers about "What is new and what it would do for the customer or what extra benefits are available in the new product" the computer and IT industry is the most innovative one where everyday something new happens and marketers want to be the first one's to introduce the product. Product life cycle of such constantly developing products is short and the marketers have to reap the benefits of high sales in shortest possible time. Hence, heavy doses of advertisements are fed to the customers.

Price changes—as is known price is normally the single most important feature of a product, which helps customers, decide about its purchase.

Price changes, discount offers, extended guarantees and warranties have become part of marketing strategy. However, unless the customer gets to know about the changes, he cannot take favourable decisions. Hence there is the need to advertise price changes.

In order to motivate the customers into buying action price changes are made. If the announcement of price reduction is made well in advance, the competitors will get time to take pre-emptive measures, negating any benefit which could accrue by price reduction in terms of increased sales. Timeliness is of great importance when firms want to announce price reductions. Maruti reduced the price of their 800 cc car and made sudden announcement, which gave a big boost to its sales during ensuing period.

New Package

When the firms feel that some staleness has crept into their product and modifications are not possible in the immediate future, they change the package, giving it a modern look, which in turn attracts the customer's attention resulting in increased sales.

A look at the FMCGs would confirm that package change is a common phenomenon. And it does tend to increase sales, provided the customers are made fully aware of the new package, else, some customers may not buy the product considering it as a new untested product. This is done through advertising.

Promotional plans—Firms face loss of market share and sometimes the market shrinks albeit temporarily. In such events, firms want to make purchasing of their products more attractive than that of the competitor. This is done by means of promotional plans. Buy one get one free, buy a car get a stereo free, get a TV set and get a walkman free; these and similar offers help firms to bring extra share of the market.

In fact, such offers amount to price reduction to an extent. Yet, while price reductions have a tendency of being of a more permanent nature, promotions can be withdrawn as and when the firm thinks it has achieved its market share. Bringing back original price gives the firm back its profit margin. However, Maruti took nearly a year before they could restore the original price of its 800 cc model.

Products sell through the distribution channels; the importance of the channels cannot be minimized unless an alternative system of sales is found out. Firms have to inform the segment customers about the location where they can get the product. Therefore they advertise the names, addresses and phone numbers of the sales outlets.

As the channel members also benefit from the advertisements, firms like to have cooperative AD campaigns where the middlemen, persons in the distribution network participate in advertising expense.

Some products are highly technical in nature and wrong or improper use of the product could make it unserviceable. Even mileage and functioning would improve if the cars were maintained properly. In sale of plant and machinery, capital goods such education of the customer is almost mandatory. Even in smaller products like domestic electric appliances, voltage and current specifications are part of the education programme, which is advertised to reach the target segment.

Sometimes firms lose business due to reasons beyond their control, like strike by workers or natural calamity. In such events, as customers needing the product have bought from competitors, it is important to advertise the fact that the firm is back in business. To further supplement their marketing efforts, firms can resort to some promotional plan and advertise it. This would be the best cover for the earlier mishap.

Most general advertising noticed is in reminder category. Pepsi and Coke advertising blitz, which often takes the shape of business war, is an excellent example of reminder ads.

Amul has been in business for a long time now. It is a well-established brand with good market share, innovative marketing and successful reminder advertising. By the way, Amul uses cartoon clips to good effect in these reminder ads.

Comic or cartoon clips can be used if the product justifies it.

Advertisements are given for recruitment of staff by firms. These could be part of newspapers classified category or these could be on special pages. These days

most newspapers and business magazines have sections devoted to recruitment by firms.

Recruitment advertising too has an indirect effect as they subtly remind the customers of the firm's existence.

Advertisements are given to appoint distributors, dealers, agents, retailer's franchisees and C&F agents. Marketers normally know the people who are in the same trade and they can opt from that list when planning to appoint a channel member. Advertising can give firms a wider selection. In case of new areas with geographic business expansion, advertisements can be a real boon.

Firms have to declare their semi-annual and annual profit and loss accounts and the balance sheet. These periodic results can help in consolidating the brand equity too.

For industrial products advertising is meant to assist the sales persons in getting appointments with the customer personnel, like the proverbial foot in the door.

Besides, since normally big money is involved in purchase of industrial products customers need lot more information in the first instant even to arouse their curiosity. Hence, industrial product advertising takes two different forms as follows:

- Advertising details of the product
- Image building advertising, which keeps the firm in constant focus of the buyer.

Firms planning to get investors to buy their shares resort to heavy advertising to create not just a ripple but a storm in the financial market so that small and big investors queue up to buy their shares. There are specialized advertising agencies like Saubhagya and Clea who have the expertise of such advertising.

With global business a fact of life firms would be neglecting international markets at their own risk and peril. Several Indian firms are already multinational companies and more are to follow. In such a situation international advertising has assumed importance. Several Multinational Advertising Agencies have set up offices in India and are providing advertising support for multinational businesses.

Main objectives of advertising are to increase profitable sales, improve market share and the brand image. Brand image builds brand equity, which in turn brings brand loyalty.

CHAPTER

7

Brand Value for CRM

In the Indian context the company's corporate brand equity or value can be compared to the value of company's goodwill. It may be recalled that in the early twentieth century, when a company was sold, extra price was required to be paid for the goodwill the company had accumulated. At times the owners sold the company's assets without its goodwill and the buyers had to pay much less. The owners could then start another company using the goodwill of the first company.

A corporation's brand has always been basically the business intangible and therefore unquantifiable. But Corporate Branding L.L.C., a Stamford, branding consultancy, has taken up the task of determining the real precise value of a brand through a proprietary calculation it calls Core Brand Equity. The results of this calculation can have important strategic and budget implications for marketing departments of corporations, according to Jim Gregory, Corporate Branding's CEO.

"We believe that companies should always be out building their corporate brand as well as their product brands," he said. "When they do that, it adds significant value to the corporation in terms of increased market value and market capitalization."

Branding consultants have been arguing that for years, but Gregory asserts that Core Brand Equity can ascertain a specific dollar/money figure for a particular corporate brand. For example, the value of General Electric Co.'s brand was $61.2 billion at the time of its assessment, making it the most valuable corporate brand, according to the Core Brand Equity data.

Following GE is another business giant, Microsoft Corp., with $59.6 billion in estimated brand equity. Third is retailer Wal-Mart, with estimated brand equity of $42.0 billion. On the business-to-business version of the list, IBM occupies the third place, with a brand equity value of $27.1 billion. (The brand equity values given here are of the period when the assessments were made and may not be the current values. Students should take these values only as indicators and not sacrosanct.)

Corporate Branding bases its calculations on data from its annual brand favourable (associated customers choice) and familiarity studies. The consultancy interviews directors and executives of the largest U.S. companies, asking them to rate more than 1,000 companies.

Using this data, Corporate Branding compares competitors and companies of similar revenues to determine the financial impact that a brand's "favorability" and familiarity have on its market capitalization.

Corporate branding determines the percentage that brand equity contributes to overall market capitalization. The highest percentage is that of Coca-Cola, whose brand contributes 19.4% to its market capitalisation, according to the consultancy.

Among business-to-business companies, FedEx Corp. has the highest percentage, with an estimated $3 billion in brand equity with 18.4% of its market capitalisation. Second is Microsoft, whose brand equity accounts for 18.3% of its market capitalisation.

At the other end of the scale, pharmaceutical company Schering-Plough has the lowest b-to-b brand equity percentage at 4.2%. Abbott Laboratories also has a low brand equity percentage, 5.2%. By comparison, Bristol-Myers Squibb's brand equity is 11.4%.

In Gregory's view, Schering-Plough and Abbott, by allowing their brands to languish, are leaving money on the table. So is Eli Lilly, with a brand equity percentage of 8.6%. as per Gregory a branding campaign could boost the market capitalization of these companies by billions.

"They don't have to increase their brand equity by much to make it very valuable," he said. "If they increase it to 12%, it's a huge benefit to the corporation at very little cost."

Brand Equity: Myth or Reality

Brands' value can be ascertained by adding the product satisfaction levels, package selection and the value additions made with the help of product quality, the company image, price and its functions. The high brand value helps the company in the following areas:

- Premium price customers are willing to pay for the brand
- Increase in intrinsic sales value and volumes
- Increase in market share for the product
- However one negative factor with the brand value is that the company has to spend on marketing expenses to maintain the market share as the competition is closely following the market leader with their own plans.

Customers love popular brands. Brands do for the products the following:

- Brands build trust among the customers who accept the product as reliable that would give them the known benefits.
- Brands focus the buyer's mind on the desired satisfaction from the product.
- Brands provide the seller's promise and guarantee associated with the product
- Brands start occupying the hearts and the minds of their satisfied customers like the famous bike, Harley Davidson.

- Brands form economic assets for the company and goodwill.
- Brands build buyers'-sellers' relationships. As the customers get the desired level of satisfaction they become brand's personal advertisers. Sellers can use these satisfied buyers for getting information on new product demand, product variants and the needed product differentiations.
- Brands promote customer relationships with the sellers as together they can create stories of the brand's success for convincing other customers, either by word of mouth publicity or through advertising.

A brand is not just a product on a shelf but is distinguished from similar products or services. Coca-Cola, Pepsi, Ivory soap are all world known brands. Thus

Brand = Product + Packaging + Added values

The added values may be:

- Quality
- Image
- Price
- Function

Good Knight that was purchased by Godrej from Transelektra has ISI mark, a symbol of quality. The good image of Godrej, availability at an affordable price, and lasting effect makes it a good brand, among the mosquito mats. Thus, Good Knight continues to improve its market share.

Brand equity became a hot topic in 1980's because companies were being bought and sold for the value of their brand names. The Pharma industry was no exception. Crocin was taken over by SKB from Duphar, Complan was taken over by Heinz from Glaxo, and Dr. Reddy's Lab took over Reflux from Sol Pharma. Thus, today in India, brand selling has come to the fore and concept of brand equity is gaining popularity.

Brand equity is short hand for what a brand is worth. It is the asset, which the marketer is building. In fact, brand equity is the asset itself, in the same way that a house is. The value of a house may depend on whether the valuation is for sale or purchase, area etc. In theory, a brand's value is the capital worth of the premium it achieves over the equivalent generic product i.e. same thing without the brand name.

Therefore, Becosules, the No.1 brand in pharma industry, Dexorange No.1 in heamatinic, and Complan command a better price due to the above four determinant factors.

Brand equity can he affected by the following factors:

Volume Business: Higher the sales, greater can be the brand equity. Higher sales signify brand acceptance and its image. The value goes up if the market size too is big. Thus, larger volume sales in a larger market can have higher brand equity than larger volume in a smaller market. For example

			Sales (Rs. Mn)	**Market**
Dexorange Plus	Franco-Indian	Heamatinic	388	Large
Beblex	Anglo-French	Vitamins	138	Larger
Becosule	Pfizer	Vitamins	680	Larger
Glynase	US Vitamins	Antidiabetic	146	OK
Cifran	Ranbaxy	Antibiotic	450	Larger

These brands definitely have high brand equity. Similarly, Becosules brand equity will be higher than Dexorange due to larger market.

Leadership i.e., ranks in the Market: Brand equity will be higher if the product is the leader. Glynase being No.2 will have higher brand equity. However, it will be less than Daonil, which is No. 1 anti-diabetic, ranked drug. Similarly, Dexorange Plus with high volume sales and No.1 position should command a better brand equity than Glynase if we consider only the first two criteria.

Market Size: Higher the market size greater will be the brand equity. Taking an example from above, Becosule, Cifran, Dexorange Plus can command high brand equity because of bigger market size compared to Glynase.

Relative Price: It is a ratio of perceived price divided by actual price. This reflects the consumer's belief in the brand especially the quality of the brand. Higher ratio indicates that perceived value is high. Thus, company has scope to increase the price, and also has scope to increase the loyal customer base. This also denotes perceived quality. It is an important factor, which can affect brand equity.

Marketing expenses to total sales: Higher the marketing expense percentage to sales, less will be the brand equity. It affects the profitability of the brand. In fact, if brand sales are related to higher inputs it can lead to lower brand equity even though the sales may be high.

Similarly, high cost of goods with high marketing expense can lead to erosion in brand equity. Becosule and Dexorange Plus are classical examples. Becousle because of high cost of goods and higher marketing expense will command lower brand equity compared to Dexorange Plus even though the sales and market share of Becosule is higher.

Actual quality satisfaction score: Today's environment requires higher image of the brand among the actual users. Customer satisfaction score can be the indicator for evaluating and affecting the brand equity. Lucas has a better brand equity compared to Merrelli in Auto Industry because of product satisfaction score. Therefore, brand equity of Lucas is higher. Similarly, Becosule can command a higher satisfaction score among Vitamins preparation.

Perceived quality, image of the company can influence title satisfaction score. However, higher the satisfaction score does not mean that brand may be No. 1 in sales. However, a potential does exist to improve the sales.

Phillips even though rated as No. 1 Company in customer friendliness is not No. 1 in Hi-fi or TV or refrigerator market. However, it can become No. 1 provided marketing activities become more effective. Thus, it can enhance its brand equity in India. High quality does not mean high brand equity but can be one of the factors to improve the brand equity.

Status of the product on product life cycle: Brand equity will be higher if product is on the late state of growing phase or in early saturation stage. Marketing expenses will be less and profit will be high. Therefore, brand equity will be higher. Similarly, brand equity in a star or cash cow category as per Boston Consultancy Group Matrix can be improved.

Price Elasticity: Brand equity generates high-perceived value. However, due to competition, government policy, market becomes more sensitive. In fact, you cannot increase the price. Toothpaste, soap, Paracetamol in pharma segment are a few examples. In these markets even though the brand equity may be high a dramatic increase in price can affect the demand and lower the brand equity. Therefore, this factor can play an important role.

Profitability: Higher the profitability greater will be the brand equity. High profit with high volume of sales can definitely improve the equity value. In fact this point becomes very important in calculating the value of the brand. For example, Becosule's brand equity can be lower due to low net profitability compared to Dexorange in pharma industry provided net profitability is the only criteria.

Scope for Line Extension: A product which can be used as a ladder to generate more sales through line extension will definitely in long term can be viewed as product with higher brand equity. Recently, Crocin was sold to SKB. Crocin can be combined with Ibu or Diclofenac to give yet another line extension in different therapeutic segment. Complan can be extended into biscuit segment and thus giving yet another opportunity to expand, Thums Up in can and 1000 ml bottles has given additional sales and profit to Coca-Cola. Thus, this can be one of the important factors.

Brand Equity Measurements

Multiple Earning Method: It is normally calculated on the basis of recent net profit. Net profit is multiplied 10 to 20 times. This gives the value of brand equity. For an example, if the net profit is 2 mn the brand equity value will be 2 × 10 = 20 mn. Multiples are decided on factors like volume sales, market size, market share, etc., which can improve the brand equity.

Brand Equity RKS Index: Under this technique the first step is to find out the index value by determining the factors, which can affect the brand equity. This has been discussed earlier.

Giving Weightage

Arriving at Index score in terms of %

The second step will be to find out the net sales and then it is multiplied by % of Index score. For example, if Dexorange % index score is 40% and sales value is 380 mn then the brand equity as per this method will be 380 mn × 40% = 152 mn.

Thus, brand equity is the storehouse of future profit. A growing brand has more equity than a declining brand. Many companies in India and abroad have started listing them as asset in their balance sheet. This improves the bargaining power of the company. The next five years will see this emerging trend turn into a reality. Therefore, an annual brand equity assessment should challenge the prevailing system and status of the brand. Consumer values shift and a brand has to keep pace with it. More scientific marketers will do more analysis of positioning of brand and create activities, which will continue to improve the brand equity.

RKS index & calculation of brand equity

Factors	Weight Score (a)	Rating Score (b)	Weighted Score (a x b)
		1 2 3 4 5	
Volume business of product	10		
Rank in the market	15		
Market size	15		
> 1%			
< 1%			
Perceived value	15		
Higher			
Lower			
Profitability	15		
Market expense to total sales	10		
Status of product on life cycle	10		
Scope of life extension	10		
Total 500	**100**		

Index Score = Total Weighted Score / 500 x 100 = – – – %

CHAPTER

8

Public Relations: Building CRM through Stakeholders

Focus is on defining PR, common objectives of PR, the PR process, and the target public for PR the PR Message. PR can be and usually is an effective form of creating positive marketing climate for the firm and thus becomes part of marketing communication methods.

Introduction

What we see on TV as advertisements for eggs, milk and diamonds is not direct marketing / advertising as you hardly find any sponsor. Drink more milk, eat eggs every day are meant to create awareness among the public and hence can be called PR Campaigns. Unfortunately, the task of PR is not appreciated by most of the persons and it tends to become a thankless job. In election campaigns, after the candidate has finished and gone his secretary remains to answer the questions regarding how the speech should be interpreted for improving the candidate's image. After the corporate Chairman has given an expose of the firm's plans, its elaboration and explanation is done by the PR persons. Press releases are part of the PR job. In case of any catastrophe the PR has to explain how the firm is coping with it and the damage control measures it is going to take. The famous oil spill in the ocean had the oil company's PR people on their toes. It may bee added that in such crises even the CEO takes the role of PR.

Public relations cover all the communications of the firm except the marketing / advertising and personal selling communications.

Public relations can be defined as: "the process of understanding public attitudes on relevant issues, interpreting these attitudes for management, and then working either to win the organizational polices and practices with those attitudes or to modify the attitudes themselves."

Publicity is only one aspect of PR job, which covers the making of press releases given regarding the firm's activities and plans. Besides PR is a useful tool in creating positive ambient.

Cue for the sale of firm's products in the target market segment.

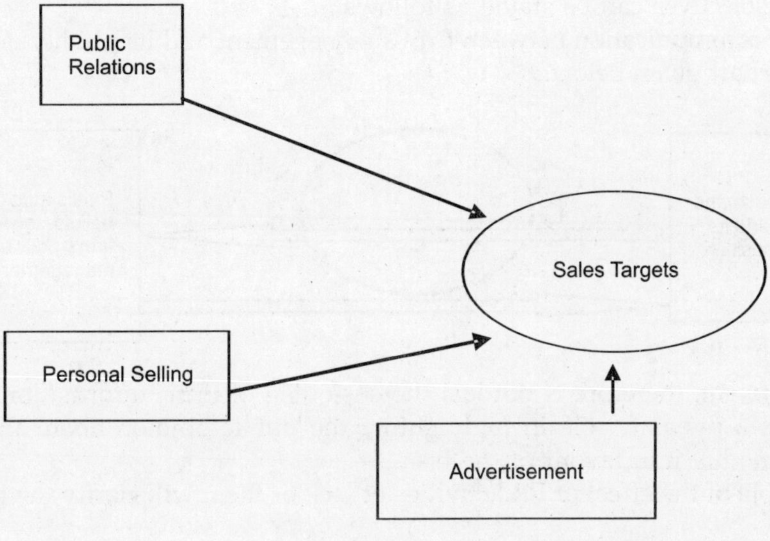

Public relations task in marketing activities is subtle. Nonetheless it is equally important, as through PR, the firm is able to build custom/ customer base not as a hard sell exercise, but with gaining customer support. This is done with great finesse and yet with bringing customers on the right side of the firm. You like us you buy from us.

The main features of PR are as follows:

When the firms arrange PR activities they do not have total control on the message being sent. It becomes the prerogative of the editors of the media and they can surely use their right. In personal selling or in marketing /advertising the firm talks all good things about the product. In case of PR the media men can express their likes and dislikes in their reports and not just what the firm wants them to do.

PR is addressed to several different classes of people, the customers being one of them. The message goes to the firm's stakeholders, the buyers, the sellers, the investors, banks, the government, local bodies, trade associations and social activists like the environment protection groups. It pays to keep these people on the firm's right side.

PR does not have any direct media cost as the PR message goes in the form of media's editorial. No media space or time needs to be purchased for PR.

PR besides assisting in improving sales also does a number of preplanned tasks like improving investor's interest in the firm. Labour relations and activities connected with labour welfare get publicity through PR.

The most visible role of PR is seen during annual general meetings of the shareholders of the firms. The entire programme is managed by the PR department.

The PR Base

Firms have plans for marketing, advertising with proper laid down objectives. Same way they have plans and objectives for PR activities. While marketing objectives could be increasing market share, enlarging geographic base or even training of their sales persons, PR Objectives can be stated as follows:

- Two-way communication between firm's management and its public, as can be seen from the chart given below:

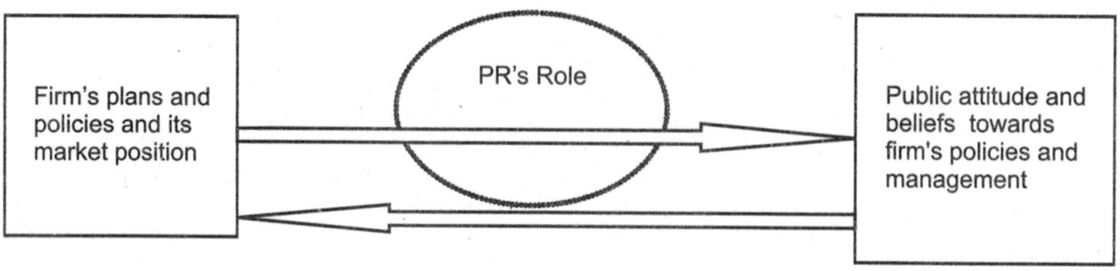

- PR department, therefore is not just the custodian of firms information base, but it also plays a dynamic role in highlighting the public opinion about the firm as it tends to modify it in favour of the firm.
- An example of the effect of PR activities or lack of them will clarify the point for the students.
- It was in 1960s that the Bangalore based excellent public sector firm Hindustan Aeronautics Ltd. had been manufacturing small aircraft used to spray insecticides in the vast expanse of agricultural land. Some of these aircraft crash-landed due to some technical problem and such a good firm went into disrepute. It took a lot of PR work to bring it back as a major technology driven firm in the Indian mindset.

As against this, about the same time an American firm operating in India came to know that its Aviation Turbo Fuel (ATF) has got a tiny trace of extra moisture than specified. The firm promptly downgraded the ATF as kerosene oil and gave prominent PR advertisements in this regard thus taking a mileage from an otherwise sure disastrous situation for the firm. The high image of the firm carried the day for the firm.

For this purpose it becomes the foremost task of the PR department of any firm to keep its eyes and ears close to the ground and plan proactive interaction rather than trying to retrieve lost ground on any account.

PR has to coordinate between public opinion and firms plans and policies. This would help even at the last minute for taking corrective action if needed. Most firms are aware of the strong sentiments of the public towards environment and pollution control. As the firms take measures in the direction of becoming non-polluting industry they should also keep the public informed about their actions in this regard. Plans and policies are not enough as the public wants to know the action firms are taking. Firms need to address themselves with other socially relevant issues like grow more trees, adopting for maintaining green areas of the town. The firms are corporate citizens of the country and it is imperative that they behave as such. It is equally important to let the people know that you are a responsible corporate citizen and this is achieved through PR.

As new competitive firms start operating they can, with a little effort develop a good public image. Even if your firm's image has been good so far, where does it stand in competition today. The best way to answer the question is to have a survey conducted and after that take any corrective measures as required.

With the advent of several reputed TV Brands like AIWA, SONY, THOMSON and LG, firms like Videocon and BPL would have taken a bigger beating but for their good public image. Hence, you can imagine that the task of PR is endless.

As a marketing mix factor PR has to come up with the most significant factor of the firm, which is promoting sales of goods. This is done mainly through press releases, which tell about the firm's achievements, plans and changes being brought about for increasing efficiency and customer satisfaction. These press releases play a vital role perhaps much greater than direct advertising as these items when published in the newspapers come under the editorial purview and hence get greater credibility than advertising. The only danger is of editorial pencil which may remove even the punch lines and make the whole thing drab.

Firms gain good mileage through their brand equity. With high brand equity firms can charge higher prices and still sell in large quantities. It is the name sells in most cases. Name provides for guarantee of quality. For the people for whom price is of no consequence, brand is what they buy. Even price conscious people buy good brand product for the value for money and the product life thus rendering them economical to the buyers.

Damage control is a major responsibility of PR. This task is usually needed to be performed once in a long while it is of great importance as not handling it properly could lead to greater disaster. Natural calamities like floods, earthquakes cause problems for firms, but how the firms deal with the problems and what becomes the public's perception about it is of importance to the firms. Then there are man made problems like the Bhopal gas leak. Smaller hazards keep on plaguing the firms and only good PR can nullify the negative effect of these on the firm's image and as a rub off on the firm's sales and profits. It is the reputation of the firm its goodwill which is at stake!

Marketing research for the effect of communication sent by the firms to the public is important as the perceptions of the message sent could be different with the sender firm and the receiver. Understanding the nature of public acceptance will help PR manager to tailor the next message according to the corrections required.

As we have seen PRs objective is different from that of advertising. PR has to project the public view of the firm in the first instant. PR managers are in constant contact with the public, the opinion leaders, the government and the customers. These contacts provide with knowledge of the attitudes of people as the PR person has to be alert to catch even stray phrase of significance to the firm.

One problem which many firms feel that they are being perceived as laid back firms Philips had this image till eighties in the 20th century. With dynamically pursuing the task of changing the image their PR department did bring about a turn around in the people's mind.

When the readers read any article from the editors it has a different effect on them then seeing the advertisements.

Earlier the success of PR campaign was measured by the column centimetre space it could get in the favoured media. Bigger the space, better the PR. It does not however tell you the effect of the space gained has had on the public mindset. The ultimate test, as in the case of advertising comes from the increase in sales figures and change for the better in the customer's attitude towards your product. For understanding the attitude changes, advertising research type research is required to be done.

Unlike advertising research where the target segment is the group of customers likely to purchase your product, in case of PR, the public consists of investors, stockholders, customers and suppliers towards whom the PR effort is directed.

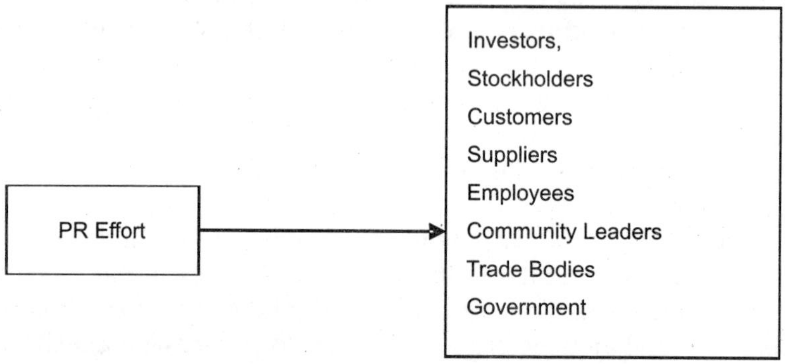

Public Relations Manager's job is to have a firm grip of the media available for transmitting the message to the public. Understanding media thus is an important aspect of his job. In this case, PR manager approaches the media editors, correspondents with information about the firm, its activities and plans. This is useful information, which makes the media and the PR interdependent.

These days a lot of advertising uses direct attack on competition, which if not refuted can create misinformation among the customers. Between two competitive toothpaste brands the difference of opinion came regarding the time one of them kept the mouth of the user fresh. Ten hours said one firm and soon the competitor said fifteen hours. A PR job would have sufficed by telling through editorial comments about the true nature of the toothpaste.

With plethora of non-banking financial institutions, to gain advantage one such firm advertised the norms public should use to assess the firms. The advertisement had a reverse effect as many persons read it out of context and felt that that particular NBFC is not good. It took a lot of effort as also their PR teams rapport with the press, which helped them in retrieving the situation and giving their side of the story as a press release.

PR too depends on endorsements to an extent!

If the firm says in the advertisement that their Matiz car is the best in its range, public may or may not accept the statement. The thinking becomes "any way it is their advertisement and who will ever say any thing bad about their product. However, if

Murad Ali Baig says the same thing or the editor of *Motoring Times* says it, the public is surely going to believe it.

Marketing efforts too get a boost with the help of marketing PR activities.

A technical short film shows how the car engine gets corroded because of friction between cylinder walls and the piston rings. Next it shows good brand of lubricating oil being used halves the corrosion. And then the film shows the firm's brand being used totally removing any possibility of corrosion. The film does a subtle job of marketing PR as the visuals leave a lasting impression on the viewers about the efficacy of the oil.

PR helps in image building. Every firm wants to be known as a good corporate citizen. When the public is shown a movie which highlights the efforts taken by the firm in removing pollutants from its effluents going in the river, it endorses the public opinion about the firm as a good corporate citizen. Such films help mould the opinion when negative opinions have already been formed. Following scenes will give other examples of PR, which incidentally create goodwill for the firm, which does get reflected in the sale of its products.

The CEO of the firm presenting a cheque of Rs. 10,00,000 for the Gujarat relief fund to the Prime Minister of India.

Marketing director presenting specially designed cars for the handicapped at a discounted price.

President of the firm sponsoring and inaugurating a sports event for the blind.

Firm offering scholarships to the deserving children of its workers for higher studies.

Such events if not given right publicity would go unheard and unsung. It becomes the major task of the PR department to ensure that the good deed does rub off on the cash register of the firm bringing in extra profitable sales.

It is said that a company is known by the men it keeps. And how? Good, happy, hard working employees do provide a good general backdrop in the public's mind. Firms go out of their way these days to keep their employees happy. Perquisites like good housing, medical aid for the family, sports activities, and children's education are a must for this purpose. PR's job is to focus the public attention on the theme of happy workmen. The firm automatically gets a boost as a good firm, as only a good employer can be a good firm. And who wants to do business with a firm, which is not good. A good example of personnel PR is the advertisement of Tata Steels; in which happy employees involved in various activities are shown. In the end the advertisement says, "We also make steel"

Firms and Society

Firms do have some dependence on the society in which they operate. They get employees, investments, and home sub-assemblers. Society too gets employment opportunities, better living standards. A factory in a backward area like Mankapur in UP State got a big boost when public sector firm ITI established its factory there with French collaboration. The entire countryside was transformed into a thriving industrial town from its earlier days of a sleepy laid-back village. ITI had the opportunity of building its image as a big benevolent corporate citizen. The fact that they did every thing to protect the environment of the area was surely a plus point.

Firms do good to the community and the society in which they operate. PR has to press home the advantage and get the right mileage, which is firm's due.

PR and the Government

In the era prior to 1992, when the government of India opened up country's economy, private business was overloaded with government liaison work. The government lowly paid staff doled out permits and licences and it became the breeding ground for corrupt politicians and public servants. With the change brought about in 1992, firms are no longer facing the vice like grip. Yet, there are areas, which still need to be smoothened, and interaction with the government becomes a primary task of the PR department of any firm.

Industry lobby, with industry trader associations like ASSOCHEM, CII, FICCI are liaising with the government to sort out their problems.

The Investing Public

Investments as equity, bonds are made in the firms you can trust. Hence, the PR task for investors is the same as for marketing PR. Investment PR is a highly specialized job which entails a thorough knowledge of money market, interest rates prevailing in the market, firm's financial position and needs. PR person has to market firm's financial status to encourage investing public in coming to the firm. Investment PR requires that information about the investors should be provided to the firm and about the firm to the investing public.

How to? What are the means available to the investment PR persons to provide accurate and fast information to the investing public?

Press Releases

These are the most commonly used methods of disseminating information. The firm selects the information to be given, and then it is written down in a language normally used in the press. You can use the reporter's format or the one used by journalists. If it is given a good news coverage then the chances of its being read by the public are high.

Press Conferences

When the firms have to say a great deal, like when they have to announce the annual financial report and balance sheet, firms have their Annual General Meetings (AGM) where press is invited. Unlike in press releases in press conferences the media people can ask questions to elicit replies to reconfirm their thinking and be objective about the firm. Besides AGMs firms call press conferences at product launches, public issues.

Crises Management

When the firms face situations like strike, natural calamity or strike the must inform the stakeholders including shareholders. Non-information leads to speculations and hence leads to mis-information with disastrous results. It is the ability of crisis PR, which helps firm tide over the crisis with the least damage to its reputation and its sales.

Summary

Public relations function deals with the public opinion and informs the firm about the same. It also tells the public about the results and plans and policies of the firm. It helps the firm in coordinating its activities to keep in tune with public likes and dislikes. It can help the firm in to moulding public opinion in its favour. PR is use to help in selling the products as also in managing crisis situations.

CHAPTER

9

Customer Relationship, Value and Behaviour

Introduction

At different times each member of the society is a buyer. And as a buyer people want to be known as sane, intelligent buyers. Buyer's skills come from an innate selfishness that when we are spending money we should get the money's worth. The term VALUE FOR MONEY is born out of this desire. To prove the rule, there are exceptions like people buying beyond their means when they have to impress somebody, like friends, fiancés. It is said that no one buys a product. They buy the benefits, which they derive from the product. If the benefits outweigh the cost the buyers have paid then they have received value for money. Let us define customer value as follows:

- Total customer value—the sum total of all the benefits the customer is likely to derive from the product.
- Total customer cost—the sum of moneys the customer is to spend while selecting, buying, using and disposing of the product.
- Product perceived value—the difference of total customer value and total customer cost represents the customer's idea of the usefulness of the product.

The product purchase decisions are taken on the basis of the following:

- Product brand image/brand equity
- Buyer's usage value
- Value of the service provided with the product
- Intrinsic value of the product
- The above add up to total customer value of the product.

The other side of decision to buy comes from the following:

- Product price

- Product search expense
- Decision time delay costs
- Cost while using the product
- The above add up to total customer costs for the purchase of the product.

In case the buyer and the user are two different persons, there is likelihood of delays or wrong purchases. Personal choice of the buyer may be based on his own personal experience with the product or he may have some relationship with the seller. In such events, the sellers do well to establish relationship with the buyers and the users as well.

People do not buy products. They buy the benefits, which the product offers them. Therefore, after-purchase value of the product assumes great importance as only those products with high after purchase value will be purchased repeatedly, which brings to the point of customer satisfaction from the usage of the product which is measured as follows:

- Actual benefit derived as compared to the benefit perception the customer had before the product was purchased
- Benefits derived as compared to those obtained from a competitive product
- Benefits get enlarged if the product costs are in consonance with the perceived benefits and in such cases the customers derive a sense of pride besides satisfaction, which in today's marketing terminology is stated as customer delight
- Customer's delight also comes from being known as an intelligent buyer among the peer group

Product innovation, product differentiation, leads the buyers into the delight zone. As the competition is doing exactly the same thing, trying to win over the same segment customers, the firm, which remains proactive to the perceived and even intangible needs of the customers, is the winner. In order to achieve it firms must be in the market research mode all the time fathoming the customer, his mindset, likes and dislikes, the perception of product benefits. Product differentiation, should however be made at those extra costs which can be borne by the market. There is no point in, as an extreme example, using gold wire in the television set instead of copper wire, because except for increasing the cost it will not improve the quality or even aesthetics of the product.

Sustainable competitive advantage in order to achieve sustainable competitive advantage the firm has to constantly upgrade its product value to the customer and product delivery systems. Buyer's loyalty can never be taken for granted and therefore to ensure it the following actions are needed to be taken by the firm.

- Differentiating the product, price, and distribution system and advertising promotion.
- Communicating the differentiation to the customer, "we know we are good, you should know it too."

Washing powder marketing looks like a battlefield where each player is trying to outdo the other by making tall claims, "washes whitest" TV demonstrations, innovative use of the media, help in achieving one aim of getting trial use by the buyer. However, it is the real value of the product, which aims for re-buys by the purchasers.

In order to increase market share the firm has to take competitor's customers. It is of use to know that value the competitor's customers are placing on the competitive products. Market surveys are conducted by firms to ascertain the perceived value of the product purchase both of their customers and those of competition. The results of the surveys assist in redefining the product differentiation, communication and service providing plans. These help the firms to keep upgrading the customer value of the products.

Satisfaction Survey—firms need to know the satisfaction or dissatisfaction factors of the products with their existing and past customers. Following methods are used for the purpose.

Personal interviews with those customers who were using the product earlier and have now stopped using the same, either they have switched to competition or stopped altogether. These interviews give an insight of the reasons and failure on the part of the firm in providing satisfaction. These apparent post-mortems help rebuild the marketing strategies by improving service standards, terms of business like payment terms, and delivery systems.

Surprise customers—firms can send some unidentifiable customers who would give correct feedback about the service provided and customer care taken by the selling team. Such ghosts customers are part of many hotel chains who are interested to know the behaviour pattern of the service team when the top management is not there to watch the team in action.

Complaint management—the firms who do not pay attention to the suggestions and complaints made by customers are likely to lose those customers. The top most authority in the firm should attend to complaints, or least he must be aware of the complaints. Suggestion boxes, complaint or assessment forms to assess the service being provided by hotels and restaurants are available in most places and they form the vital link between the customers and their satisfaction.

Customer complaint and suggestion surveys—one telecom firm in India in the private sector is continuously on the customer's trail understanding their varied and increasing demands, their dissatisfaction levels and they are able to find instant remedial measures for the same.

Pricing strategies can help in making the customers loyal. A value for money product stays with the customer and helps in making purchase decisions. Price changes, like lowering price can be helpful in penetrating the market. The inherent danger is the customer mindset, where many times a lower price product is considered having lower value.

Michael Porter has evolved value chain a method for evaluating the customer value being built in the product through the management process. The value chain looks at the different functional areas of business from the customers viewpoint, underscore the fact that if the customer is forgotten in any action or activity of the firm some value to the customer may be getting lost. The value chain is given below:

A represents the support functions and B represents the primary functions.

Suppliers							
	A	Infrastructure					
	A	Finance					
	A	Human resource					
	A	Information					
	B	Inbound	Operations logistics	Outbound logistics	Marketing /sales	Service	Customers

As can be seen from the matrix success of the firm depends on the way the activities of each functional area are conducted and coordinated with each other.

As an example, if purchasing does not care to order the raw materials in time there will be delay in production and delivery to the customer. If the human resource management gets the wrong kind of person for operations the quality of products may suffer ultimately affecting the sales and profitability. If the outbound delivery uses an ineffective transport system there may be delays or even damages to the goods, hampering customer satisfaction. Each activity should be carried out and cared for as it is going to add value to the customer. If it is not performed well it will take away some value from the customer resulting in loss of the customer to the firm, and the competitors are ever ready to grab dissatisfied customers all the time.

Service to customer is of paramount importance and this is one area, which most firms in India tend to neglect. To a customer, the firm's service is the only visible face of the firm. Therefore, the service must represent the firm correctly by involving the customer to the extent possible in the service delivery process showing the finer points like selection of transporter.

Michael Porter's value chain, as stated earlier, has a major drawback inasmuch that it does not render itself to cross-functional analysis in a firm. Hence, cross functional work processes and teams lend themselves for better understanding on the total customer approach of the firm, which is given below:

Defining new product—firms keep bringing new products in the market. New products, which are brought out based on understanding of the market through marketing research, have better chance of success. The activities include, beside marketing research, technology through R&D, or purchase of technology (in some cases through reverse engineering process, if it is not illegal).

Production Process—including purchasing, inventory management of raw material, components, semi-finished goods and finished goods with the Just in Time (JIT) Technique for keeping current assets to a minimum, quality management with TQM.

Marketing and servicing the customers—including continuous market research, distribution channels management, advertising and sales promotion, from getting the purchase order to supply and billing and finally getting paid for the supply. Next, the same order to payment cycle restarts.

Service—the importance of the service to the customer can never be overemphasized as only the service provides the firm with sustainable competitive advantage, as it cannot be easily copied.

Firms strive for profitable sales and growth. These come from customers who become loyal to the firm due to the satisfaction or delight they get from the product usage.

Loyal customers normally buy more, accept new products from the firm, become spokespersons of the firm and take up advisory role in the firm's operations, like new promotional plan, new advertising campaign and some customers can be the part of advisory panel or focus group with the firm.

Understanding customer satisfaction is therefore an absolute must in these days of severe competition.

Speedy complaint redress, complaint cause removal and complaint statistics are a must to survive for the firms.

Customers who are loyal to the firm must be retained as, over a period of time the firm's selling cost on such customers reduces as lots of activities become routine; the newsletter, direct mail promotional offers can be sent without having to bother about finding where are the new customers. They help the firm with word of mouth publicity in getting more customers.

A lost customer can become a major liability if he chooses to vilify the firm. Firms need to interview these lost customers and even if they become non-buyers of the firm's products they should remain friendly or at least neutral with respect to the firm.

The process of selling of the early twentieth century has given way to relationship marketing of today as can be seen from the following:

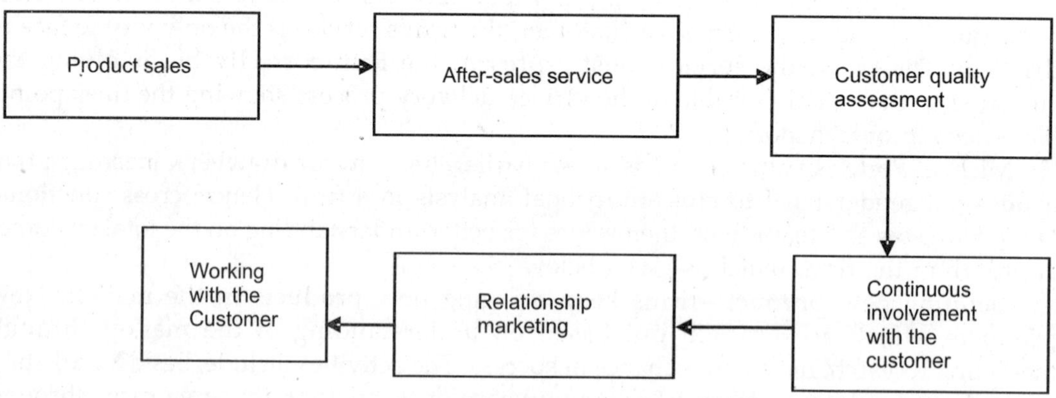

In the 20th century beginning there was hardly any competition and sellers had to just place the product in the market and it was sold. Then came the fifties of the twentieth century and products, which needed service, were provided with after-sales service through service engineers of the firm. They also demonstrated the product if it was needed, informed the buyer's ways of optimizing the use of the product and methods of saving possible through the use of the product like lower down time.

In the third phase in the second half of the twentieth century, customers were becoming quality conscious and the firms started quality control programs in their manufacturing operations. From just testing the quality, the firms started checking the quality of purchaser raw materials and components, and the quality of sub-assemblies inside the factories.

In the next phase the customer became the focus of marketers and the products had to meet the expectation levels of the customer. The seller made phone calls after the sale was made to ask about the quality assessment and ease in usage of the product. However, as most products had little or no competition manufacturers were in fact giving only lip service to improving product quality. A classic example is the Ambassador car. A new model of Ambassador was introduced with only, minor changes of putting ashtrays on the back door. After a few years, gradually the ashtrays were removed. Again to be reintroduced as a newer model. This game was obviously known to the customers but as they had little option, they had to buy the car. Only some bought a Fiat the only other option.

Relationship marketing—it is the new mantra of marketing today. It works well only when the seller is able to overwhelm the customer with so much of importance that he cannot just think of going for competitive product. Newsletters, new product information, samples for trial, cultural activities invitations go a long way in building relationships.

Working with the customers—the seller does not leave the customer after the sale has been made. The seller keeps engineering support, maintenance support with the buyer to keep reassuring about the benefits he is going to derive from the use of the product. This is especially true of the industrial products like power plants, air-conditioning units.

Seller's profitability comes from the profitability of his customers. An oil company advertised "Use our lubricating oils and increase your machinery life by twenty per cent. Additionally servicing downtime gets reduced by ten per cent. The total saving for a machinery of million rupees would be ten thousand rupees per annum. (The best way is to actually calculate and give the saving figure along with the calculations, which will make the offer authentic to the buyer).

Ostrow and Smith have defined consumer behaviour as actions of consumers in the marketplace and underlying motives for those actions. The study of consumer behaviour is the study to understand how consumers spend time, money and effort on consumption related items. It includes what they buy, why they buy, when they buy, where they buy, how often they buy and how often they use it?

We are all consumers and we behave in the marketplace in different manner, sometimes logically and at other times irrationally. Study of consumer behaviour helps to predict with a high degree of accuracy how a particular person will behave under certain circumstances. This gives rise to more scientific approach to business communication.

Philip Kotler has designed a consumer behaviour model, which offers the variety of stimulus present for consumer for their decision making for purchase action.

Model of Consumer Behaviour

Market Stimuli	Other Stimuli	Buyer Characteristics	Buyer Decision Process	Buyer Decisions
Product	Economic	Cultural	Problem Recognition	Product choice
Price	Technological	Social	Information Search	Brand choice
Placement	Political	Personal	Evaluating Alternatives	Dealer's choice
Promotion	Cultural	Psychological	Purchase Decisions	Purchase timings

Market stimulants—the main marketing mix factors, famous four Ps, Product, Price, Placement and Promotion can provide stimulus to buyers. We have seen how can particular product just by being in the market makes us buy the product. Listed below are influencing factors. Detailed discussions about the same will be taken up later on at the appropriate place.

Social Factors

Reference groups—they are the community leaders, religious gurus, professors, councillors and others.

Family—includes, parents, children, grand parents, siblings, uncles and aunts.

Roles and structures—role of head of the household, the breadwinner, in the family, which could be a new one, just husband-wife, or with small children, teenage kids, or grown-up children who have left the household, needs to be defined in the buying process.

Age and stage in life cycle—with better medical facility the average age of Indians has greatly increased. There is a large group of senior citizens. With lower rate of child mortality the population of teens and preteens has increased manifolds giving rise to needs and products to satisfy the same.

Occupation and economic circumstances—standard of living of people differs because of size of regular income as also on the occupation. A white collared worker would like to project an image of a well-dressed person as against a small businessman, who would not be bothered with appearance.

Lifestyle and psychographics are used to understand the mindset of people and for measuring and categorizing life style

Good resource people—with financial backing

Actualizers—those who have achieved their desires, who have become somebody

Fulfilled—are the satisfied people

Achievers—are the people who have targeted their dreams and fulfilled them.

Experiencers—are those who have gone through the struggle and come out successful

Low resource people—with low finance

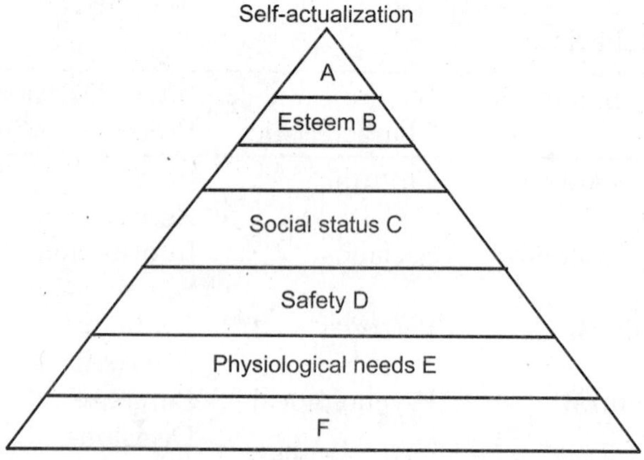

Believers—are optimists who feel their time will come soon
Strivers—are hopefuls about their future
Makers—are busy people who are into nitty-gritty of making a success
Strugglers—are not so optimistic about their future

Personality and Self-concept

People have physiological needs like food, clothing, shelter and psychological needs like need of love, esteem and self-actualization. Maslow has propounded that people's needs follow a hierarchy, in terms of importance of needs and their place in the person's life.

Maslow's hierarchy of needs

Perception—Select, organize, and interpret information to obtain a meaningful understanding for selecting and deciding in favour of a product.

Attitudes and beliefs—attitudes are a person's evaluation of emotional feelings and tendencies for action towards some object or an idea.

Buying roles can be described as follows:

- Initiator—the person who puts forward the idea of obtaining a certain product
- Influencer—is the one who gives his opinion about the suitability of the product
- Decider—is the one who has the authority to decide whether the product should be purchased or not
- Buyer—is the person who places the order
- User—is the one who puts the product to use.

Thus, we can develop complete buyer behaviour as given below:

- Believe in the product
- Develop attitudes
- Make thoughtful choice

Habitual Buying Behaviour

It can be seen from the following matrix:

Major difference in brands	High involvement Complex buying behaviour	Low involvement Variety seeking buying behaviour
Less difference in brands	Dissonance reducing buying behaviour	Habitual buying behaviour

When, for example the difference in brands is large like in cars and the involvement in buying is also more, the buying process becomes complex. Conversely if the brand differences are low like in shampoos, and purchase involvement is low, most purchases are done on the basis of habit only.

Stages of Buying Decision Process

- Problem recognition is defined by obvious or inherent need of the consumer
- Information search
- Evaluation of alternatives
- Purchase decision
- Post-purchase behaviour

Sources of Information

- Personal—Family, friends, neighbours
- Commercial—Advertisements, salespersons, dealers, packages, displays
- Public Sources—Mass media, consumer rating organizations
- Experiment—Handling the product, experiments, using samples of products like shampoo sachets.

Evaluation of Alternatives

Problem-purchase of a computer

Identify decision criteria is as follows:

- Price
- Manufacture/Model
- Support
- Repair record
- Warranties
- Reliability

Weightage to criteria allotted by consumer:

- Price 70, manufacture/model 60, support 40, repair record 75, warranties 50, reliability 70.
- Alternative choices—Wipro, LG, HCL, Compaq, IBM, Local assembly.
- Now for each of these six computers, put weight, e.g., Wipro-Price 30, manufacture/model 50, support 40, repair record 60, warranty 40, reliability 60
- As can be seen price weightage is inversely proportional to price. In other words higher the price, lower the weightage.
- Select the one where the numbers add up to highest. Then implement the decision, make the purchase.

Post-purchase behaviour comes from satisfaction, use and disposal after use.

Buying behaviour results from ethics in marketing as well marketers are required to sell products, which give value for money to the customers. Non-standard products defective goods, prices that give wrong impression to the buyers (hidden charges like transport, taxes duties not mentioned in the beginning) short packing are some areas of unethical practices. Such deals can give only short term small benefits and in the long run even if the law does not catch up, the customers eschew purchasing such goods and dealing with such marketers. In the bargain even good products of the marketer are discarded. A few examples will make the subject better understood by the students.

- Food items mixed with unhygienic wrong products like wrong non-food grade preservatives.
- Fake branded products
- Products like video and audio tapes which are pirated
- Quoting different prices to customers for standard products, unless quantity discounts are being offered.
- Advertising five-star hotel when it does not have even three-star facilities
- Advertising contraband goods like liquor, drugs
- Cheating in annual sales where the prices are jacked up from original; then the discounted price still remains almost as original.
- Incorrect or misleading advertising should be firmly avoided. In can cause untold harm including legal action, which has become one of the deterrents of such ads today.

Market Segmentation

Markets are such a heterogeneous place that unless we get to understand each part of it we remain ignorant of the market. There are people buying Mercedes cars and in the market people are buying low cost bicycles as means of transportation. Marketers of Mercedes communicate with the rich elitist class to sell their product. These people reside in certain section of the town; visit one club or the other, read a few business magazines like *Business India*, *Business Today*, and *India Today*. The cycle buyers go to cinema halls for low cost entertainment. Cycle sellers can show film advertising clips and slides to communicate to the segment. Both elite class and lower class persons would get the right message without too much clutter and in a language understood by them. Therefore, market segmentation helps both, the buyers and sellers.

Market segmentation is done on the following lines:

- Geographic factors
- Demographic factors
- Psychological factors
- Socio-cultural factors
- Use related
- Benefit segment
- Combination of some of the above mentioned factors

In India Tanishq watches have the following segment:

As the price starts from Rs. 20,000 to Rs. 125,000 high income, elite life style fashionable locality form the segment. Market communication, advertisement can thus be written in the language easily understood by the segment and placed in the media seen and read by them.

Geographic segment is for the region like south northwest and east of the country. Each region has its own peculiarities in customer needs and therefore consumer behaviour too is different for each. In each region there are metro large areas, large cities and smaller towns, besides villages. Urban, semi-urban and rural divide provides a market segment.

Demographic segment is by age, sex, marital status, income, education and occupation.

Age segment is important as with growing population of senior citizens and a large teenage group, product needs for these segments are increasing. Healthcare products, vacation time products are needed for elder citizens. Teens need coffee bars, discos, and video game parlours.

Income separates people in their buying pattern and product groups. Marketers can decide to cater to one income group or the other, make products needed by them and then advertise in media most seen and read by them. Low cost readymade garments for low-income segment can be advertised best on radio and local language press. Likewise Rolex watches for the rich segment can be advertised in business magazines and TV channels such as Star Plus.

Male and female customers have some specific products for each, like shaving creams for men and lipstick for women. With age the use of cosmetics change for women and marketers can make use of this change by offering products of their need. Young girls need cosmetics to enjoy mutual attraction with boys and for flirtation. Married women use cosmetics to keep their husbands happy and senior ladies use them to feel young.

Education and occupation segments—customer who are well read would buy books of their interest. A professor of management would buy books on management.

Psychological/psychographics segment—peoples needs like shelter, food, safety, affection and self-actualization makes for different segments. These are the hierarchy of needs as per Maslow. The person who is self-actualized, graphics given below has different needs than others.

Psychological/psychographics segment divides customers around their mindset. People need ego boosting and certain products like fashion garments, designer watches and accessories make them feel good when they can have their heads in the cloud nine. Persons can be motivated to buy a car just because they have been selected to test drive it. Today's business executive is extremely busy and his/her involvement in buying daily need products is low. The target customer therefore is the buyer and not the user, may be the servant or some retired member of the family. The involvement increases with the value of purchase or some personal preference. Please buy only Godrej. Shaving cream for me is a way in which the involvement manifests itself.

Socio-Cultural Segmentation

Family—starting life the young persons are unmarried. They need household goods, like cleaning equipment washing machines, cooking equipment, TV set.

Married couples initially need to go on honeymoon and later on according to their status and income needs keep adding up to car, house, and soon baby foods, diapers. Once the children grow then music system, books games and sports equipment are needed. As the children start their own life, the aging parents now alone again require, health products, medicines.

Society—social groups originate from parity in income, occupation and education. Lots of purchases especially of consumer durables are made because the neighbour has purchased it. "Keeping up with the Jones" is the phrase used to describe this tendency of copying common in one social segment. Advertising based on targeting one social group becomes easy as the group members speak the same language, understand the same subtleties, the same comic situations and have the same attitudes and beliefs.

Cultural and sub-cultural segmentation—our country boasts of unity in diversity. Cultural differences are quite pronounced as we travel from north to south, east to west. In the north for instance when guests are visiting offering them any thing three in number is considered inauspicious, while in the south it is the done thing. Traditional women keep their heads covered in the north on auspicious occasions and in the south they have heads uncovered.

Sub-cultural segments come from areas like the north Punjabi culture with exuberant dances, music, extrovert lifestyle, as compared to Rajasthani segment, more conservative, traditional, although they also have their own dances and music. Each area in India has a fund of cultural heritage, which drives the segment members to behave in a certain manner. Durga Puja sees Bengali's buying dresses decoration material and the like.

With global marketing becoming important in India cultural diversity around the world, has to be learnt. Simple things like favourite colours become important; cycles exported to Iran can come back to India if they do not come in Iran's favourite green colour. The subject will be discussed in detail in international advertising chapter.

Segmentation on the basis of usage: Imagine a person who buys a cell-phone and uses it only to see the number calling him and then goes to the nearest land phone to call back. Another guy uses cell-phone the whole day, making STD and ISD calls to his foreign clients and collaborators. Or, a person stays in a five-star hotel only for one day in a year, eats out and just pays for the room rent of about Rs. 6,000 as against the person who stays at least for a week in a month, throws parties uses the hotel facilities and his yearly bill exceeds Rs. 10,00,000. While it is understood that the customer is the king, we can now see that some customers are emperors, others are kings, some are princes, and yet others are just buyers. That is why to lure big buyers; firms have special treats for them, including the frequent flyer programme of many airlines, room upgrades of big hotel users. It may however be remembered that today's prince can become tomorrow's emperor and hence firms can ill afford to neglect to provide the best possible service to him.

Usage situation segment: Situational usage is prevalent for greeting cards, flowers, gift items that are given on occasions like Christmas, Deepavali and Eid. Card maker's gift suppliers focus their advertising effort towards the customers.

Benefit segment people are looking for benefits all the time, like the calorie conscious person wants tasty food with low calories, and insurance people sell insurance promising life long benefits. In fact the entire marketing is based on making customers aware of the benefits the firm's products provide as value for money and which are unique.

Demographic and psychographics analysis guides firms in their advertising communications by making them understand the following:

- Who are our target markets?
- What should we tell them?
- Where this communication should be made?

Media too arranges such research and information so that firms know which media to use for which segment. In India ABC gives the circulation figures of different publications and an idea of their readers. For TV, research organizations arrange for Television Rating Points (TRPs), which give area-wise idea of viewer-ship of TV channels and their programmes.

Segmentation and Its Usage in Advertising

To be of use to effective communication the segment should be clearly defined. It should not be two small or too large, should be growing and should have access to advertising media.

Locating and identifying segments is easy for geographic or demographic segments. For psychological psychographics and user segments need market surveys with properly designed questionnaires and good reliable team asking questions, which are aware of the objective, methodology analysis and report writing.

For products like an expensive watch, segment in a town like Delhi would be in thousands, for Mercedes it may be in hundreds only. A segment for special type of trout safari may be too small.

The segment should be stable and increasing. Persons trying out new brands all the time are unstable buyers and cannot be counted for the segment.

Marketers have to communicate to the segment and availability of suitable and economical media becomes a necessity.

Motivation is the inner urge, which propels people to act. Seeing and smelling food people get motivated to eat while they may not be even hungry. Graphically it can be shown as on the next page.

When the need is felt and till the time it is not fulfilled, the person suffers from anxiety and worry which forces him to understand the nature of the need and its fulfilment propelling him into purchase action, which reduces his worry.

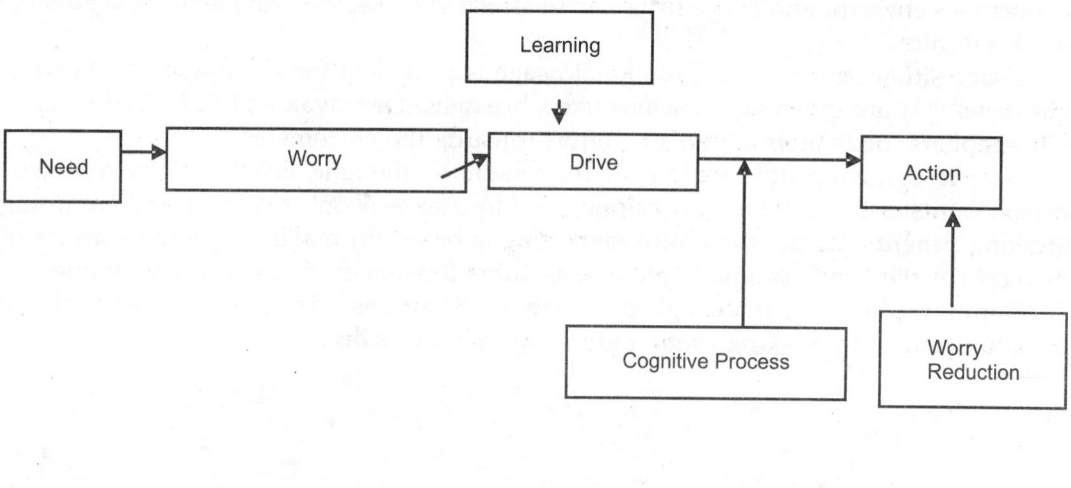

(From the *Consumer Behaviour* by Schiffman and Kanuk)

People have two types of needs, physiological, i.e., requirements of their bodies and psychological needs of the mind. Food, water, clothing and shelter are the primary physiological needs, and needs of power, self-esteem, affection love are the secondary ones. House may be the primary need but a bungalow where you can entertain guests becomes psychological secondary need.

Changing nature of goals and needs—When a particular goal or need cannot be fulfilled, a substitute goal emerges. Similarly, after fulfilment a new goal or need arises. In any case needs can never be fully satisfied. When a person becomes Vice President of a firm, he changes his goal to becoming the President. Product updates, newer technologies help the firms to use this urge as a springboard for launching innovative products.

Once the basic needs are fulfilled, people want to achieve higher goals. After getting a good house to live people would like to be community leaders.

As the saying goes, "Nothing succeeds like success". Success gives extra fillip to people for going to higher level goals. Failure, on the other hand make people redefine their goals, by either lowering the standard or taking a different road altogether.

Goal substitution occurs on non-attainment of goal. If you cannot buy Honda City car, buy a Maruti 800. Some people go in to a dream world devoid of reality.

Non-achievement causes people to go into depression, which can result in behavioural changes like sulking and going into a shell, anger, rationalization of failure which is bad as it makes a person complacent, and frustrated.

Behaviour is oriented towards achieving personal goals. People have general types of goals and then they have product-oriented goals. We will travel to the hills once I purchase my Ford IKON car becomes a product and action oriented goal. We can see that everyone has rational and emotional motivations, with purely objective or subjective criteria.

Motivational research is conducted as psychoanalysis of consumer's mind to understand, sometimes not so apparent reasons for their motives. The subconscious mind works for reasons of its own. Some product personality types have been profiled as a result of motivational research as follows:

- Baking conveys motherhood, feminity, love and caring; subconsciously the baking process is a substitute for the childbirth process.
- Ice cream is subconsciously associated with love and affection
- Home maintenance kit is defining the man and machismo.
- Beer represents active alive people

Personality is the sum total of individual traits of character, bearing and behaviour. It allows us to fine tune the differences among various people. With effort people can change their personality; from introverts they can become extroverts, from careless types they can become caring types.

Sigmund Freud developed the psychoanalytical theory of personality. He says that human personality consists of three overlapping areas—Id, Super ego and ego.

Id is the primitive animal-like instinct, which drives persons hunger, thrust, and sex urges. Lots of advertising is based on using this animal force to advantage, and that is why female form is used to attract the males and vice-versa.

Super ego is the mind's control on Id, the animal instincts, so that people can live within social norms.

Ego is the balancing force between id and super ego helping people to keep to the right path between id's drive and societal norms.

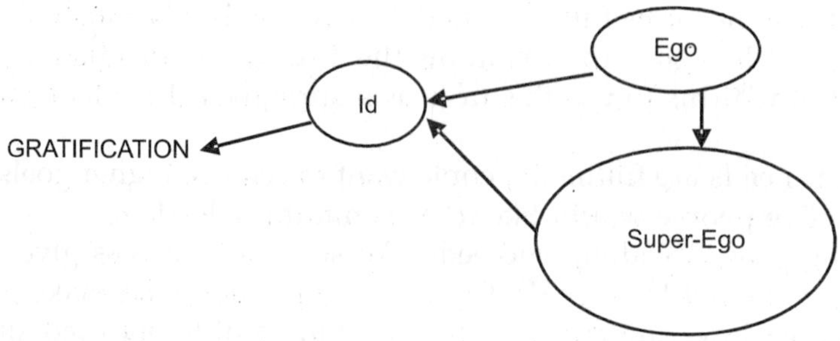

Freudian theory and brand/product personality—Some products are best represented by a celebrity, like Shah Rukh Khan can be called Mr. Santro, the car he is successfully advertising. He can also be named as Shah Rukh Mayur Khan when he personifies Mayur Suiting. Customers tend to associate the brands with the brand personality. Hence marketers need to use a personality who can be fully identified with the product. Hritik Roshan is promoting Coke, and yet as there have been many coke promoters, it is difficult to name Hritik as Mr. Coke.

Personality Theory of Post-Freud People—unlike Freud, other social scientists felt that motives cannot be confined to basic and sexual instincts. Social interaction and life style too gives motivation to people to act.

There are four types of personalities as follows:

(a) Thinking and sensing types are rational logical, objective and fast decision makers
(b) Feeling and sensing types believe in their own selves, are subjective and they consult others in decision-making
(c) Thinking and intuiting types take broad view, look for wider range of options and take decisions for long range of time.
(d) Feeling and intuiting types take broad view, are people oriented take subjective decisions for long time zones

Karen Horney proposed that people can be classified in three personality types:

- Compliant types who seek company, want love and appreciation
- Aggressive types go against others and try to excel to gain admiration
- Detached types who remain away, want independence from interference and are keen to be solo winners

Let us discuss consumer materialism and compulsive buying. Materialistic people enjoy buying valuable goods and showing them off, which makes them egocentric and self-centred. They believe that their possessions would project their lifestyle and yet no possession gives them real satisfaction because the more you have the more you want and there is no end to wanting. "My Swiss villa proves that I am a successful person."

Compulsive buying behaviour makes people buy things, which either they do not need or cannot afford. Sale offers, mail order people, catch those people who are on a buying spree.

Consumers get an image of the product on their mental screen. Marketers have to position their products in the right market segment to ensure that positive mental image is formed and that it stays. Repetition of advertisements is meant to fix the product on the mind's screen.

Pepsi has been positioned as a drink for the youth and to counter it (as youth remains the biggest segment Coke is positioned there too.) Maruti 800 is positioned as the common man's car while Honda City has the slot of upper class car. Raymond Suiting is in the top position for the elite while Mayur Suiting is for the middle class.

Perceived price can be, high, low or fair. Then there is differential pricing like lower air ticket for senior citizens. There are sale prices when heavy discounts are offered, like save up to 50%, buy more at less price. Such offers can be deceptive, as the correct picture is not given to the consumers. While people feel happy at making purchases and acquiring products, if the price is the same as imagined by the buyer, then it does not give any pleasure. However, if the perceived price turns out to be more than the actual price then the transaction becomes interesting to the buyer. For example, buying a 200-litre refrigerator would cost the buyer Rs. 14,000 and it costs him as much then there is no joy. In case the purchase price is Rs. 13,500 only it gives mental satisfaction and pleasure to the buyer.

Most often, especially for consumer goods price and quality of a product get associated with each other and reduction in price can create doubts about the reduction in quality of the product. Similarly, product, country, quality and price are perceived by the customers as a package, as can be seen from below:

- Made in the USA best quality high price
- Made in Germany, solid in technology medium price
- Made in Japan, elegant, not sturdy, price quite high
- Made in Korea, almost as good as from Japan lower in price
- Made in India, low labour cost low price inconsistent quality. (This perception is not correct any more but Brand India needs to be strengthened to overcome this perception.)

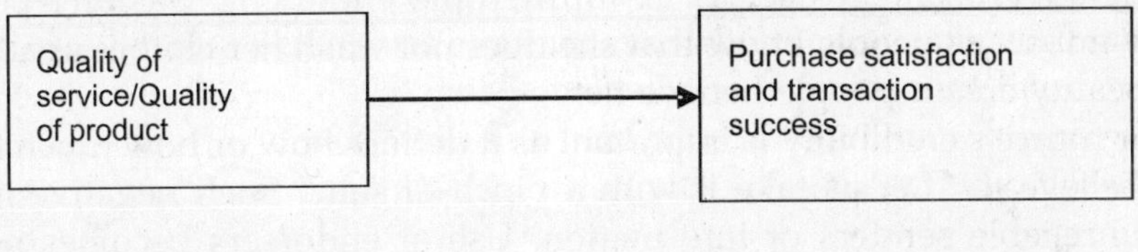

Price and Quality Relationship: Takes into account that each product has some service attached to it.

There are different types of consumers with unique personalities. There are consumers ready to experiment and they buy products in the introductory stage of product life cycle. Computer note pads, palm top computers find a good market among this type of personality, who is always ready to innovate and experiment.

Dogmatic types have rigid behaviour pattern. When this type buys a new product it is contrary to their belief. Therefore, they have to be on the defensive and are uncomfortable with such purchases. They can be persuaded by authoritative, dramatic and dynamic advertisements, which help them overcome their basic negative attitude.

Open-minded consumers take to new products easily.

Social "type sets"—self-centred persons look for answers within themselves while extroverts are ready and at times eager to find out what their peers and seniors have to say, (who says what becomes important and a significant purchase decision tool).

Stimulation levels are important guides for consumer behaviour study. Some consumers lead a sedate life and minimum level of curiosity arousal is enough for them to become interested in the product. There are hard-core consumers who look for being shaken out of their slumber and for them heavy dosage of stimulation is needed. These persons can practically psyche themselves into the purchase mood.

Attitudes are predisposition levels people have towards a product or an idea. These positive or negative attitudes are based on, earlier experience, odd remark heard from a known or even unknown person, from persons like salesmen connected to the product, the environment or mood in which the message about the product was given to the consumer.

Attitudes are normally consistent for a particular product. If a thing is not liked then it is not to be purchased. Housewives may not even think of purchasing a twin drum-washing machine with the known benefits of single drum machines. At times attitudes change for reasons like, "let us economize" or non-availability of favourites brand in the shop visited and imminence of need. "Let us buy Godrej soap as Lux is not in stock." Such decisions for FMCG purchases are taken easily as the cost of replacement/ or repurchase is not heavy, unlike a consumer durable product like a car or TV, which cannot be purchased, everyday.

Communication process is planned taking into account the target market segment and the mindset of the people of the segment. One communication model is given below:

In communications the credibility of source, or who is saying it, matters a lot. Firm's brand equity can authenticate what is being put in the advertisements. Most firms use endorsers to talk about their products, which make the target segment believe in the product. Wrong endorsers can cause harm to the product or can have no impact rendering the advertisement useless. A top heroine endorsing washing powder may not have any impact as people know that she does not wash her clothes at all. When she endorses a beauty cream people believe her.

Sender or source's credibility is important as it defines how or how much the receiver is going to believe it. "Let us take it with a pinch of salt." Such negative impressions come with unreliable senders of information. Use of endorsers becomes necessary in such cases. Source or sender has its own need for sending the message. How right is

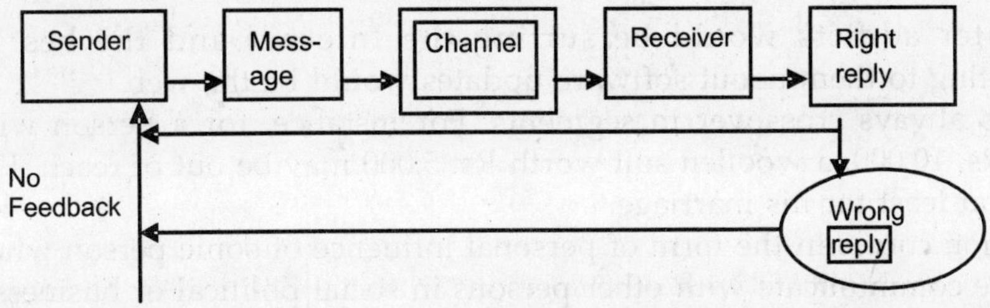

that need? For example, many firms resort to having yearly sale of their products. People want to know if it is a genuine sale, and if yes, why the firm is selling good products at heavily discounted prices? Is it that they have odd size unsold products, heavy inventory as their export order got cancelled, or, is it that the discounted prices are in fact the same as original? The firm increased the prices first and then declared the sale. Increase of prices was of 20% and discount offered is 17%. Such types of sales lose their impact in no time and bring bad name to the sale and to the seller.

Personal involvement is the key factor on the interest the customer is going to have in understanding and correctly interpreting the message. Sachin Tendulkar will like to go through the exact specifications of the cricket bat, while a non-playing cricket TV commentator may just take no notice of the bat.

Moods of persons at the time they are receiving the message govern how well they will receive and accept the message. Watching a tragic sob story movie on TV would make people less willing to accept the positive aspects of a product. It calls for proper selection of media; sitcoms, news bulletins, and movie-based programmes are viewed on TV with a happy frame of mind, generally.

In order to monitor customer response to a message and its media pre-testing is done where the advertisement is shown to a select group of the market segment to gauge their reaction and get their feedback. In case of poor response, corrections in message and media can be made.

After the advertisement has been released, post-testing is done to find out how effectively the advertisement has met its objectives.

Persuasion strategy -for proper impact of the message, selection of the market segment to be catered to, creativity of the advertisement and objectives associated with the communication are key elements of strategy. Some examples are given below:

Housewife, family income Rs. 20,000 pm, urbanite, graduate would be reading, Famina, Cosmopolitan, Star Dust magazines, watching afternoon soap operas like, Saans, Santa Barbara, Dynasty.

College student's family income Rs. 40,000 pm would be reading sports, motorcycle and car magazines, listening to FM radio.

Achievers, family income Rs. 80,000 pm, would be reading business magazines like Business India, Business Today, Financial national and international newspapers and watching news on Star TV.

Senior citizens family income Rs. 20,000 pm would be reading health and investment magazines, watching travel related TV programmes for enjoying vicarious adventure and thrills.

Computer addicts would be surfing the Internet and the best media for communicating to them about software updates would be the web.

There is always crossover in segments. For instance, for a person with monthly income of Rs, 10,000, a woollen suit worth Rs. 5,000 may be out of reach. However, he may buy it at least for his marriage.

Persuasion comes in the form of personal influence of some person who counts. In daily life we communicate with other persons in social political or business situations. A good communicator listens more than he/she speaks. When in doubt, we seek advice, or sometimes we get advice totally unasked for. In both cases, it is stored in the brain from where it can be restored at the time of purchase decision-making. We normally go to people whom we consider as more knowledgeable then us. These people are the opinion leaders. Buying a set of golf clubs it is best to ask the golf champion, rather then a layman. For cameras and films, the professional photographer, not the camera salesperson would be the best bet.

Opinion leaders being experts on their subjects can be trusted to give correct opinion on their subject of specialization. Marketers, on the other hand would invariably give only the positive aspects of their products.

Several times customers seek only information, and sometimes they ask for advice. Can we trace which of the following statements of opinion leaders is information and which is advice.

Which is the best gent's shoe for formal wear? "In my view, Bata is still the best"

How to use the vacuum cleaner? "I use it once a week to clean the carpet, the curtains, the floors and the ceiling. You could do the same."

Where to take my Maruti for servicing in Delhi? "There is no better place then Competent Motors, my dear."

Where can I get a gift for my girl/boy friend? "Try Giggles in CP and you will not go wrong."

As can be seen opinion-leaders are mostly "product" specific. You will not ask your milkman where to buy computer software. In case of doubt, people take second or even third opinion until they are satisfied by the opinion. People with set ideas, often stop after they have got an opinion, which agrees, to their own thinking. Such subjective opinions can be misleading resulting in wrong decisions.

Advertisers extend the theory of opinion leadership in advertising by using the leaders as product endorsers.

Self-image is the some total of a person as he thinks about himself and it is a guiding factor in purchase decision along with wisdom of opinion leaders. "What type of person am I? The image I project to outsiders, how people view my personality" make for the self-image. There are several types of self image:

- How people view themselves?
- How they want others to view them?
- How they would like to seen in the future?

Self-image and products purchased has an interesting connection, as the industrialist buys Mercedes to project the self-image of a successful person. Actors and actresses want to look good and attractive to their fans and their clothes, makeup is meant to focus on that image. Marketers take advantage by using this concept while communicating to them.

Consumer perception is the consumer's view of the things including messages and stimuli seen / focused on him. These perceptions are given or acquired by visual stimulus, like seeing pictures of products in advertisements, hearing about the products from friends and looking the retail shops, point of purchase (POP), VISUAL Impact.

To heighten the impact advertisers use sensational gimmicks including adventure sports, pretty women as sex objects to make the impact. The level of minimum stimulation, which can attract is called the threshold level. For two different stimuli the minimum difference, which becomes noticeable is known as JND, (Just Noticeable Difference).

Weber has given the law, which stipulates that, "an additional stimulus equal to JND must be added for majority of people to perceive a difference between the resulting stimulus and the initial stimulus."

Car polish makers add some ingredients in the product that it keeps the lustre for a week as compared to competitive product where the shine lasts for four days. The danger in making it better, to the extent that the shine lasts for a month or even a fortnight, would increase the gap between purchases. Marketers and advertisers use the JND to good use in their product development and advertising strategy.

Subliminal perception considers even below the JND stimulus as psychologists have found that even such stimulus leaves an impression on the subconscious level and while it remains dormant it may manifest itself at the right time when product purchase is being considered. Years before a friend had said that the best TV set is from Sony and today finalizing the purchase it comes as bolt from the blue and the decision is made in its favour.

Hence, the decision process is based on the complex nature of human insights, which the marketers find ways to stimulate and bring to surface in their favour.

Marketing and communicating to the target market segment, of new innovative product calls for sustained efforts of advertising, personal selling and word of mouth appreciation of product for a period of time.

Market based new product, which the market considers as new. When Airtel company introduced cellular phones in Delhi, they were new to the market, and consumers took it as such.

Consumer based new products are the one's which the consumers find totally new.

The innovative or the new product is seen by the firm as new to it and the firm becomes buoyant about it. The firm ignores the fact the product may not be new to the market as competitors may already have introduced the same.

Product innovation takes into account the features, which are unique to the product. One refrigerator manufacturer is claiming novel door cooling system, not available in other refrigerators.

The new product development can be on a continuous basis or on one-off base. Telephone industry has had both types of innovations as can be seen from the following table:

Discontinuous development	Dynamic continuous development	Continuous development
Telephone	Answering machine, voice mail	Auto-dialing facility, memory phones
Pager	Nationwide paging, two-way paging, sports scores	Message displays, alarm clocks
Fax	Fax modem, mobile fax	Speed dial, delayed dispatches

Consumers look for relative advantages in each product. Also the expense of making change and product's compatibility with other products with the consumer too plays an important role in buying new products. For example, the modem, and printer should be able to work with the computer before they are purchased.

Organizational Buying Behaviour

Organizations or firms involved in manufacturing goods purchase, raw materials and components needed in the manufacturing process. They also buy consumables like electricity, water and gases, which are consumed, in the manufacturing process. Such purchases by the firms have the following characteristics:

- Fewer buyers but large quantity buyers
- Close supplier and buyer relationship
- Geographic concentration of buyers
- Derived demand
- Inelastic demand/fluctuating demand
- Professional purchasing
- Several buying influences

Firms produce large volumes of products and hence need large quantity of materials. An individual will buy a TV picture tube only as a replacement only if his TV set's picture tube has become defective. A TV set manufacturer will be buying picture tubes in thousands for putting them in the TV sets. Yet as compared to individual buyers, TV set manufacturers will be far less in number.

In most cases industries are established near the source of one or two major raw materials needed for manufacture. Hence, most industries are concentrated in that area. Gujarat has lot of cotton, which accounts for large number of textile mills in that region.

The demand of raw materials is derived from the plan of manufacture of products, which use the material. The tyre sale is dependent on the number of cars manufactured in a particular period.

For such intermediary products the demand remains inelastic over long periods of time with only marginal changes. However, it could also be grammatically changed in case the buyers find different usages of the product when the demand will increase. If the product becomes obsolete, the demand could just disappear, as happens often in fashion garments.

Purchase in such cases becomes a professional discipline. Depending on the value in money terms and also in availability terms, the importance is given to purchase decisions.

Buying situations can be classified as follows:

- First buy is when a new firm makes the purchases or an old firm tries out a new product
- Re-buy takes place when a satisfied buyer buys the product again. This happens when besides the product other factors like firms after-sales service, the buyer accepts behaviour of its sales people.
- Modified re-buy is made when the manufacturer accepts customer's suggestions and product is suitably modified to suit the firm.
- New task purchase depends on the launch of new products and is planned accordingly.

System for buying in the organizations consists of the following persons:

- Initiators are the people who place the requirement of the product before the firm's authorities. In most firms they would be either R& D persons or purchase executives
- Users are the people who define the product with specifications and would ultimately use it. They would be R&D engineers, production engineers
- Influencers are the people who influence the purchase decision, which brand; model to buy, from which dealer. These could be R&D managers, consultants.
- Deciders are the authorized people who can decide spending of money for making the purchase. They are of the rank of General Managers.
- Approvers are the people with power of approving the purchase like Chief Executive Officers and Managing Directors
- Gatekeepers are those who filter information and see to it that only relevant information reaches the decision-makers about the product. These could be receptionists, purchasing agents.

Consumer behaviour in organizational buying therefore becomes complex, with a number of persons involved in the decision-making. Therefore, unlike in consumer products the role of advertisement in organizational buying is limited to: a) image building of the firm and b) providing detailed information to the buyers about the products.

Environment factors are also major influencers in organizational buying as follows:

Environmental factors	Organizational factors	Interpersonal factors	Individual	Business buyer
Level of demand	Objectives	Interests	Age	-do-
Economic outlook	Policies	Authority	Income education job position	-do-
Interest rate	Policies	Authority	-do-	-do-
Risk of technical changes	Procedures	Status	Personality	-do-
Political and regulatory developments	-do-	-do-	Attitude for risks	-do-
Competitive developments	Organizational structure	Empathy	-do-	-do-
Social	Systems	Persuasiveness	Culture	-do-

- Environment factors like market demand of the product influences the quantity of purchase as also the purchase frequency.
- Economic outlook of the country gives the information on the money supply situation, interest rates for leasing and it has influence on purchase decisions.
- If the firms know that a new technically superior product is going to be available in the near future, they would not risk large purchase of materials.
- Political environment deals with the political will which allows or restricts trading, like the anti-dumping laws of the USA.
- If the market is swaying towards a better competitive product, the firm may make only cautious purchases.
- If the sociological changes force the market towards decline then also purchases get reduced. With the availability of packed wheat flour no one is buying wheat and getting it ground in a mill.
- Organizational policy changes, changes in hierarchy levels, promotions, procedural changes and systems could alter the purchase pattern of the firm.
- Factors connected to individual members of a firm like inter-personnel relations, people's authority, personal interests, empathy with suppliers and persuasiveness of marketers are important for purchase decisions.

Organizational buying decisions are taken by purchase committee consisting of:

- CEO, who only wants the best in the line product.
- R&D Manager, who wants the state of the art product.
- Financial Manager, who wants value for money, economical products.
- Purchase Manager, who wants the usual product, to avoid inventories hassles.
- Production Manager, who wants no change in assembly process unless new product helps in major cost reduction

Each one is a customer in his own right and his needs must be satisfied. It calls for communication excellence to put same points in different words to conform to their perception of need as follows:

To the CEO, "Our product is top of the line as can be seen from our specifications, which incidentally, exceed the specifications given by competition and you can see the testimonials from our national and international customers which speak for themselves."

To the R&D Manager, "you have heard of the latest proven technology in microprocessors based on fibre optics, you can open the equipment and see it for yourself that we are giving you the state-of-the-art product."

To the finance manager, "our product pricing is based on volume business and that is why we can give you the price of our product with latest technology comparable to the price offered by competition for their older generation product."

To the purchase manager, "we believe that by the time our product reaches you, your old inventory would be almost exhausted and it would be easy for you to standardize on our state-of-the-art product, which we are sure would make you even more respected member of your firm."

To the production manger, "you would be able to reduce manufacturing time after the training we will provide to you people, thus reducing the cost of manufacture considerably. Besides, with reduction in quality problem, the firm will get a better brand image and after-sales service team would become practically redundant."

It would be necessary to test the product before making the claims as mentioned above.

Consumer behaviour and firm's responses find that firms do take care of how the consumer will behave.

ITC agro introduced their branded Atta, Health World first in the south India, as their study showed that south Indians are more quality conscious than north Indians in the matter of a product like Atta, in spite of the fact that the Atta consumption in the north is nine times more then in the south. Once the brand gets established in the south, they will move to the north as well with region specific brands and tastes to suit different palates.

Dwarka men's wear offering cool cotton trousers and shirts, chose the month of March 2000 to launch the product just before the onset of summer. They have successfully marketed their product in the West Asia and European markets.

Targeting their cell phones for the youth of the country, Ericsson has introduced FM Radio in the phones which come in a range of bright colours to capture the fancy of the youth.

Consumer Behaviour: Positivism and Interpretivism

Positivism: Prediction of consumer action—Quantitative-consumer rationale, weigh alternatives. With market study, it can be predicted that *x* per cent customers would buy the product.

Interpretivism: Understanding consumer practises-qualitative-reality is subjective, each usage experience is unique, and research findings can be subjective. Cannot be generalized, like it is not easy to predict how many first buyers would go for repurchase of the product.

Attitudes play an important role in purchase actions and it is necessary to understand as to how they are formed:

- Direct experience from using the product, "the soap is too hard"
- Influence of family and friends, "Son, buy only Honda motorcycle, it is the best value for money"
- Direct marketing, Eureka Forbes salesman in your house, "see for yourself how easy it is to use the vacuum cleaner Sir"
- Exposure to advertisements, wife to husband, "see the mixer grinder ad on the TV and you would agree it is the best value for money"
- Personality factor, "I cannot buy a motor cycle, only a car would do for me"
- Attitudes - four functions
- Utilitarian function—brand utility
- Ego-defensive function—product enhances self concept
- Value expressive function—consumer values, life style are reflected
- Knowledge function—fulfilling need to know

Also, there can be a combination of several of these functions.

The task before buyers is one of resolving conflicting attitudes as given below:

- Tasty v/s healthy food, pizza or fruit cream
- Quality v/s price, Wipro PC or the assembled one
- Sturdy v/s elegant, jeans or silk

The decisions are taken on purchases on the following considerations:

- The Family
- Economics
- Emotional support
- Life style
- Family socialization—manners, values, goals

Family Consumer Roles

- Husband/wife
- Children
- Teens
- Family life cycle, where lifestyle keeps changing as can be seen from the following:
- Bachelor-mostly carefree
- Honeymooners need affordable luxuries
- Parents' young children-need baby products
- Parents' teenage children-need teen fad products, like FM Radio
- Parents with children away from home, healthcare products
- Dissolution—old age homes

Feeling and Emotions

These can be measured on a scale. Let us try out a skin cream and get reactions of women after they have used the cream on a scale as follows:

A-Like it very much—B-like it—C-nothing special—D-do not like—E-do not like it at all.

The survey can be done on the following parameters:

Skin felt	A	B	C	D	E
Relaxed					
Beautiful					
Tight					
Smooth					
Supple					
Clean					
Refreshed					
Oily					
Pampered					

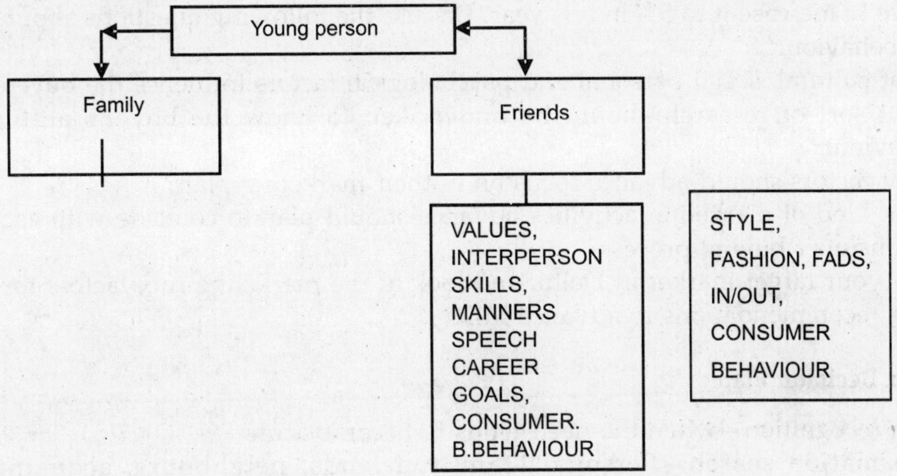

- Designing persuasive communication
- Proper market segmentation
- If product transcendent segmentation—umbrella messaging for all audience
- Good PR
- Media plan—consumer profile to match with media audience profile
- Each media is effective for some products, audiences and advertising objectives
- WWW
- Overlapping audience

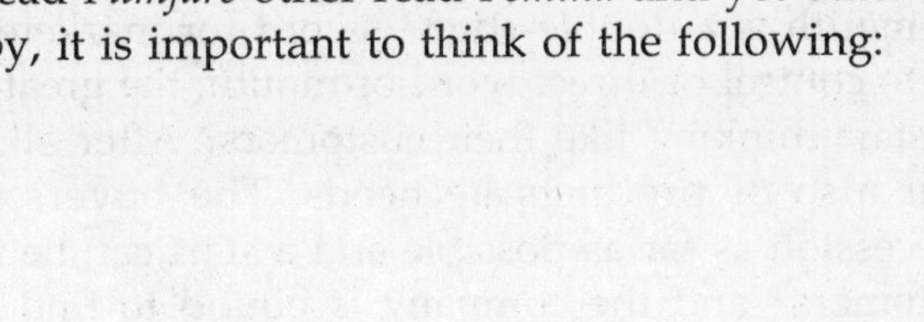

Some customers read *Filmfare* other read *Femina* and yet other read both
In advertising copy, it is important to think of the following:

- Copy appeal
- Copy length
- Endorsements
- Visuals
- Time limit offers
- Free trial offers
- Pricing
- Example

You are the marketing and advertising manager of advance stereo systems with five competitors, Philips, Videocon, BPL, AIWA and Sony. Your market share is 3%.

You have to increase it to 5% in one year. Discuss the following questions about market and its behaviour:

- What cultural, social personal and psychological factors influence the buyers most? What sort of research should be undertaken to know the buyer's attitude and behaviour?
- What factors should advance focus on in their marketing plan?
- What kind of marketing activities advance should plan to coincide with each stage of consumer buying process?
- Plan your target market in Delhi, and look at the marketing mix factors for giving your recommendations to advance MD.

Purchase Decision Plan

Problem recognition—when the need tends to become acute.

Information search—Personal—family, friends, neighbours, acquaintances, Commercial—Advertising, Salesmen, dealers, packaging, displays, Public source-Consumer rating organizations, Experiential-handling, examining, using the product.

Evaluation of alternatives with weightage given on parameters decided by you, cameras—size weight, auto-focus, zoom, speed, price, Hotels—location, cleanliness, atmosphere and price.

Purchase decision—There can be a situation where after deciding to buy you delay or even cancel the purchase. Sometimes if people close to you have a negative attitude towards the product you may not buy it. Secondly, there may be a change in situation.

Customers depend on their family and friends and at times even unknown persons before taking buying decisions. With internet becoming prevalent lots of people are selecting products to purchase through the, "chat route." Increasingly buyers want to have a first hand feedback on the product usage. Companies need to build a customer network or have a strong CRM (Customer Relationship Management) as a built-in thrust to keep their customers with them. The word of mouth publicity, both positive and negative work wonders. The best is to have the positive publicity for your product, while the opposite can be for the competition.

Today, consumers have more ways to wield their influence and opinion than ever before, but word-of-mouth is a double-edged sword for marketers. Unfortunately, the more companies try to control or direct word-of-mouth, the greater their risk of failure.

Can companies start thinking like their customers? After all each one of the team members is a buyer also of products he needs. The buyers mindset needs to be understood with precession as far as possible and a start can be made by interviewing the employees "customers" and the company is bound to find highly educative and revealing insight into their psyche. The method of product selection, brand approval will become apparent.

Customer do not need information, the product benefit story till they are ready to buy and yet all the advertising addressed towards them is not going waste as it enters their subliminal memory that tends to surface when the buying decision has to be taken. Ideally companies would like the influencers of the actual buyers get trapped in their personal elevators till they are ready to become their brand ambassadors.

Customers do assume the role of brand ambassadors provided they get the following from the company:

- A useful product
- At reasonable price
- With comparative ease of purchase
- And the product offers the benefits sold with it and more
- It is easy to dispose of the product once it is of no use to the buyer, if possible with some money reimbursed.
- The product adds to their status and enhances their life style quotient.

Post-purchase decisions:

- The product could satisfy you.
- If you are not satisfied then you could try to reverse the purchase action. Or sell off the product
- Let us discuss Indian buyer's purchases of some common FMCG products.
- Washing powder sells about 30% less than washing soap cakes.

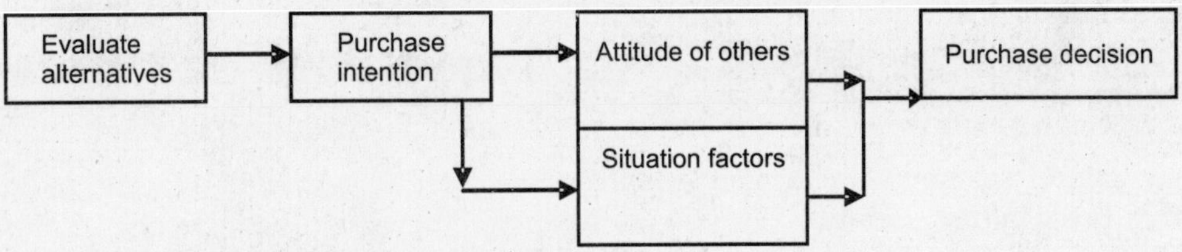

- Toilet soap sells about 59% of washing soap cakes.
- Electric bulbs sell six times than the tubelights.
- Nail polish sells about the same as lipsticks.
- Leather shoes sell 50% than the casual shoes

Product penetration in urban and rural India is as follows:

S. No.	Products	Urban%	Rural%	Total%
1.	Tooth care	90	50	60
2.	Washing powders	100	90	98
3.	Tea	90	70	80
4.	Milk powder	9	3	5
5.	Butter	10	2	4
6.	Salt	100	95	97
7.	Chocolates	10	2	4
8.	Ice cream	25	10	14
9.	Shampoo	25	9	13
10.	Hair oil	90	85	87
11.	Wristwatches	45	20	28
12.	Talcum powder	45	25	30
13.	Lipsticks	22	12	15
14.	Nail polish	40	30	32

Religions Practised

S. No.	Religion	%
1.	Hinduism	81
2.	Islam	12
3.	Christianity	2
4.	Others	5

CHAPTER

10

Ethical Marketing, Reinforcing CRM

Gandhi laid great stress on personal integrity. It is this characteristic in human beings, which takes them far ahead of others. However, no one can just hang it on his chest as a medal, proclaiming his integrity. Integrity is also of thoughts, words and deed. Integrity is not only about taking bribes, but also much more than that.

Given below are a few examples of integrity or lack of it:

- A person sitting in his office, during office time, in his busy schedule, writes a personal letter. He even uses office stationery for the letter.
- A person promises his colleague something of corporate importance in private and in office meeting he just denies ever having given the promise.
- A person knowingly gives a torn note (cash) while buying a product at a busy sales counter.

The Board of Directors with the help of functional staff runs firms and each of the functional has its own peculiarities with regard to ethical problems faced by them. The executive authority of day-to-day functioning of the firm is vested with the CEO, who is supported by the departmental heads and other staff for executing the plans laid down by the Board of Directors. The main functional areas are given below:

Following are the possible ethical issues in each of the functional areas:

Marketing consists of the following sub-divisions:

Sales

Sales deals with the actual action needed by the firm for obtaining the customers purchase order. The following are the areas, which require safeguards against unethical behaviour:

- Supply of product not exactly as per the order or the sample shown
- Keeping hidden costs like cost of transportation, accessories shown before getting the order

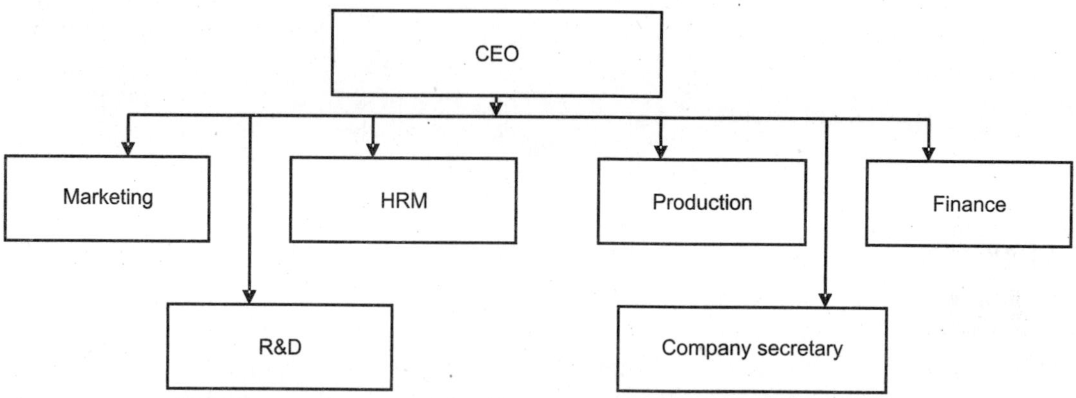

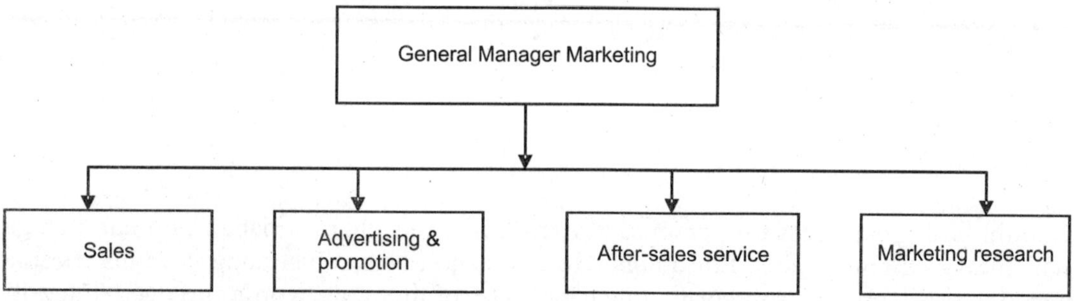

- Not accepting the responsibility of defective product by some obscure small print condition
- Changing product specifications without prior intimation to the customer
- Changing terms of business without taking the customer's approval
- Delaying the supply of goods without proper reason and not communication the delay to the customer
- Treating two customers differently without any reason
- Using superlative adjectives to describe the product when the actual product will not stand the customer's scrutiny.
- Not providing the needed after-sales service as per original sales contract
- Playing favourites between two customers regarding price or priority in supplies.

Some of the above stated ethical issues may not appear as violation of ethical norms and yet these have a profound impact on the relationship firms have with their customers. These are enough to rattle even the most loyal of the customers and could end in the firm losing them to competitors.

Advertising and Promotion

These are the major methods of communicating with the customers, especially for mass markets where personal contacts need reinforcement of advertising and promotion. The following areas are prone to unethical practices in the communication methods:

- Exaggerating the product benefits to the customers or overselling through puffery
- Supplying products, which are different than those advertised
- Giving wrong price idea in advertisements by not including the necessary add-ons.
- Increasing the price of the product before starting its promotional plan with price reductions when in fact only the price has come back to the original price or maybe it is still a shade higher than the starting price.
- Not supplying the promised gift in the promotion campaign
- Making snide references to competitive products without any truth in them
- Making comparative advertisements by using only selected parameters, where the firm scores over its competition
- Giving wrong testimonials to the prospective customers of the product from its users by adding and subtracting it with the help of selected words
- Hiding major flaw of the product
- Not providing the advertised service to the customers as a part of the promotional plans (like not upgrading airline on board seats even after the customer has fulfilled the required criteria.)

After-Sales Service

After the purchase has been made its continuous usage depends on the benefits the product provides to its user. This can be fully ensured by the firm by providing proper after-sales service to the customers. Some of the lacunae in the service are given below:

- Service engineers not going by the priority fixed and playing favourite for personal gain
- Using substandard material during service and charging for the real material
- Using wrong outmoded service equipment, which endangers the product itself during its service
- Not taking service calls if the location is not easy to reach, while free service was promised before the sales at the location
- Making only temporary adjustments in the product so that it can be used temporarily and the customer is forced to bring it up again for repeat service at his cost.
- Not keeping proper service records of major products for future use, as it will help in easy diagnosis of the problem in the product next time around
- Over billing the service charge when the customer is not aware of the rates
- Using rejected or substandard components for customer's temporary relief while he has to shell out major amounts when he comes to get the product set right again
- Refusing to service the product under some pretext or the other like, please do not bother us. As you can see we have no time for your product. Cheating the customer by writing in fine print several reasons for not providing the service.
- When the product comes for service, exchanging a few healthy parts with substandard parts. These removed parts can be sold to other customers.

Marketing Research

Marketing research is done to ascertain the market needs, its trends and competitive activities. However, if the research is conducted purely to sanctify the manager's viewpoint then the entire research exercise goes waste. Following are the reasons why research can fall into the ethical trap:

- Research is conducted only to substantiate the manager's viewpoint
- Research is focused on areas, which need not be covered, as the manager does not want the truth to ever come out.
- In-depth research is undertaken when only preliminary research would have satisfied the research objective
- Some old research is dug up by the researcher, camouflaged and served as new research report for getting paid
- Biased research report to suit the Marketing Manager
- Selling the research report to competition as well.
- Entrusting the marketing research to a novice, because the manager wants to oblige him
- Getting a good report, but not using it as it does not follow the manager's thinking
- Suppressing the important facts of the research report from the leader as these do not confirm to the leader's thinking
- Diluting the impact of the research by telling that the manager has been in the know of the findings of the report because of his vast experience

Critical Success Factors

The companies have to understand that customers are in the market to buy but not necessarily their product. The following, therefore, becomes critical to the success of a company in spite of the fickle nature of the customers. As customers each person has done a lot of impulse buying, consulted a large number of people, known and even unknown before buying his expensive buys. As marketers' people forget their own idiosyncrasies and lop-sided purchase motivations. It is therefore all the more important to realise the critical factors as given below:

- Salespersons attitude towards the customers comes from a spirit of service and dedication and cannot be induced by mere training or ordering about
- Product quality needs to be entirely in consonance with the declared ones and if possible should go beyond the written word to not only provide customer satisfaction but customer delight
- Easy access to product purchase lends a definite edge to the seller
- Price needs to be the perceived value in the customer's mind
- Business terms must take care of the sensibilities of the customers and must be tailor-made to find the right fit with the customers, including payment terms, delivery options, guarantee terms and long term availability of spares if required
- Good disposal value of the product after it has completed its utility

Balance Score Card

Managers need to evaluate the effectiveness of their strategies for winning and influencing their customer. And this exercise cannot be deferred as it could easily lead to losing customers in no time. The evaluation can be done using the following matrix:

Rating	Service for customer satisfaction	Quality for customer delight	Ease of product purchase	Perceived value of the product in customers mind
Superior				
Good				
Average				
Poor				

The best evaluation is done by customers themselves and after studying the pattern of a cross section of customers corrective action can be initiated by the manager.

While the sales figures give the hard numbers they do not in effect tell about the range of customer satisfaction and re-buy plans, because there can be several reasons for increase in sales as given below:

- Competitive reduced offerings due to production problems
- Seasonality of business
- Price changes of the competitors
- New customer influx in the segment

The real test of success comes from the soft numbers as given below:

- Customer becoming brand ambassador without provocation
- Improvement in "Top of the mind recall" of the brand amongst the segment customers and prospects
- Improvement in re-buys
- Customer referrals for prospective customers

Marketing Audit

Winning customers and influencing them remains the most important part of marketing activities and, therefore, the marketing strengths of a firm are the most important single factor for its success. Firms selling the entire produce at a reasonable profit, increasing sales of the same product portfolio, selling at a higher price or successfully developing new products and selling them too profitably would not face serious problems. This is in fact the ideal scenario as competition too is, all the time sharpening their tools to conquer the customer. Therefore, it becomes imperative for companies to keep evaluating the marketing strengths of the firm on the following areas:

Marketing environment—markets, customers, brand equity, competition levels, economic trends, money supply position in the market, legal issues, and social developments, causes and problems besetting the market.

Marketing action—products, pricing, distribution channels, advertising and promotion, and personal selling, publicity.

The real questions to be asked during audit are summarized below:

- Customer's primary and secondary levels of satisfaction derived from the product; the idea of product as sold by the firm and the customers viewpoint about what product he is purchasing.

- Environmental issues shaping the markets, competition and the customers
- Firm's special skills as compared to competition in market
- Marketing problems and opportunities the firm is facing today and may have to face in the future.

Environmental Threats and Opportunities

In the dynamics of country's economics, firms must understand that the changing conditions will make some markets more amenable than the others. Firms need to have constant vigil in the following areas:

Law and politics—government regulations can change product emphasis in the market; a recent example being the stopping of sales of cars not conforming to the Euro-emission norms. Other examples are, Government of India's disinvestments in some prominent firms, their Voluntary Retirement Scheme, the famous VRS, price regulation of some commodities and at times deregulation of prices. These affect the business of some firms or the others.

Competition—competitive action needs continuous attention, especially if the market is an oligopoly one. Remaining proactive on competitive product launches, new pricing, advertising and promotion would help the firm in retaining their market share and in even increasing it.

Suppliers—oligopoly supply firms tend to have the edge and they keep changing the prices (always to the higher side), and other terms of business to their advantage. Firms, which have diversified vertically, are at a distinct advantage over others. It is therefore necessary for firms to keep a constant vigil on supply scene and always keep more than one supplier for vital raw materials.

Demographics—population composition is changing; there is a large teenage group, a large population of senior citizens and migration of workers from villages to towns is a continuous phenomenon.

Alternatives are available with better technology (electric shavers became popular for a while in the 1970-1980 period); lower air fare prompts train travellers to go by air.

Understanding the product location in its life cycle is important to understand the behaviour of competitors who could be market leaders or market laggards. Their firms have their own priorities with regard to placing the product in a particular segment. Competitive information can lead the firm to a vigilant proactive decision in terms of its own products business plan.

Understanding the consumer—consumer needs, their buying patterns and habits, purchase decision triggers, and the answers to the five W and one H questions is required—what they buy, why they buy, where they buy it from, when they buy, which price they buy at, and finally, how they buy. In the normal circumstances, when the firm is making a profit and selling its entire produce these questions become irrelevant. It is only when new competitive product swamps the market, the firm does not know what hit it. Maslow's hierarchy of needs and the Freudian theory of desires must be addressed to plan market policies. A car is just not a means of transportation alone; it could reflect the owner's status. Mercedes is bought more as a status symbol than for any other purpose. Firms do better if they understand consumer behaviour in their selected market segments for the product.

Market Segmentation

In the first half of the twentieth century the firm's focus used to be on production and whatever was produced was sold, competition was either not there or it was just not enough, with market for all the players in the field. With severe competition from international players, each selling multiple brands and models, it would be futile for firms to sell in the mass market. The segment variety needs different selling techniques, advertising messages as what works for one segment may not work for the other. Product, price promotion and placement all need different strategies for different segments. Segmentation is done on the following lines:

Demographic variables	Geographic variables
Age	Country
Sex	Climate
Family size	City size
Children's ages	State
Occupation	Population density
Income	Country's main religions
Education	
Religion	
Social status	
Psychographic variables	**Product usage variables**
Lifestyle	Heavy users
Personality	Light users
Product loyalty	
Product awareness	

Strategic audit should trace the firm's growth and standing in the marketplace, which can be done on the following parameters:

Market growth:

(i) Same product increased sales through penetrating prices and increased efforts of the marketing team

(ii) Same product sales increase in extension of geographic areas

(iii) New or improved product in the same geographic area.

Acquisitions involves investments of available funds of cash-rich firms in product or business diversification by acquiring other firms, business. Diversifications can be vertical or horizontal depending on whether the firm has bought into its supplier or a product with which it has some synergy.

Distribution channels—ability of selection of the type of distribution network as also the actual dealers of the product to cover the geographic segments is of vital importance for the success of the firm, especially for consumer goods. It is the last link in the chain connecting the manufacturer to the consumer and the only one which gests the buyer money in exchange of goods supplied.

Pricing policy is governed by the following considerations:

Elasticity of demand—does the price change affect the product demand or not; the firms if they are marketing in multiple segments must be fully aware of the demand changes in each segment on variation of price.

Government price regulations—in some products the government has its own price mechanism, especially in the food and drugs, and the firms must take this into consideration while fixing the price.

Competitors—price becomes a function of competitive pricing, unless the firm can claim a higher price based on their better brand equity.

Pricing and promotions—short term extra benefits are given to customers, which reduce the profits for the firm, but gain additional market share. Such increases are mostly short-lived as they invite competitive reaction nullifying the increase in the market share. At times the commission given to the channel members change as the firm expects the channel members to pass on the benefits to the customers, putting a smoke screen before the competitors, giving the impression that they are not involved in any price war on their own.

Price and quality—for premium quality goods high prices can be kept with high brand equity, for low quality goods keeping high prices could be the means of getting quick profits before competition catches on. Keeping low prices of high quality products would mean generic product, high growth market and firm wanting to improve its market share. Low quality low price would be for bargains and discounts often to unload extra inventory.

Product strategy—it should take the product's brand equity, stage of its life cycle, competitive products, production capacity/or product availability (heavy advertising and promotion will fall flat if the product is not available, unless the firm is trying to create artificial scarcity to increase demand.

Advertising and promotion—creating product awareness, leading to interest in owning it can be generated through intelligent use of advertising, which does not over-sell the product and remains in the realm of plausibility. Besides, personal selling, publicity and promotion have definite roles to play in market communications. The audit judges the efficacy of these communications with the market segment.

Case Studies

Understanding Case Studies

Case studies help the students and the readers to relate to the practical aspects of the theories given in the book. In fact the students can analyze the information given, find alternative solutions, assess the best option and then give their recommendations on the case. It would be the task for the teacher or the guide, to steer the students on the right path enabling them to arrive at the best recommendations. The following method is suggested for arriving at the recommendation stage:

- Read the case cursorily in the first stage
- Study any figures or tables provided in the case.
- Analyze the figures
- Study the case in detail again
- Use the tools available for analyzing the case
- Write down rough report
- Discuss the rough report with your guide
- Make final report on the basis of the discussions

Final report should have the following elements in it:

- Title page
- Acknowledgements where you express your gratitude to those who helped you in the case analysis
- Table of contents with page numbers
- Executive summary of the recommendations on the case
- Brief information on the case
- Tools you are planning to use in the case study
- Case analysis
- Recommendations (with possible expected results, if possible) and conclusions

- Glossary of important words used
- Bibliography of written matter used in the case study

The students must understand that while solving case studies there is no absolutely right or wrong answer. The areas to look for are:

- The student has understood the case, its problem areas well
- The student is using the right tools in solving the case
- The student has analyzed the figures and tables given in the case (if any)
- The student has presented his recommendations in a forthright unambiguous manner
- The recommendations need not be many, but they should be hard hitting and direct
- The recommendations must arise out of the case analysis, the tools used. Any major deviation, which is not explicitly mentioned in the case, must be stated clearly wit reasons for the same.

CASE STUDY 1

Force Tyre Company

Relationship Sales

Ram had just joined the Force Tyre Company as the head of marketing. He had to make friends with the automobile manufacturers purchase managers. His major customer was the large vehicle maker Zed cars. Zed cars purchase manager Madan was a tough customer, very upright and a hard taskmaster. He wanted every thing as per his own ideas and any change or delay could result in force losing the business. Ram had been advised by his MD, that he should handle Madan carefully else there will be major problems for the firm as also for Ram. He decided to make a personal visit to know Madan better and took an appointment with him. The following conversation took place after the initial pleasantries.

Madan, "So you are the new salesman at Force. Frankly I have been losing faith in the Force Company. The deliveries are delayed, billings are wrong. In fact the list of my complaints is virtually endless. Anyway, since you are new I cannot possibly put the blame on you. I will give you just two months to amend the situation. Otherwise you know there are other better tyre people in the market."

Ram, "Perhaps you are right. Anyone who gets such treatment as you have described to me would feel let down. Let me just reassure you that while I am not a wonder worker, you will, in the next three months, get the best service any tyre company can provide in the country."

Madan, "What about the defective tyres we have returned to you? In the first place why should you be sending such tyres to us? Secondly, what about replacements, or at least a credit note to cover the cost of the tyres?"

Ram, "Sir, permit me to put some facts before you. When we explained the latest development in tyre technology to your quality engineers, they have not only accepted all the tyres, but given us a green signal for using the same technology for future dispatches too. I am sure you too must have read about the bubble barrier technology prevalent in the west."

Madan, "Good. Now I would like to discuss new prices for our next order for the next year supplies. Are you ready for the same? Incidentally, tomorrow, the salesman from Keats tyres, your main competitor is coming to see me."

Notes for the Students

Where do you think the tyre salespeople have been missing out on the customer to make him almost inimical towards the firm?

When there is a change in marketing personnel, what sort of guidance, introduction, and orientation should be given to the new salesperson?

In B-to-B what are the options available to the sellers for building relationships with their customers?

Guidelines for the Students

Marketing person should take prior appointment for meetings with the customers irrespective of the level of person they have to meet. This gives the person importance, a little ego boosting, while it helps, in most cases the marketing person getting undivided time and attention of the customer.

Marketing person should always be on time or a few minutes early for the meeting. This spare time lets the person become composed, collect his wits and arrange his talk properly.

Marketing person should be wearing clean dress, not flashy but sober business suit, should be well-groomed and impeccable in manners.

He should be a good listener to become a good conversationalist.

He should carry the required documents, testimonials, and sales records and not leave anything for the next call. Most of all he should be carrying his visiting cards.

If the buyer has become friendly it may be a good idea to invite him for a dinner or luncheon meeting. Take him away from his office in a neutral more friendly, peaceful place and it would add to building the relationship. If the marketing person is meeting the customer for the first time, it is a good idea to do some background research on the customer, his habits, likes and dislikes. Genuine praise helps while flattery may create a barrier between the two.

There is a thin line between bribery and gift, and the customer's perception of the difference between the two. Marketing person should know it and use to his advantage.

Newsletters, yearly calendars, dairies are worth considering. At festival time gifts are exchanged between friends and relatives. These opportunities can be exploited as in many cases the customers are expecting the gifts.

Trying to be a genuine friend, who helps when help is required, can make a big difference between being one of the sellers and being the friend and a seller.

Let us categorise the customers as follows:

- Users of FMCG Products
- Dealers in FMCG Products

- Buyers of consumer durables
- Dealers in consumer durables
- Industrial buyers
- Industrial distributors
- Services buyers

Customer and client—the difference between a customer and a client can be defined as follows:

When there is only one-to-one relationship between the user and the supplier, the user is the client and not a customer. On the contrary, if there are large numbers of users or buyers, they are the customers. In relationship marketing the idea is to try and convert as many of the customers into clients as possible, as individual attention can be provided and the buyers become more loyal.

Now let us demonstrate the methods by which firms can conduct relationship marketing for the customer groups:

FMCG Users—since these are in large numbers, it is the most difficult task to build relationships with them. However, in these days of cut-throat competition, firms have devised ways of doing just that. Product promotion like, "open the package and you may be the lucky winner of a gold earring." Those who get the earring become loyal customers and others remain loyal in the hope of getting the earring. Hence, relationship, although a weak one is developed between the seller and the buyer. For heavy users, "buy two and get one free" becomes the binding force.

Dealers in FMCG products—relationship between the seller and the channel member for FMCG products are based on the profit the dealer/retailer can make by selling the product. Sales depend on utility value, quality and availability of the product. Hence, if the seller can provide a product, much in demand of good quality and having value for money, it would surely build good custom as also a good relationship between the channel and the seller. Better discounts, handling of complaints, effective advertisement in the right media help build business for the channel member. Next, the seller can train the salespersons of the retailers to build the relationship.

Buyers of consumer durables—as consumer durables are not purchased often; it is of great importance that the buyers keep a good healthy attitude towards the product. This is possible by using the following plan:

- Supplying quality product
- Offering speedy after sales service to the satisfaction of the customer.
- Making accessories and spare parts available when and where needed
- Publishing and distributing free newsletters to the customers giving them new product information, new researches in the area
- Organizing special events like cultural programmes where the buyers are invited
- Making them special offers, promotional programme offers before offering them to the public.

Dealers in consumer durables—profit and profit potential are the two motivating factors for the dealers in consumer durable goods. Turnover discounts, target based incentives can play a vital role in building relationship with these dealers. Firms are known to give interesting and expensive gifts to the dealers. Dealers could be multi-brand sellers and the firm offering greater incentive will get better business from them. Paid foreign holidays, luxury cars or equivalent cash are some of the methods used by the sellers to keep the dealers loyal to them.

Industrial buyers—industrial purchase decisions are often taken by a team consisting of, the purchase manager, technical manager, R&D Manager, finance manager, the ultimate user of the product and the CEO of the firm. A good brand image/equity of the firm helps in building relations. Frequency of visits, timely redress of complaints, JIT supplies, help a lot in building the relationship. Additionally, dinners with the families, outings, picnics, and gifts on birthdays of the spouse and children, assistance in any official or personal problem go a long way in that direction.

CASE STUDY 2

Jagdish Electronics

Jagdish Electronics is a large manufacturer of electronic and telecom products. They have a workforce of three thousand and yearly turnover of rupees one thousand crore. Besides three factories, they also have a major research facility. Jagdish have a rule that any new vendor or a new product must be approved by the research engineers, before it is inducted in the products.

Megaton is a producer of components and other products like test instruments needed by Jagdish. Megaton was having a difficult time in getting any approvals even though their products were not only acceptable but also just right for Jagdish. Marketing Manager Ram was in real dilemma as to what should be his next action.

One morning after taking an appointment with Dr. Kapil, Ram had reached the R&D Labs well in time. There was no sign of Dr. Kapil. After waiting for nearly half an hour he was about to leave when he found Kapil, red in the face with two-day beard, running towards his chamber.

Ram said, "There seems to be some problem. Can I be of some help?"

Dr. Kapil, "Oh, so you have come. See, I am in great hurry. I came here only to take some cash lying in my office and may be borrow some from my friends. My son is seriously sick in the hospital and of all days only today my car had to conk out. Anyway, please allow me to proceed and we shall meet again."

Ram, "please stop. I think I have the answer to all your problems. See I am free today and my car is in your car parking. I am carrying extra cash of about forty thousand which I can loan to you without hesitation or problem."

Dr. Kapil, "are you sure? Then what are we waiting for? Let us get out of here and head for the hospital."

For the next three weeks Ram attended the hospital daily till Kapil's son became all right. On the day he was being discharged Ram brought flowers, pen set, chocolates school bag as gifts for the son which were not be refused by Kapil.

Need it be said that in all future cases Ram's products were taken up for quick approval and seldom rejected. Even when they were rejected it was only for a temporary period for minor changes.

Questions

- Was Ram right in neglecting his other assignments for being with Kapil and his son?
- Was it ethical to loan his company's money to Kapil?
- Was it ethical for Kapil to take Ram's help and later on gifts for his son?

CASE STUDY 3

Mode Freeze Ltd.

Mode Freeze Ltd. after setting up manufacturing plant in Noida near Delhi, Mode is ready to start sales of its refrigerators. The range of products is given below:

- Refrigerators in sizes from 70 litres to 450 litres
- Deep Freezers for both domestic and commercial use
- Car refrigerators with 25 to 70 litres capacity

Next summer they are planning to introduce window and split air-conditioners too.

As the plant is near Delhi, Mode wants to start the sales in Delhi initially. The CEO of Mode Rashmi is with the Marketing Manager Gauri to discuss the distribution arrangements for their products.

Gauri, "I think initially we should go for the traditional route of distributors, dealers and retailers. Later on we can think of alternative channels as well."

Rashmi, "Please tell me what have you done so far in this regard?"

Gauri, "We have received applications from prospective channel members against our advertisements. We have three applications from area distributors, twenty-five from dealers and hundred fifty from retailers. Our team has us their report on each of the candidates regarding the suitability to be with us my plan for the arrangement in Delhi is as follows:

- Appoint one area distributor each in north, west, east, central and two in the south Delhi.
- Appoint dealers in the peripheral areas around Delhi, which we have already identified.
- Let the distributors and dealers appoint retailers in their areas after getting our approval in each case to avoid the wrong people joining us. We can think of a tripartite agreement between us, the distributor/dealer and the retailer to bind each one with us.

Rashmi, "It is all very good. You have also to think of the stronghold or virtual stranglehold, which our competitors have on the distribution channels."

Gauri, "OK, we will work on this angle and get back to you in a day's time."

The statement Gauri's team made is given below:

Total sales per annum of the products in Delhi is Rs. 500 crore as follows:

	East	South	North	West	Central	Total
Refrigerators	35	110	70	55	90	360
Car refrigerators	2	15	3	18	2	30
Deep freezer	15	40	10	25	20	110
Total	**52**	**168**	**83**	**88**	**112**	**500**

The market as per present trends is growing at the rate of five percent per year.

Study of various channels, the area coverage, coverage density, firm's control and selling expenses in each case is given below:

	Geographic coverage %	Coverage density%	Firm's control%	Expense per unit sale in Rs.
Distributor/dealer/retailer	100	60	45	3000
Only retailer	100	60	30	2600
Firm's own shops	30	100	100	1800
Direct sales—Eureka Forbes style	100	30	100	1200
Internet	100	5	Nil	200

Today, Gauri and Rashmi have to decide about the distribution strategy.

Question for the Students

Which in your opinion is the best distribution channel or more than one channel is required? Discuss the merits and demerits of each channel and give your recommendations on the case.

CASE STUDY 4

Zena Hotels

Zena Hotels was started by Silva in Goa as a five-star property, a tourist's haven, ten years ago. Now with the decline in international tourism Silva has expended his hotel to cater to the local tourists also. Objective of the hotel is to sell the rooms at good rates for maximum occupancy.

The new expended hotel is based on the airline concept of having three classes in aircraft, the economy, business and the first class. At Zena the rooms are also in three categories as follows:

- Budget rooms for Indian travellers as also foreign travellers on a budget
- Deluxe rooms for business executives
- Super suites for industrialists

Zena has the required five-star facilities, like health club, which comes free to the suite guests, but others have to pay for them.

Till two years back, Zena had a good occupancy rate, averaging eighty per cent year round. Mostly travel agents based in different countries in the world did the bookings. Now Silva has to rethink his strategy of marketing his hotel. He feels that with the expanded hotel his clients should include the Indian businessman, Indian holiday makers, business executives, besides the foreign tourists. He is not sure that the travel agents would do justice to his hotel. He has the following options:

- Sell his hotels directly to Indian business by offering discounts, which go to the travel agents
- Frequent guests discounts and extra facilities like room upgrades, lower rates.
- Sell some rooms en bloc to the best bidder either from a travel agent or a business house who would get a low rate for year long booking.
- Start a Hotel Management School where he can use some of the rooms as classrooms (on the lines of Medical Colleges in the hospital campus)

- Revise cost estimates to get to the variable costs only for modifying the tariff.
- Organize road shows in major towns to attract customers from there.
- Focus on Indian industrial sector and try to use their Administrative Managers for getting their bookings; maybe by providing them some official/ personal incentive (debatable issue as it may tantamount to offering bribe to them).

Zena owners are engaging a consultancy firm to recommend them the best alternative to come back as a leading property in Goa.

Task for the Students

Plan a short-term and a long-term marketing strategy for Zena Hotels.

CASE STUDY 5

7-11 Stores

7-11 Stores—the store caters to the general public living in the store's vicinity by supplying the following products:

- Meat, seafood, vegetables
- Confectionary and bakery products
- Health and beauty products
- Gift items
- Toys both mechanical and electronic

As new super market has started operating in the area the store is facing major sales problems. Earlier it was growing both in sales and profits as can be seen from the following table:

1980	Sales Rs. 10 million profit Rs. 0.7 million
1985	Sales Rs. 15 million profit Rs. 0.9 million
1990	Sales Rs. 18 million profit Rs. 1.0 million
1995	Sales Rs. 25 million profit Rs. 1.1 million
2000	Sales Rs. 34 million profit Rs. 1.1 million

From the year 2000 the decline started which has now become a major problem for the store. From the statistics it can be seen that the total sale of the items sold by the store amount to twenty-three per cent of the retail sale in the country. The sale is growing at the rate of seven per cent perhaps the highest growth rate of any consumer product group. The store sells more products but gets less profit for the same and the situation is going to worse soon as more stores are coming up in the area.

As more people are getting the health conscious they are buying branded products, even items like salt, sugar, flour and condiments. This has given rise to the prices of the branded products. With the recession setting in, the commodity sale is again picking up at least in the middle-income group. Heavy advertising directed towards the health awareness, children, teenagers is making the life of an average Indian quite miserable, as he wants to, but cannot afford to buy the branded products.

The other danger is coming from the Internet sellers. In Delhi food items can be ordered on the net and fresh vegetables and fruits are delivered against payment within ten hours at home. However, as only the elite has Internet connection so far the threat is more imaginary than real.

On an average expenditure on store products is 12 per cent of the disposable personal income.

Five force competitors analysis:

Rivalry—one super market is already in competition. With bigger space they are offering larger variety, more imported goods. They have kids play area and even a coffee bar.

Threat of new entrants is real as international super market chains are eyeing the Indian market, which will come with a well-known brand and marketing expertise.

Substitute products—one could not imagine that there can be substitute products for food items, but now many restaurants offer home delivery service, which obviates the need of cooking to an extent.

Bargaining power of the buyers—usually the stores sell products on fixed prices given on the product and displayed in the store. The customer shift takes place only due to indifferent service or the distance they have to travel to come to the store. Price is seldom the cause of the shift as the stores keep prices low and work on volume business.

Bargaining power of the suppliers—manufacturers want to sell in the markets with the best volumes and margins. Hence, the super markets get better terms in price and delivery.

The store has to revitalize itself. Frequent buyer programme, joint advertising with the manufacturers, and better buying of goods as per market demand and foreign tie-ups are being planned.

Tasks for the Students

Plan short term and long-term strategies for the store to remain a profitable venture. Can penetrating price be useful in the case or do they need to build the brand equity further? Are promotional plans required at present?

CASE STUDY 6

Kelvin Appliances

Kelvin Appliances started by Mohan began operations in 1975. The first product was a refrigerator. Kelvin stayed with refrigerators till 1998, while offering a full range of refrigerators and deep freezers. In 1991, it was apparent that unless Kelvin diversified it couldn't retain its market share. Kelvin planned to sell microwaves, air-conditioners, coolers, heat radiators, washing machines, and vacuum cleaners. The idea was to include dishwashers as well at a later date.

Product plans—setting up manufacturing facilities for the product range called for huge investments and the returns were not guaranteed. Hence, the management of Kelvin decided to buy and sell the products and thus supplement their existing product range of refrigerators. For this purpose Kelvin signed an agreement with Vitas, which had the following salient points:

- Vitas will manufacture the products as per international standards
- Kelvin will maintain a close watch on the quality of Vitas products
- Vitas will acquire ISO 9000 Standards in one year's time.
- Kelvin will have the option of posting their own quality engineers at Vitas
- Kelvin will have the option of pre-shipment inspection of goods on random basis
- Vitas will provide free guarantee and warrantee service to Kelvin customers. Vitas will also have the option of signing annual maintenance contract with the customers.

While the life expectancy of refrigerators was at 16 years, Kelvin has felt let down by the life expectancy of other products, which is as given below:

- Microwave 10 years
- Air-conditioners 7 years
- Coolers 5 years
- Heat radiators 3 years
- Washing machines 9 years

- Vacuum cleaners 6 years
- Dishwashers 5 years – only estimated as the product was introduced only in 2000.

The life expectancy of competitive products is at least 20% more and because of this reason Kelvin is losing sales to competitors. Kelvin has realized that 65% of the sale price is the manufacturing cost. However, Kelvin's agreement with Vitas does not get over for the next five years.

Cost elements of home appliances are given below:

Selling price	100%
Manufacturing costs	65%
Transport and storage	5%
Selling	5%
Advertising	6%
Service	4%
R&D	3%
Overheads	13%

There have been cases of Vitas neglect of complaints from the customers, which is bringing a bad name to Kelvin. Marketing, advertising and sales promotion are purely in Kelvin's hands.

Since the R&D is not Kelvin's hand they are not able to upgrade the product.

Product	USA	Europe	Japan
Microwaves	85	35	80
Refrigerators	99	92	99
Dishwashers	52	30	NA
Washing machines	75	88	99
Vacuum cleaners	98	82	98
Deep freezers	35	45	NA
Water heaters	99	NA	30

Task for the Students

Students should plan sales directly to large builders, hotels, hospitals and other bulk buyers. Can these products be customized or custom built? Would Kelvin need its own R&D for realizing the objective or is it possible under the present arrangement? How much impact does the brand have on the sale of these products?

Plan Kelvin's strategy for marketing the products taking the following into account:

Should Kelvin stay with the Vitas Agreement?

How can Kelvin improve their brand equity?

Should Kelvin reduce the number of products or plan product portfolio better?

Should Kelvin take over the service from Vitas and get a price reduction from Vitas as also get their own engineers trained at Vitas?

Distribution channels have been the strength of Kelvin so far but with addition of Vitas products the channel members are not comfortable with Kelvin. Should Kelvin plan new channels, new in variety or in numbers?

Should Kelvin plan overseas forays with their products only or with their total product range, including bought out items? The international market of the products, as per cent of households owning the products is given below:

CASE STUDY 7

Crown Apparels Ltd.

The famous Crown group of India started Crown Apparels Ltd. in 1975. Initially they were only importing readymade gents suits from England. In 1980, they decided to start their garments factory in the hope of meeting the growing demand as also to provide the products as per customer's demand in the country. The move was not successful at all due to the following reasons:

The elite buyers were tuned to the English styling and design. Even with better cloth, Crown suffers from not so attractive cut and styling of the suits.

With indigenous production the quantities to be sold were huge and most Indians preferred to get their clothes stitched by their local tailor.

In mass production the quality of stitching suffered.

Some suppliers were still importing from England and they even started importing from the fashion centres of Europe, France.

From 1991, with the liberalization of Indian economy, imports got a fillip and the sales of Crown suffered further.

The total demand of readymade suits for gents' in the year 2000 was Rs. 250 crore. It is estimated to grow at the rate of about 10% per annum for the next five years.

	1998	1999	2000	2001	2002	2003	2004	2005
Crown	105	110	100	100	100	105	105	110
C-1	40	40	60	65	65	65	65	70
C-2	35	35	30	35	35	40	40	40
Imports	20	25	60	75	100	120	150	180
	200	225	250	275	300	330	360	400

Customers' perception of brands in the market is as follows:

Crown brand is well established with several loyal buyers.

Crown is known for the quality of cloth, which is, in most cases better or equal to the quality of imported suits.

Crown offers a wide range of products; even the odd sizes, which are usually, slow moving products.

Crown has a strong network of dealers and retailers. However, in the last two years, many dealers have opted out of Crown's operations to tie up with foreign brands.

Crown has presence in forty cities of India and their suits are sold in many more through their network. They have offices and godowns in the four metro cities of the country. Imported suits are being sold only in four metro towns at present but seeing the market the importers are planning to enlarge their network and are targeting Crown's dealer network to sell their products by ousting Crown from there.

In pricing Crown has positioned itself just below the imported suits, and they are above the other Indian brands as can be seen from the prices given below:

- Crown price range Rs. 4,500-12,000
- C-1 price range Rs. 4,000-6,000
- C-2 price range Rs. 3,500-5,500
- Imported suits price range Rs. 6,000-30,000

Crown is keen to ensure that they get back their market share and also not lose their dealer network. The prices quoted now are about 15% lower because of the local competition. Profit margins have reduced quite a bit. Advertising and promotion expenses have shot up.

Crown has only a few options with them, like boosting their brand equity to the level of imported brands, increasing production to enjoy economies of scale, improve the design and cut of their suits.

Task for the Students

Using the four Ps plan a marketing strategy for Crown to help them achieve their objective of market share and improved profits.

CASE STUDY

8

Honeymoon Hotel Nainital (HHN)

Located in the Kumaun region it boasts of a wonderful lake surrounded by the town. Boating, yachting, horse riding, skating are prominent activities available to the tourists who come here, besides sight seeing, for which there are numerous places for trekking picnicking in the town and in the surrounding areas. During summer months the place is full to the brim as people who can afford leave the torturous heat of the plains for the cool climate of Nainital. In winter months, during marriage season the honeymooners throng the place to enjoy the solitude and sight seeing it offers. Raja Gupta started the HHN in 1974 to cater to the honeymooners and therefore selected a plot of land on the upper climbs of the town, which has a fantastic view of the snow-clad mountains almost year round.

Raja has several other businesses and to control them he stays in Delhi about 300 kilometres away from Nainital. He has appointed Ravi Pant a local hotel management graduate as General Manager of the hotel and he has been running it from its inception.

The hotel boasts of the following facilities:

- Pizza Hut restaurant given on lease to Pizza Hut, Delhi
- Mughal restaurant serving mughlai dishes is popular with honeymooners
- China Town caters to the clients interested in Chinese cuisine.
- Mongrel bar is popular with locals as well as tourists

The hotel has 60 rooms; they had started with twenty rooms and extended to 60 in 1999, when despite poor condition of rooms they were fully occupied for eight months in the year. The lobby, checking and reservation desks were well kept and heated during winters. The hotel's outward appearance was remarkably good which attracted the visitors and the Delhi office took care of the room bookings.

Hotel staff—as is common to hotels run on seasonal basis; the permanent staff was a mere skeleton one while temporary hands were hired during the season. The organization structure of the hotel is given below:

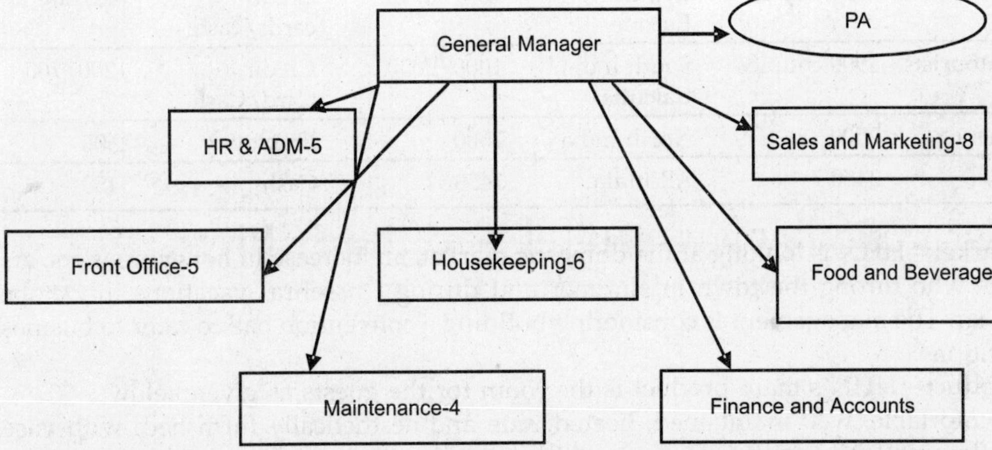

Each department has a number of employees as given in the blocks.

Ravi Pant has built a reasonably good core team and he keeps them happy by praising their work and giving them right advice when needed.

Present scenario—as many more hotels have come up near the Mall Road, which have easy accessibility for tourists coming by buses, HHN is losing its appeal even to honeymooners.

The Marketing Plan

Mission—HHN's mission is to deliver the maximum return on investment to the shareholders by assuring quality service, best rooms in town and tasty, hygienic food round the clock through restaurants and the room service. The quality of service to be guaranteed by qualified trained and motivated employees. To keep the tariff in consonance with the quality expected and delivered by the HHN.

Marketing objective is to maximize the hotel revenue with expenses kept to a minimum. The rule to guide expenses is "cut costs till it hurts but not hinders the hotel operations" and the entire team is committed to the objective.

Revenue target for the year 2001 is:

Room revenue: Rs. 600 @ 70% occupancy	Rs. 6500,000
Telephone revenue	Rs. 325,000

Purpose of staying at HHN:

Honeymooners	1252 couples	North India, Calcutta	40/12	Credit cards/cash	30/30
Foreign tourists	175 couples	UK, USA, Europe	100/50/25	Credit cards/cash	145/30
Indian tourists	1900 couples	South India/ Calcutta	1000/9000	Credit Card/Cash	1200/700
Business	2500	North India	2500	Employers	2500
Others	3450	All India	3450	Cash	3450-

Market—HHN is looking at the domestic market, an increase in honeymooners, and tourists who throng the town in summer and during Dussehra vacations in October each year. The management is considering building a convention hall to cater to business conventions.

Product—HHN's main product is the room for the guests as given below:

- Comfortable, well maintained, heated, safe and aesthetically furnished, with vases of flowers, fruit baskets
- Clean toilets attached with the rooms, well stocked with toiletries
- Restaurants and a bar with a variety of foods, drinks, efficient service by trained waiters and prompt room service
- Evening entertainment, live band during season
- Daily cleaning of the rooms by well-mannered staff and replenishment of toiletries.
- Well maintained lawn, rock garden and jogging trail
- Provision for sightseeing trips in cars with knowledgeable guides at extra cost
- Travel desk for the convenience of guests for outward reservations, pickup and drop from the railway station and the nearby airport.

The GM has plans to further improve the hotel revenue but first he wants to invest in the following areas:

- Training of front office staff, housekeepers, maintenance staff, waiters in the restaurant, room service boys
- Training of managerial staff
- Control system improvement

GMs SWOT analysis has brought out the following aspects of the hotel:

Strengths

- The hotel has a good reputation with its clientele
- It is well located, accessible by car
- Honeymooners get the privacy they look for
- Room rent is in line with the hotel facilities and is competitive
- Food and drinks, cocktails of the hotel are generally well liked by the guests

Weaknesses

- It does not have a big enough hall for large parties and conventions
- During season it gets crowded for the comfort of honeymooners
- The name of the hotel takes away some clients as it gives the impression of a leisurely, laidback place

Opportunities

- With bifurcation of UP, Nainital is the only hill station worth the name in UP.
- India as a tourist destination is becoming important in the west and Nainital is close to the Corbet Park the famous tourist attraction
- Indian tourism has been on the rise in the last five years
- Government of India is keen to develop the tourism industry in the country

Threats

- New hotels with better and modern facilities like computerized booking worldwide, better furnishings and modern toilets are springing up in the area.
- USA is not considering India as a tourist destination at least temporarily

Marketing Plans—the GM of the hotel has placed the following ideas before the owner regarding the hotel, its reputation, profitability and its ability to compete with the new hotels in the area.

Pricing—the GM wants to have flexi-pricing policy, which would give him the leverage to accommodate the middle class travellers in case there is vacancy in rooms. He also wants special privileges to be offered to frequent travellers to the hotel.

Promotion—GM wants to promote the hotel through the travel agencies by giving a few agencies authority to give bulk-booking rates even to single bookings. He wants to invite the representatives of the agencies to the hotel, showcase it for them, give them the latest literature and announce extra discounts for bulk bookings.

GM wants to buy a fleet of luxury cars and mini coaches for sightseeing for the guests.

GM also wants to start small guesthouses in Bheemtal, Almora and Kausani to give the guests a variegated experience of the Himalayas, in one package.

Given below is the Profit and Loss Statement of the hotel

Revenue	Rupees	Expenses	
Room rent	6500,000	Purchases	1000,000
Telephone	325,000	Telephone	350,000
Restaurant/Bar	250,0000	Salaries and wages	5250,000
Miscellaneous	300,000	Insurance/Interest	700,000
		Depreciation	650,000
		Miscellaneous	1 350,000
Total	9625,000		9300,000

Profit before tax is Rs. 325,000

The profit is likely to go down further and hence the anxiety of the management towards bringing the hotel back at its feet despite the competition.

Task before the Students

Plan a complete recovery package for the hotel, taking the swot analysis existing plan in to account.

CASE STUDY

9

Airlink India Ltd.

The airline was started in 1995, when the government opened the Indian skies to private sector. Promoted by Capt. Ahuja, who had worked in the Indian Airlines for the last fifteen years, as a senior pilot, the airline was financed by the Singhal group of companies, who had made a mark in the country's tourism industry as they owned six five-star hotels one each in Delhi, Kolkata, Chennai, Mumbai, Ahmedabad and Bangalore, besides having a travel agency covering the entire country and having offices in the UK, USA and France.

There was much jubilation in the airline on the 31st March, 1998, when it showed a cash profit for the first time. Ahuja said, "We have arrived, finally."

How it all began—Ahuja had read about the privatization plan of the government of India before he went to play golf with Rajesh Singhal of the Singhal group, who was his school friend from Doon school. Sharing a bottle of beer, Ahuja mentioned his desire of setting up an airline, which brought Singhal on his feet. "Yes, let us do it before others steal our idea"

Airline India was registered with a capital of Rs. 3 crore, with plans of offering extra benefits to Indian fliers while charging the same fare as others, including the government operators were charging. By1997, a few other airlines came into being and the battle for gaining customers started in right earnest. What followed can best be described as a race for offering add-on to the customers on a continuous basis. Fashion shows, in-flight auctions, latest movies from Hollywood and Bollywood were screened daily.

Airline India started with a fleet of seven Boeings-202, since they have added twelve more Dornier Aircraft to the fleet. They have managed to remain low-cost carrier by optimizing the use of aircraft, better maintenance of aircraft and small payroll. They have a small group of highly paid, motivated people who perform their tasks with total dedication.

Airline India has acquired seat miles over a period of time, which is reflected in the statement given below:

	1999	2000	2001	2002
Seat miles in millions	3.0	3.3	3.5	4.0

Cities served by the airline are given below:
Profitable sectors—
Mumbai-Delhi
Kolkata-Delhi
Chennai-Delhi
Delhi-Bangalore
Kolkata-Mumbai

Loss Making Sectors—
Lucknow-Varanasi
Goa-Chennai
Kanpur-Delhi
Chandigarh-Shimla
Kolkata-Dibrugarh

The GM wants to close the non-profit routes but is finding it difficult in view of the pressure from the staff and the government alike.

SWOT analysis of the airlines is given below:

Strengths—the airline is young in terms of fleet, personnel, it provides the state of art service with total computerized operations and on line reservations and check-ins. Its MD is dynamic, clear thinking who gives total freedom of action to his team.

Weaknesses—its lack of experience in crisis management. Dearth of ground staff, services, and separate lounges for first class passengers.

Opportunities—with open economy of the country, the travel, within and from overseas has increased and is slated to increase at the rate of 12% per annum, barring inclement political climate.

Threats—some foreign airlines are planning to enter the growing Indian market. Also, the political instability and growing violence in the country could inhibit foreigners from visiting the country.

Financial statements are given below to understand the functioning of the airlines:

	2001	2000	1999	1998
Revenue passenger in lacs	1300	1150	970	825
Revenue freight	25	20	15	15
Total revenue	1325	1170	985	840
Expenses	1200	1100	925	790
Income	125	70	60	50
Taxes	40	25	22	20
Net income	85	45	38	30
Return on assets	1.5	3.2	5.1	5.0
Return on equity	4.0	8.0	12	10
Debt % of equity	50	35	38	30

The airline is hoping that the major airlines of the world would abstain from entering the Indian market, because if that happens, it would definitely put a big strain on the airline and they will have to increase their marketing, advertising and promotion expenses to counter the brand advantage of international players. The airline itself has been toying with the idea of joining hands with a foreign airline but they fear that it may turn out to be a takeover bid ultimately. Captain Ahuja being a flyer is keen to keep the Indian flag flying on the carrier.

Airline business in India has been on a seesaw for the last five years. In 1996 there was less tension on the country's border, new foreign firms had entered the market in the area of automobiles, telecom, readymade garments, shoes, power, and with good harvests the country was definitely on road to prosperity. The cable TV revolution had already made a big impact on the advertising world and the famous Cola war; the war of the detergents had started peaking.

On the minus side the financial scams; irregularities on stock market had taken a toll on the investment and saving sectors. People in general were becoming wary of the social evil which had been invading politics as well, that of bribery and corruption.

The government at the centre comprises fifteen party alliance which makes it a hotchpotch and decision making keeping all the factions happy is really a tight rope walking. Some factions of the government want to further encourage private enterprise while others are not so enthusiastic about the same. Foreign investors have been cautious in bringing moneys in the country as it gets about one-tenth of what China gets annually as Foreign Direct Investment.

The government of India took such a long time in permitting Singapore Airlines to join hands with Tatas to operate in India that both the parties lost interest in the venture. For the MD of Airlines India this proved to be a blessing.

India, with a population of over a billion people, rising GNP and per capita income is surely going to improve the market condition for national airlines. The question is the time frame in which it will start. Till then can players like Airlink India keep putting up a brave front, hoping that their bitter pill would work in their favour to dissuade foreign players from entering India despite the government's open door policy for such overtures?

Tasks for the Students

To plan a marketing strategy to ensure profit and growth of the airline in the era of growing competition.

Should the Airlink go for product diversification, new pricing strategy or plan improving their services. As time elapses their flight and ground crew would become old and jaded. Also, as they are known for having the smartest crew it is also in danger of losing them to present and future competition, as has started already. Holding on to the team would need a good profit picture to enable the airline to provide increasingly interesting cash incentives to the staff.

CASE STUDY 10

Wisdom Freezers Ltd.

A study in selection of distribution channel:

Wisdom Freezers Ltd.—WFL a world player in refrigerators and deep freezers are planning to bring to India their products and they have chosen to start from Delhi. They have studied the distribution pattern of the existing players and have found the following options for their products:

Wholesalers-dealers-retailers

Own shops

Products

Refrigerators come in the range of 165 L., 230 L., 280 L., 325 L., and 450 L. The prices in rupees are given below for single and double door models:

165 liters	10,000	Not available as double door model
230 liters	15,000	17000
280 liters	21,000	24000
325 liters	32,000	36000
450 liters	55,000-four door only	

The weighted average price of refrigerators is Rs 20,000

Deep freezers come in two sizes, 320 liters @ Rs. 56,000 and 410 liters @ Rs. 75,000, with weighted average price at Rs. 60,000.

The business is seasonal, with March to September being the prime time and October to February being off season when all the firms offer exchange plans and cash discount to their customers, which could go up to twenty-five per cent.

Distribution Channel—WFL has thought of three types of channels as follows:

- Sole distributor for Delhi who will get a flat discount of 4.5%.

- Distributors for north, east, west south and central Delhi, who get flat 7% as commission.
- Own shops, east Delhi 1, west, 2, south 4, north 3 total 10 shops with expense @12%.

The target market sales in 1995 in Delhi is given below:

	Households	Refrigerators	Deep freezers
East Delhi	1.1 lacs	13000	1000
West Delhi	1.2 lacs	15000	2000
North Delhi	1.7 lacs	14000	500
South Delhi	1.5 lacs	18000	3500
Total Delhi	5.5 lacs	60000	7000

Coverage through the different channels is given in the following table:

	Area coverage %	Market penetration in the area covered %
Sole distributor	70	40
Area distributors	90	40
Own shop	50	80

Hence the three methods have weighted value as given below:
Sole distributor—28%
Area distributor—36%
Own shop—37.5%

Besides, there can be other methods of distribution like, tele shopping, door-to-door, kitty parties, and road shows.

Task before the Students

The students should identify the best methods possible in Indian conditions taking into account the coverage, expenses and market acceptance of the channels, as there can be more than one depending on the market.

CASE STUDY 11

Citi Mobiles Ltd.

Marketing research for of introducing innovative product.

Citi Mobiles Ltd.—CML has been in the business of manufacturing and marketing two-wheelers both scooters and motorcycles since 1970 and enjoyed leadership in the market with 34% share. They are also into exports to Europe, Middle East, South America and Australia. They export thirty per cent of their production. In 1991, CML planned to diversify into cars. They had been trying for the past few years to gauge the market for cars and had discovered that in case they can come up with a small car they could convert their two-wheeler customers into four-wheel car buying. The price could normally be twice that of the mobike price, double the number of wheels doubles the price. The mobike was selling at Rs. 35,000; hence car price ex-factory was pegged at Rs. 75,000.

CML had in 1991, the following marketing department structure:

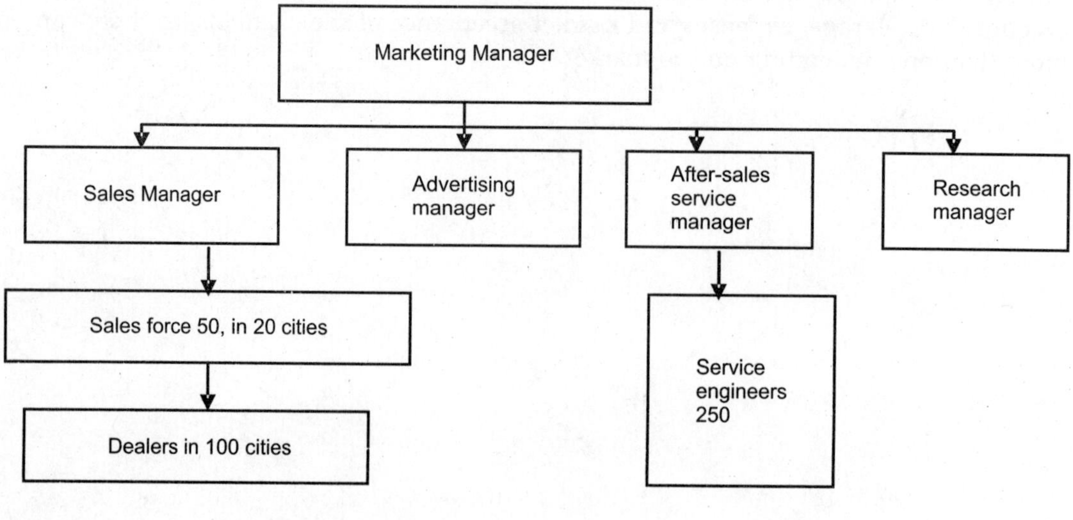

- CML hopes to retrain their selected personnel in sales and service of cars. Likewise they would upgrade the able and willing dealers for selling cars.
- CML signed an agreement with Renault of France for their sub-compact 500cc car which could be sold in India at ex-factory price of Rs. 75,000. The subcompact car Smily was liked by a small group of mo-bike owners as possible replacement for their bikes as they were under extreme pressure from their parents for going in for a car, at present price of cars they could ill afford the same.

CML decided to arrange a market survey for Smily as follows:

- Research problem—unknown buying process and factors influencing buying decisions for a new innovative subcompact car.

Objectives of the research

- Factors influencing buyers
- Stages of buying decisions
- Occupation, income levels and vehicle ownership at present
- Attitude towards the subcompact car—the Smily

Information needed from the research:

- Is there a need for subcompact cars in India?
- Will it be a first car, a substitute for mo-bike or will, it be second or third car in affluent homes?
- How the buyers get information about cars?
- Who initiates the buying process?
- Who is the decision maker?
- What interests the buyers most, in order of their priority?
- Economy in running the car
- Styling
- Comfort
- Price
- Brand
- Service availability in the country
- Durability of the car
- Easy availability of genuine spares in the country
- Luggage compartment size
- Ease of getting loans

Further information required is as follows:

- Buyer's view on dealership: dealer's location, reputation, availability of service facility, quality of service
- Role of the dealer in the buying process
- Role of credit and guarantee
- Post-purchase opinion

Research methodology:

Primary research

- Sample size 3500-stratified random technique for selecting the sample (rich and upper middle, middle class segments.)
- Findings of the research
- Need was felt @44% by housewives, 36% by teenagers
- The need was influenced by increasing levels of pollution on the roads of Delhi, increasing number of accidents involving mo-bikes and household income.

	Total response %	Total response
Family member, mother, wife	36	1300
Peer groups of teens and young adults	14	500
Relatives	6	200
Teenagers	44	1500

Factors influencing purchase are given below:

- Status symbol 58% – the mo-bike owners felt they would notch up a few rungs in the status ladder
- Economy 80%, with fuel prices always on the rise, the subcompact was advertised as giving huge fuel economy
- Safety 100% – the subcompact was sure to give much higher levels of safety than the mo-bike
- Comfort-70% – driving a car in all weathers on a comfortable seat was definitely more comfortable than riding a bike, especially when distances in Delhi are generally greater than other metros of India.

CML had advertised in the newspapers, magazines, they had set up hoardings and shown the advertisement on the TV network, besides they had used some other media like pamphlets.

The respondents were asked as to how they got to know about Smily, 52% saw the advertisements and 48% had not seen it.

The advertisements were seen on the following lines:

- Newspapers 55%
- Magazines 22%
- Hoardings 10%
- TV-30%
- Others 10%

The respondents were asked the reasons why they remembered the advertisements and they gave the reasons as follows:

	Impressive advertisement	Saw it many times	Appeared in many channels	Appeared in many magazines	Total
Newspapers	2	14	Nil	Nil	16
Magazines	Nil	4	Nil	4	8
TV	8	8	8	Nil	24
Hoardings	Nil	4	Nil	Nil	4
Totals	10	30	8	4	52

Therefore it can be concluded that TV and newspaper are the appropriate media for the product.

Later on the respondents needed more information and they got it from the following sources:

Profession	Literature	Dealers	Users	Firm's staff	Friends	Totals
Business	300	600	600	200	400	2100
Executive	200	Zero	300	Zero	400	900
Student	500	400	500	Zero	400	1800
Rank	Three	Three	One	Four	Two	

The respondents wanted information in the following areas:

	Price	Capacity	Durability	Servicing	Reputation	Totals
Literature	200	100	300	100	300	1000
Dealers	300	600	200	200	300	1600
Users	600	300	500	700	600	2700
Showrooms	100	100	200	100	100	600
Friends	400	300	300	400	400	1800
Totals	1600	1400	1500	1500	1700	7700
Rank	2	4	3	3	1	

As can be seen the respondents considered the brand reputation the most important information. Second was the price of the product. In buying decisions, the ranking of preference was as given below:

- After-sales service
- Guarantee period offered
- Price
- Discounts
- Credit offered/credit terms
- Possibility of putting air-conditioner in the car

Decision to buy was taken by the following persons jointly their influence area being:

- Head of the family 50%
- The other spouse 12%
- Teenage children 38%

Number of cars in income groups was as follows:

- < 20000 rupees a month = one car
- 20000–50000 rupees a month = two cars
- > 50000 rupees a month = two or more cars

Decision time for making the purchase was as given below:

- < 2 months 45%
- 2 months to four months 35%
- > Four months 20%

Among the buyers of Smily, during test marketing period those who had purchased the car six months back 70% were satisfied with the car.

To sum up the buying process is given below:

- Feel the need
- Become aware of the product, the Smily subcompact
- Search for information
- Share the product knowledge with the family
- Accept the impact of family and friends influence
- Decide to buy
- Post-purchase behaviour

Decision Options:

Own a bike

Motorcycle
No bike

Will buy a bike

Subcompact car

Brand . . . . Maruti or Smily
Capacity for seating, luggage
Price
Engine power
Number of cars the customer has or wants to own
When to buy the subcompact
Where to buy it
When to buy
How to pay—cash, instalments, leasing

Task for the Students

Select the market segment; build the buyer's profile and process of purchase decision, actual purchase action. Also plan out advertising media, promotional plans for Smily. How should Smily go about building its brand identity and brand equity? Where should it be positioned in the market place and why?

The students should analyze the market research presented in the case to determine if the research was conducted with right objectives in mind. Should they have arranged for more than one research with separate objectives to make them exhaustive, to the point and useful?

CASE STUDY

12

ABC Inc.

ABC Inc. an oil company registered in the USA—Credit as a sales tool.

ABC had been in operation in India since the beginning of the twentieth century. It was dealing in petroleum products with a vast product range, including petrol, diesel, and kerosene oil, lubricants for automobiles industry and greases. The company had offices, storage depots, and petrol pumps all over the country. The sales were organized directly to the large industrial and transport buyers and the government buyers and through a network of distributors, dealers and retailers for the general consumers of the products.

The company had appointed a major distributor XYZ suppliers to look after the sales of part of the state of Uttar Pradesh, in 1935 and they had been giving good business to the company. During the twenty-five year period, XYZ had been taken over by the young people, (headed by Madan the eldest son of Somani the original distributor). Of the family who had virtually, put the old guard on the shelf. The old people were required only for high level contacts with the ABC, who had a great regard for them and who did not care much for the young people, who, they felt needed time to mature to be successful in the venture.

XYZ was doing sales worth Rs. 160 lac per annum, which in the year 1960 was considered large. They had their own depots at their headquarters town Kanpur besides at five more locations. They had a sales force of fourteen who were carrying on the business. The biggest asset of XYZ was their relationship with ABC, who accepted them as partners in business and hence worthy of being consulted for major marketing decisions.

In 1960, the oil business was growing at the rate of ten per cent per annum and most firms in this product range were planning to expand their activities, distribution network and product range. The firms had established refineries in the country although crude oil was being imported from the Middle East.

At this juncture Madan's brain started working overtime hoping to encash the demand advantage in the country. After a lengthy discussion with his brothers he developed the following plan.

XYZ—To upgrade their offices, depots and their salesmen to be as good as that of the company.

To increase their purchases from the company by twenty per cent and try push strategy to increase their sales.

XYZ was able to achieve the target in three months time.

At this point, Madan got his father involved in the scheme. He asked the elder Somani to participate in organizing the Silver Jubilee of their firm as distributors of ABC. The following actions were immediately taken in this regard.

Invitation cards were sent to all the directors of ABC in the USA, top brass in Mumbai, Delhi and Lucknow. Along with the invitation cards air tickets for two-way journey were sent.

The best hotel rooms were booked in the town for the guests.

Traditional Indian reception was to be given at the airport, railway station to the guests.

Cultural programs, cocktail and dinner parties on lavish scale were planned.

Sightseeing trips to places of interest were planned.

Gifts for the guests were chosen with care; for the Americans, typical Indian gifts were purchased.

The chairman of ABC was to felicitate the senior Somani and give him a plaque commending the services of his firm.

Speeches from the senior members and vote of thanks were planned to be given by Madan.

On the last of the three-day programme a farewell party was arranged on a grand scale.

Still photography and movie of the main functions were planned:

On the entire programme, Madan was to spend Rs. 10 lac, which was a big amount in those days, when the best hotel room with air-conditioning was available for Rs. 300 in Kanpur.

As the chairman of ABC accepted the invitation so did most of the invitees. The entire celebrations went off. The chairman was extremely pleased with the entire organization and commended the same to the Indian management.

Soon the main offices of XYZ and ABC in India and the USA were prominently displaying the photographs of the function.

Aftermath of the silver jubilee:

Prior to the function XYZ were getting credit for Rs. 3 lac for a period of sixty days. In the first month they bought products worth 6 lac and paid much before the due date. In the next six-month they increased their purchase from Rs. 3 lac a month to an average of Rs. 30 lac a month and Madan used to ring up the manager in Delhi to say that he should not worry about the payments which would be coming in no time. The first Rs. 30 lac came promptly and afterwards the managers in India and later on in the USA kept waiting for the payments. After seven months with overdue balances touching

Rs. 120 lac the firm closed down, Somani Madan and the entire clan disappeared taking with them the entire product stocks overnight. When ABC, went to XYZs depots and godowns with the local police they found nothing there. The Con Game played by XYZ came as a big blow to ABC.

Besides fixing the blame for the disaster, ABC had to reorganize their credit policy to ensure that the Kanpur episode is never repeated. In future any member of the distribution channel wanting credit facility had to pledge their immovable unencumbered property to ABC to at least 150% of the credit asked for. The credit period was limited to a maximum of one month, with extension up to two months only in exceptional cases with equivalent increase in value of the pledged property. The result was temporary setback to business, which soon came back to normal.

Moral of the case is that credit is good for increasing sales if adequate safeguards are kept while offering the credit facility to the distribution channel members.

Task for the Students

Analyze the case. Find out if the local salesman was at fault or his boss in Delhi. At what point of time ABC should have taken some corrective action to have achieved some limited damage control at least?

CASE STUDY 13

Hindustan Aluminium Company (Hindalco)

Like most Indian firms, Hindalco, more than forty years old firm belonging to the Birla group, faced the impact of liberalization. The firm believes that the liberalization has thrown up big challenges for Indian firms and yet it offers several opportunities too. How the large organization belonging to one of the biggest conglomerates of the country is facing the challenges and cashing on the opportunities is an eye-opener.

Hindalco's USP—It is perhaps the lowest cost producer in the world. This has been achieved in the following manner:

- Courage to expand its capacity despite government ruling against expansion in 1989.
- Innovation in the face of import restrictions for capital goods in the period under review was a must
- High capacity and high capacity utilization became the creed of the firm
- Low machinery downtime by improved maintenance schedules
- Cost reduction with new innovative technology
- Marketing practices were the key to the success, where the emphasis was on good customer relations. Hindalco became synonymous with reliable timely supply of quality aluminium
- Providing quality after-sales service was the key element in the firms marketing strategy
- Customer satisfaction was enhanced by obtaining ISO 9002 and ISO 14000 certification and induction of TQM.

Tasks for the Students

Discuss how the firm planned to overcome the onslaught of country's liberalization policy and can other firms use their plan to achieve success?

CASE STUDY

14

Verma Garments

R.P. Verma established Verma Garments (VG) twenty years ago in Delhi, to manufacture and market readymade garments for men, women and children. As its Managing Director, Verma has brought the firm from a small beginning with a turnover of Rs. 30 lac to one having a turnover of Rs. 200 crore. Till the last four years they were making a net profit of 11%. However, in the last four years competition from both Indian and foreign firms has increased depleting the profits of the firm. In fact several small firms have closed down because of the severe competition. VG has however, now a net profit of only 4%.

VG has the following organization on the top:

M

|

CEO

|

VP-PROD | VP-MARKET | VP-FINANCE- | VP-HRD

Chander 50 is the VP Marketing. He has been with the firm for the last ten years. He has a good grip on the market. His market intelligence is becoming weak as he lost a big overseas order to Indian competitor through lack of knowledge. He has built his team strictly by discipline and has few friends there.

Rajan, VP Finance is 45, has been with VG for over three years. He has been blamed for poor cash flow although he blames it on marketing. He knows his job well. Tends to inflate expenses to show lower profits. His MD knows that he is doing it on his bidding.

Vyas is 47 and has been VP Production for the last 5 years. Last year there were some quality problems, which he had solved in three months, but marketing had put the blame of lower sales and profits squarely on him. Chander even claimed that due to quality problems they lost the overseas order. Vyas is not much for product innovations and wants status quo to prevail. He has been MDs pet so far.

Kumar is sixty and has been VP HR for the last twenty years. He was the first employee to join Verma. He has been training Verma's son Som to take over from him in the next five years when he is supposed to retire.

Three months back, Verma inducted Kamal, as the CEO of the firm, ignoring the claims of the VPs. Kamal 35, is an MBA with ten years experience in garment trade. He has a good track record of achieving success in short time.

Task for the Students

Discuss the situation in the firm if the marketing person was to be promoted as the CEO. What are the advantages and the disadvantages of having a marketing person as CEO?

CASE STUDY 15

Picture Tubes Logistics

One firm making TV picture tubes had to send the tubes all round the country from a centre in the west India. The normal mode was by trucks carrying the goods for long haulage of even a few thousand kilometres. With bad roads, battered trucks, inevitably ten percent of the cargo was damaged in transit due to accidents, or transhipments. TV picture tubes being fragile were easily damaged. While insurance firms were reimbursing for the physical loss of the product, the loss of production of TV sets could not be compensated.

The answer was found by calling railway authorities. They suggested use of container service, which also provided door-to-door service. The containers would come to the factory on special trucks, get loaded and then they would go on the trucks to the railway yard to get connected to a goods train meant for the destination needed. In one stroke, the problem of damages to the goods was solved. Additional benefit came by way of less expense on packing as the containers were of the right size to fit in the required number of tubes with no extra space for the tubes to have any moving space. Besides it also brought in saving in transport costs and with the same money the customers could buy more tubes.

Task for the Students

Look around to find out other transport methods and see if they can be profitably used by the firm.

CASE STUDY 16

Sugar Mills Logistics

Look at the plight of a Sugar Mill. The mill runs usually on seasonal basis, as the sugar cane is cultivated during a short period. The most important raw material in a sugar mill is the sugar cane. Each sugar mill has a limited capacity to use the cane. At times the sugar farmers bring huge amount of cane which the mill cannot use as also the space for cane storage gets filled up. And at times there is a dearth of sugar cane at the mill. In order to regulate the flow of cane, the mills have provided the farmers, with walkie-talkie systems and they can bring in the trucks just at the right time when they do not have to wait for a long time in queues and the mill is also happy that they get the cane just at the right time when they need the same.

Tasks for the Students

Find out a suitable system of logistics, which would help the firm in overcoming the problem. With cell phones can there be further improvements made. Discuss.

CASE STUDY

17

Women Shoppers over the Years

1960—A housewife plans a shopping trip. Mrs. Rita Sinha is married with two teenage kids; husband a manager in a private firm. Sinhas are upper middle class family. After sending husband to work and children to school, Rita takes off her apron, puts on lipstick, picks up her shopping list and carry bag and is off to the nearby market. She makes the shopping list once a week, which includes grocery, toiletry, washing powder and occasional chocolates for the kids. She walks half a kilometre distance to the market. On return journey she will take a rickshaw, as she would be carrying her shopping too.

At the market she goes to her favourite shops, orders the items, waits for the shop assistant to get her things with impatience, then she moves to the next shop. She is keen to react to any price variations and would haggle over the price even with a threat of changing shops. Getting a lower price gives her great satisfaction. She does care about the product quality, but rationalizing her cheaper purchase by saving money is easy.

The big day comes once a year, when she wants to buy things for the larger family, in-laws, cousins friends, when she forces her husband to accompany her and the children on a shopping expedition. Normally, they end up buying things for children and going to a restaurant on being pressurized by the young ones.

The shopkeepers and shop assistants know her needs, whims and fancies and they try to humour her to the extent possible within the time constraint, both for her as also for the shopkeepers.

On coming home she tries to figure out how and where she over-spent, as the next pay cheque comes much later and day-to-day expenses have to be met.

Women shoppers 21st Century

Working Women—They plan shopping well in advance. Holidays are meant for shopping, house cleaning and visiting friends. Today Mrs. Reena Verma is planning a shopping expedition. She calls her friends Prema and Kimi on her cell phone in conference mode. They decide to meet at 11 a.m. at the Shoppers Stop. Let us do some window shop at first and then we can decide to go for the real thing. They enter the cosmetic area and get busy trying out different shades of lipsticks, eye shadows, and nail polishes. Prema buys some items and flashes her credit card to make the purchase. Next they are in store for ready-to-wear dresses. Here Reena wants to buy a dress to wear at the next kitty party. Dress is selected after she has tried out a dozen dresses. Next, she must get matching shoes and accessories, which are luckily available in the same shop at different counters. Time for a coffee break, MacDonald's is the next stop. In the air-conditioned shopping mall the friends have forgotten that it is time they reach home to be with their kids at least on their holiday. Not to worry, the maidservant is there to give food to the kids.

Questions

- Discuss the change in consumer behaviour and needs over the years.
- What socio-cultural changes have occurred as per the case?
- How have the marketers met the situation?

CASE STUDY 18

Kinetic Honda Case

Before Kinetic Honda 100 cc scooter was introduced in the Indian market, all the other scooters looked almost alike. Kinetic was a different scooter, because of its sleek looks, aerodynamic styling and its manufacturers felt these attributes were enough to outsell other scooters in the market like Bajaj, LML. However, the scooter sales did not pick up the envisaged volumes in the market.

In April 1986, the position was as follows:

- Kinetic Honda had sold 11,000 scooters with 21% of market share.
- Bajaj Auto lead with 3,80,000 scooters sold with 73% market share.
- LML sold 1,09,000 scooters with market share of 21%

Kinetic had launched their scooter with unique features:

- Electronic start
- Automatic gear shift
- Automatic choke
- Built-in turning indicators
- Wind tested streamlines design
- Plastic bright colours

The market survey conducted by the marketers indicated that the reasons for poor market acceptance were as given below:

- Unfamiliar design
- Was considered lightweight and therefore flimsy
- Power of the scooter at 100cc was considered less than Bajaj's 150 cc scooter
- Electronic start was also looked at with suspicion as it was taken only as a ladies scooter.

To correct the misconceptions the marketers, had to physically demonstrate to the buyers:

- Scooters body was metallic and not that of plastic
- In 1988, several scooters including, Bajaj super 150 cc, LML, Kinetic Honda, Vespa 150 were put on a gruelling 20,000 km test run
- Kinetic Honda was adjudged the best scooter in that test.
- Massive advertising campaign was launched with facts of the test and the sales increased.

Main objectives of advertising are, to increase profitable sales, improve market share and the brand image. Brand image builds brand equity, which in turn brings brand loyalty.

Kinetic Honda won three more rallies and reached the high Khardungla pass

Kinetic Honda got established as a premium product for a customer who is a social somebody with age group 25-40 years, income of Rs. 15,000 pm.

Customers of Kinetic Honda are different from the customers of Bajaj and LML as they are upward mobile, quality conscious not willing to settle for less than the best. Market share has improved to 11%.

NOW THEY SAY THE FUTURE BELONGS TO US!

CASE STUDY 19

Crystal Cassette Company

Introduction

Let us take a hypothetical firm Crystal Cassette Company (CCC), operating in the business of music in India. The firm offers a good variety of music cassettes, both from their own collection and from the rest of the Indian firms. You want good music; rare music like some old songs of fifty years, just write to CCC and it will be delivered to you by courier against cash or on credit card. The main segments of music are the following:

- Indian classical vocal
- Indian classical instrumental
- Karnataka classical vocal
- Karnataka classical instrumental
- Folk music of different states
- Film music

CCC prided itself of being able to locate the most difficult old music and for this purpose they had on their roles music lovers and connoisseurs who had an ear for good music. They also offered music albums of assorted classics on the basis of their well-designed catalogue. Marketing Manager of CCC made the marketing plan for you.

Market Analysis

CCC had a rapid growth till 1996 with sales of Rs. 1900 lac with average price of Rs. 18 each. Given below is the growth of sales in the past few years and projections for the future:

The music sales were divided as follows:

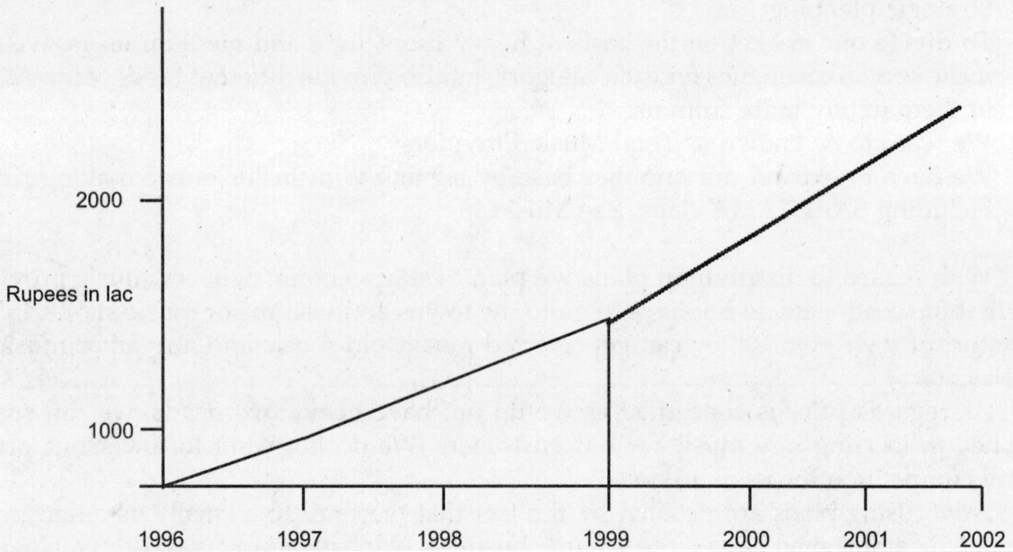

Indian Classical Music Vocal	21%
Indian Classical Music Instrumental	10%
Karnataka Classical Vocal	14%
Karnataka Classical Instrumental	9%
Folk Music	8%
Film Music	38%

Our customers come from practically all walks of life with different age groups, income levels, education and location in India and overseas. Film music which is the most prominent segment, also comes in different languages. Besides there is a small business of western music.

People living in small towns do not have access to big music stores and they love to buy cassettes from CCC.

From the point of advantage to the buyers, we offer the following benefits:

- Being small we move fast to deliver the goods
- We have the largest variety of music of the rare kind
- We look after customers from the small towns
- We have the expertise of advising the customer which music will suit his tastes.

Now other large networks including web firms are eager to make inroads into our small but well-defined market.

Marketing goals:

- Provide difficult-to-get music
- Quick correct and low cost delivery of products to the customers
- Keep our prices at par with other sellers
- Increase our product awareness through advertising plans

Strategic planning:

- To divide our market on the basis of heavy users, light and medium users. We can make special catalogues for each category, as also provide different types of incentives to them to buy more from us.
- We want to be known as Total Music Providers
- We have to expand our supplier base by signing with major music making firms, including SAREGAMA, Tips, Zee Music

With regard to distribution plans we plan to stay as home delivery music provider so that the customers do not have to go to the towns and visit major music shops. In the comfort of their homes they can get selected music, old music and any other music of their choice

As regards price is concerned as we do not have heavy overheads, we can spend money in locating rare music for our customers. We do not want to lower our prices until competition forces us to do so.

Advertising plans are decided by the fact that we cater to a small customer group unlike big stores who have large volume business. We have to focus on our catalogues, sales, and mailing list and continuously update them.

The advertising plans are derived from the marketing plan and are more narrow and focused. It highlights the objectives and strategies specific to advertising. It has its own action plan, list of alternatives and budget. It can be made for the entire year or for just one solo advertisement. Since this is only a specimen plan it is having too many details as a real plan would have. The assumptions made here are as given below:

- That we have all the information needed which is never true in the real world. Budget also keeps changing due to vagaries of market, competitive reactions, and not so ethical approach of several players in the competition.
- The playing field is fair and uniform.
- Day to changes are needed to be made in any plan to succeed.

The specimen provides a guideline, a general direction and tells you what all is required to be done.

A SWOT analysis is done to understand the ground reality.

Strength - CCC has the largest number of cassettes in their category of music. CCC has the ability to provide its customer with rare music from the past. Our customers are from outstations who want good music not available in their towns. We have experts who know good music and who can locate the most difficult old music from whichever archive it is available.

Weakness - our main weakness is our small size. Large music dealers could take away our business in no time.

Opportunities - popularity of folk music is our big opportunity as we are in that niche market. Music videos are adding to this trend.

Threats - CDs are a major threat. Will people buy CDs through catalogue sales we have to understand, before we launch it.

As stated above we want to keep our market segment as the upcountry music lovers who crave for the type of music we supply, including connoisseurs of classical and folk music.

We have placed our product offering in the niche market of usually unavailable music, especially by the people living in smaller towns.

We are wondering if we should expand our product portfolio.

Plans for increasing the sales:

- Marketing on the TV
- Telemarketing
- Web Marketing
- Sales Promotion
- Advertising

On the TV we can demonstrate the type of old forgotten music which we can supply. Telemarketers can persuade the buyers with our promotional plans to place orders on a time bound basis. Websites are being seen by a variety of buyers. With opening of e-commerce, purchase can be made through the web as well.

For new customers we want to have a promotional plan of giving a cassette free of their choice when they buy three cassettes. Also for them we want to have on line listening facility of the cassettes they want to buy before they place the order. They will get a discount if they log on to our site and order a cassette after listening on the web.

Advertising–we want to target 20% more customers and sell 10% more to each customer.

TV advertising will be based on live shows on TV, music videos and interactive information about availability of any old song.

Radio advertising will have the present top artists singing remixes of old songs to bring out nostalgia in the music lovers.

Our major source of business has been catalogues so far. We want to improve our catalogues with colour pictures of our present and past singers. We want to bring about a CD of our catalogue too!

Our Media Plan is given below:

		TV	RADIO	PRINT
Target	New customers	1,000	500	500
Insertions needed	Per new customer	150	200	300
Total insertions needed	Target × insertions per new customer	1,50,000	1,00,000	1,50,000
TV viewership	Average music viewership	7,500	2,000	10,000
Needed insertions	Total insertions/ average viewership	20	50	15
Cost per telecast	One telecast cost	50,000	10,000	10,000
Media TV Cost	Cost per telecast × needed insertions	10,00,000	5,00,000	1,50,000
Cost Per New Customer	TV Cost/New Customer	1,000	1,000	300

In promotion budget, the cost of making the TV, radio and press advertisement is taken into account plus cost of music promotional CDs, salaries of telemarketing people. Besides the cost of new catalogue, and music videos need to be added up.

Media Plan can be made as follows:

Pr-sample CD making	Feb-March
Printing press release	March
Mailing the press kit	April
Personal selling—hire telemarketers	Jan
Train telemarketers	Feb-March
Telemarketing on line	April-December
Sales promotion—design promo	Feb
Modify ads as needed	March
Promo in progress	April-May

Task for the Students

The students are requested to work out a plan regarding the monitoring process.

- Find out if any other area could be included in the plan
- It is important to constantly remind your customers and prospects that in your niche area of operation you are the best and can be totally relied upon.
- It is always a good idea to have your patrons (long time customers), to endorse your claims, as they would appear unbiased and therefore more credible.
- Looking after our existing customers better provides a major word of mouth publicity, which can be significantly helping us in achieving our goals. *Reader's Digest* does it all the time as they keep sending gift vouchers for their old faithful.
- Articles written by eminent music authorities with a subtle hint of our firm can be a big Public Relations exercise, which if handled well, will surely produce dividends for the firm
- Analyze the case and find out all possible alternatives and then focus on the best one.

CASE STUDY 20

General Insurance Corporation of India

General Insurance Corporation of India was incorporated as an apex body for general insurance, leaving out life insurance to the Life Insurance Corporation of India.

GIC started with its vision or motto as, "We shall help you in distress."

GIC made the following its mission and goals:

- Policy direction to its subsidiaries
- Plans and standards of operation
- Investment decisions
- Making subsidiaries autonomous firms
- Operate as a holding company
- Organize direct insurance in the aviation sector

With its four subsidiaries in India, and one Singapore GIC has had a monopoly run of the market of general insurance so far. Now with the private sector coming into the fore, GIC will have to gear up to face the challenge of competition. The only stipulation for the foreign players is that they have to sign an agreement with a joint venture Indian partner. A few firms have already opened their offices and are launching their operations. In the GIC fold the following five firms have been operating in India (one in Singapore):

- National Insurance
- New India Assurance
- Oriental Insurance
- United Insurance
- India International Singapore

These firms operate independently competing with each other, on the basis of better services as the rates of each firm is the same. They have so far a level playing field.

The insurance firms offer fire, marine goods carriage and cover of goods and services. With premium as low as rupees 150, it is quite affordable by the people. The problem areas are the settlement of claims. Being in the government sector, the usual official apathy towards the customers is very visible.

The government of India fixes the rates of policies and services and the firms have no liberty to make any adjustments in the same.

GIC can claim the following advantages in respect of private new firms:

- Wide experience in each of the areas of general insurance
- Large network of associates and agents in the entire country
- It has 4,200 offices in every nook and corner of India
- Representatives in each district of the country
- 85,000 employees
- Offices in 30 countries
- GIC has a large investment base of rupees 17,000 crore
- GIC profit before tax of rupees 2,285 crore
- GIC profit after tax of rupees 1,256 crore

GIC has promoted the following firms/institutions:

- GIC Mutual Fund
- GIC Housing Finance
- Loss Prevention Association of India
- National Insurance Academy

GIC also has got a joint venture firm in Kenya (along with LIC):

- Kenindia Assurance Company Ltd. Kenya

It is a good idea to see the comparison of GIC with some foreign firms given below:

	Germany as on 31-12-95	USA as on 31-12-96	France as on 31-12-96	Japan as on 31-3-95	GIC India as on 31-3-98
Premium/net worth	230%	190%	196%	141%	43%
Return on assets	2.7%	6.7%	1.8%	0.6%	14%
Expense ratio	22.3%	23.6%	27.5%	34.3%	26.8%
Rating	AA+	AA	AA-	AAA	Not available

GIC accepts that with competition coming they will have to provide better service. So far they have been having Lok Adalats and Grievance Cells, which are not adequate at all and which give their customers a negative feeling that they do expect to be giving problems to them. Let us discuss what the GIC needs to do now.

- GIC needs to improve the morale of its people with better incentive schemes
- GIC should use Internet for faster access to their customers
- Improve PR both within and outside the country

- Lay stress on comprehensive personal selling
- Advertise in a catchy language
- Increase their product portfolio in line with international products and some extra too.

How would you plan to counter the onslaught of foreign collaborated firms? What should be highlighted in marketing plan of GIC? Their customer image is of a firm which, alongwith its subsidiaries does not bother about them.

Should GIC advertise the percentage of claims settled in a given period in comparison to the international firms? Yes, but only if the figures are to their advantage.

Hence, the first thing they need to do is to put their house in order and then they can inform the customers of their success stories, which, should be easily verifiable.

Prepare a print Ad and a TV story board to improve the public image of the GIC.

CASE STUDY

21

Competent Motors

Maruti car dealer and service provider.

Competent Motors are the authorized dealers (dealer term is in many businesses becomes synonymous with retailer). They are housed in a sprawling area close to the east Delhi residential colonies. They stock all the various models of Maruti car and have a good display of the models. A shade card nears the models tells the customer the number of colours available in that model. Next, there is an in-house accessory shop from where the car buyers can have the accessories fitted of their choice. The sales department takes the order and money. On the delivery point, the technical persons are present to show to the customers all the salient features of the car and its working.

Just before delivering the car, the salespersons give the options of licence plate numbers. These plates are already in stock and are fitted on to the car in no time at all. If the customer is looking for leasing option or car purchase finance, the salesperson will guide him to the people from finance firms who are stationed there.

Competent Motors Service Centre—the same building houses the service centre also. They provide three free services to new cars as per the schedule laid down by the manufacturer. Afterwards they provide services for which the customer has to pay. As technicians have been trained by the technology people of the car, Suzuki, and only genuine spare parts are used during servicing and repairs customers prefer to get their cars serviced there only.

Recreation facilities—in case a customer has brought the car for service or repair, the Competent people offer to have him dropped in their own vehicle within a reasonable distance. However, if the customer wishes to stay on and take the car after getting it serviced, he can sit in a coffee shop and have snacks or, he can sit in the lounge where a library, an indoor sports area and a TV has been provided for customers entertainment.

Task for the Students

Compare the facility provided by the Competent Motors with the services provided by car sellers of the first half of the 20th century. Discuss the reasons for the changes you find. Can something more be done to further improve customer satisfaction/ delight?

CASE STUDY

22

Activity Base Corporation

ABC is a multi-product firm with all India sales networks. While the firm has been growing at the market rate of growth, its profit picture has been rather dismal. The management has appointed a firm of consultants to recommend to them the action they should be taking to improve their bottom line. Some details of the firm are given below for student's perusal:

Annual sales	Rs. 145 crore
Raw material cost	Rs. 50 crore
Fixed costs	Rs.15 crore
Available revenue	Rs. 80 crore
Product costs	Rs. 65.5 crore
Profit before tax	Rs. 14.5 crore
Total	Rs. 80 crore

The next table gives the product-wise picture of revenue generation, share of cost, net revenue value, cost to profit coefficient.

S. No.	Rev. value	Rev% of total	Cost value	Cost % of total	Net revenue value	%of net revenue value	Cost-profit coeff	Remarks
1.	19	24	18.2	28	0.8	5	0.25	
2.	14	17.5	16.7	25.5	-2.7	-12	Loss	
3.	14	17.5	7.2	11	6.7	4.7	3.3	
4.	11	14	5.2	7.5	5.8	40	3.8	
5.	7	9	5.4	8	10.6	11	1.5	
6.	4	5	3.4	5	0.6	4	1.0	
7.	4	5	3.6	5	0.4	3	0.75	
8.	3.5	4.5	3.3	5	0.2	1.5	0.5	
9.	2	2.5	1.85	2.5	0.15	1	0.5	
10.	1	1	1.5	2	-0.5	-0.5	Loss	

The next table gives the management support as it exists for each product. Students can use the table to diagnose the problem in each product and plan strategies accordingly.

S. No.	Revenue	Working capital	Management support	Technical support	Sales service support	Remarks
1.	19	15	Very high	Very good	Very good	
2.	14	4.5	Very high	Very good	Very good	
3.	14	5	Very high	Low	Medium	
4.	11	3	High	Low	Medium	
5.	12	0.5	Nil	Low	High demand	
6.	4	Nil	High	High	Best	
7.	4	Nil	High	High	Best	
8.	3.5	15	Spl.task force	Very good	High pressure	
9.	2	5	Low	Low	Low in sale high for old products	
10.	1	Nil	High	High	Nil	

Product one is in the maturity stage of life cycle and for some reason it is well supported by the management. It could be the management nostalgia of its hay days or it could be the boss's ego. The product appears to be on life support system. The students have to decide what should be done with it; phasing out, niche marketing?

Product two is in the decline stage of the life cycle and yet it is too well supported. Is it responsible for helping sale of another product or is it only an ego product? Should the product be removed from the portfolio or is there a chance for it in its present state?

Product three and four are giving good profits, in the cash cow or star stage. These need to be nurtured with better technical and service support from the management. (Unless the product itself does not need the support.)

Product five appears to need constant technical support. The management should arrange some research and development to make it a better product or else drop it what is the view of the students on the product?

Product six and seven are well supported by the management and they do not need working capital; they are fast selling technical products needing technical support, which is being provided. Students should decide if they should continue to get the support or not. Which stage of life cycle they belong? They look like consumable products, like oil, resin.

Product eight is a well-supported product with a special task force to get better results. It could be in question mark stage of the life cycle and therefore needs the support.

Tasks for the Students

Formulate strategies for each product taking its position in the BCG Matrix considering revenue generation and support given and needed. Working capital needs give you a clue to the monetary support provided to each product. Can you find out which products are in the star, cash cow, question mark and dog stages of the BCG Matrix?

CASE STUDY 23

Bhat Electronics Ltd.

Case Focus—Market Share and Brand Equity.

Facts file—Sale of Semiconductor Devices-period 1972.

Product—a pack of 5 transistors and 1 diode, called the silicon radio pack (SRP).

- Price of one pack Rs. 28.
- Market Share 85%

Brand Equity—while BEL had Philips Holland's technical collaboration, the fact was not well known. Also BEL being a major supplier of Defence Electronics, had kept a low profile.

Then, in 1972, the market share went down to 55% in a period of three months. On investigations the reasons found were as follows:

With glut in Japanese market firms like Toshiba NEC were off-loading their semiconductor devices at throwaway prices, which were reaching India, and their packs were selling at Rs. 3 in Delhi, which was the biggest market in India.

Transistor radios being made at that time by the assemblers in Delhi had no quality control. As long as the customer could hear some sounds, music even a little jarring, the transistor would sell.

Problem for marketing—How to bring back the market share? Could price reduction be resorted to? If not then what could be done?

Analysis and findings:

- To make customers quality conscious
- To communicate with the customers about the transient nature of Japanese products
- To help upgrade the quality of customer's finished products
- Help customers develop better newer products of international quality

How was it Done?

Organization of a national seminar on semiconductor devices; the highlights of the seminar were a manufacturing process with all the care and intricacies involved, quality assurance programme and the functions of the applications laboratory which was started for the benefit of the customers.

Setting up of an Applications Laboratory, the circuits already developed by the Lab and the assistance it was planning to provide to the customers by way of improving their circuits. (This brought indirect benefit to the company as in the improved circuits; our engineers installed our own components in the circuits).

Newsletter—a quarterly newsletter was started to inform and educate the customers of all the new devices and circuits the company was introducing and how our customers could take advantage of our efforts.

Customer database—the attendees in the seminar were asked to fill a form to give their name, address, phones and other details.

Assistance in circuit upgrades at no cost—as the applications lab team stayed back they started looking at the customers' circuits and making major visible improvements in the same. In fact the lab became so popular that it was decided to keep a cell of the lab permanently there.

Complaint handling cell directly under the Head of Marketing; this gave enormous credibility to the entire marketing operations.

Result—Market Share back to original in one year's time. Smugglers must have changed their product if not given up smuggling altogether.

Task for the Students

Please highlight the points learned in the case. In your opinion could the firm had done it differently and with better results?

CASE STUDY

24

Flying Giants (FG)

(A National Airline in Private Sector in India)

FG was formed in the wake of open sky policy of the government of India. It started operations in 1989. By 1994, FGs 13% flights were to neighbouring countries. In the next six years, FG planned for 6% increase in annual growth.

The growth is expected to come from acquiring sick airlines and second from strategic alliances with international airlines.

Most airports in the FG's destinations are overcrowded. FG has two options, one to start using satellite airports, away from the main airports, lying neglected which can be rejuvenated at a cost. The other option is to build new airports designed for short takeoff and landing facility. This will need government approval as also large sums of money. FG could recover part of the money by loaning the airport to other airlines.

For short distances up to four hundred kilometres, the fast and modern trains are also competing with the airlines. With even faster trains the competition is going to become even more severe, as the air charges are high as compared to train fares.

To maintain its market share and increase it, FG has to innovate in both ground and air service, including the following:

- Easy ticketing
- Airport transfers
- Special lounges for business passengers with bar and snacks facilities
- Easy check-ins
- Fast and easy luggage retrievals
- Better connections to more destinations
- In-flight entertainment
- Better liaison with tour operators and travel agencies
- Relationship marketing for the consumers

Students can find more areas of importance and arrange for marketing research. Please do the following:

- Define the management objectives and objectives for MR.
- Decide the type of research you would like to conduct. How would you select the sample and its size.
- Build a questionnaire for the research.

You could also define the market segment for the airlines.

CASE STUDY

25

Complete Retail Plan

Considering the importance of retail marketing this case study is devoted totally to retail marketing. How the marketing team can transform non- or profit-making retailers into dynamic businesses? As the students study the case they will get involved into the nitty gritty of retail trade and how firms can profit from the same. In easy to understand steps the reader is taken to the intricate mindset of the retailers and how they can be motivated into making profits.

It may look obvious to students that the retailers must be keen on making and increasing the profits and yet several anomalies are found. Hence, this exercise would greatly benefit the students and others handling retail trade. The case is divided into following areas:

- Objectives of the case
- Benefits from the case
- Retail philosophies and concepts
- Development of retailers for success
- Gathering retail data
- Evaluating the data
- Locating opportunities
- Prioritizing the opportunities
- Plans for retail improvement
- Select best approach
- Improvement factors
- Business model
- Retail assist
- Personalities

The next area to be covered is business communication for the retail trade:

- Communications towards retail trade
- Retail viewpoint
- Retailer's motivation
- Retail trade communication plans
- Calling on the retailer
- Objectives of the call
- Retailers benefits from the call
- Retailer needs
- Retailer resistance
- Retailer oriented communication
- Adding impact to the communication
- Follow-up action needed

Now let us discuss how the retailer's organization can be analyzed to enable the marketing team tailor make the plan for individual dealer for maximum impact and profitable results both for the retailer and the firm.

Objectives of CPR:

- Firms philosophy and concepts for the retrial trade
- Marketing team's confidence building
- Help in increasing retail sales
- To make the marketing team more efficient in the job, who will have better job satisfaction, increased recognition in the firm, better retail support
- The retailers will benefit with bigger profits, better management and enhanced customer visibility
- The firm will benefit with better profits, satisfied retailers with an edge on competition and happy marketing team

The firm's philosophy and concepts (as generally accepted) are given below:

- To make increasing profits and to grow
- Increase market share and improve brand equity
- Supply quality products, advertise and promote its products, get retailers cooperation in the same for achieving retail goals
- Support the marketing team in doing an excellent job

Improving retail performance is essential to the firm as the sale and financial gains are made here only. Firms spend a lot of money in developing the retail outlets, advertising the same, providing service for retail customers and training their sales and service staff. Retailers help in firm's brand building efforts too through their word of mouth publicity. The retailer, on his part must benefit with improved returns on his investments to ensure he is not tempted to invest elsewhere. The retailer should earn enough from selling the firm's product to keep him totally involved in it. He emerges as a successful businessman in the area.

The marketing team benefits come from increasing number of retailers looking for help from the team. The team gets time to devote into marginal retailers with undeveloped potential. The team's success ensures rewarding career growth for its members.

Retail reluctance for change comes from the following factors:

- Owner busy with day-to-day working of the outlet
- He does not have the finance needed for the change
- He feels changes are too sophisticated for his customers
- He feels his own team will not accept the changes.

Firm's marketing team is not just for getting the orders from the retailers, but for helping the retailer in building the trade, sales and profits, providing a permanent bridge of relationship with the firm for trust and confidence. The marketing team needs to become the retailers' professional counsellor and for doing it well the tram needs to at as follows:

- Understand the retailers growth potential
- Define the retail sales and profit goals
- Calculate the retail expenses
- Establish the retail business expansion plans

At this stage it is required to define the retailer's improvement opportunities (improvement opportunities are just the problem areas thus called as no retailer would like to be told that he is having problems, while every one accepts that they all have opportunities for improvement):

- Not meeting the sales targets
- Not getting profits as possible
- High on expenses
- Stilted growth plans
- Staff with low morale

As Retailer Counsellor (RC), the job would entail helping the retailer set up long range program to meet his targets, suggesting merchandising, service and sales techniques; help plan control on expenses and for arranging low cost finance.

For the task, the RC needs to have,

A positive frame of mind, with the following attributes:

- Belief that the retailer can make profitable business with the firm's products
- Ability to understand the retailer's viewpoint and see his problems
- Vision for locating retailer's improvement opportunities
- Ability to provide training and other resources needed
- Belief in himself that he can solve the retailer's problems
- Open to suggestions from the retailers
- Desire for self-improvement
- Zeal for achievement

RC also needs the following:

- Knowledge of the retail trade; ability to analyze the retailers situation and financial results, which would help in locating opportunities
- Developing plans for using the resources properly for improving performance
- Ability to get retailers acceptance for the plans

The RC must therefore be aware of the motivating factors of the retailer, existing practices followed by him and methods of improving the same. Besides he must develop skills for analysis, evaluation, planning, communications and motivating the retailers into accepting his plan. He should know how retailers' resistance could be converted into action. Besides for long-term relationship, there has to be long term RC counselling to the retailer. RC should be able to persuade the retailer into things like extending outlet hours, arranging better displays, play house for kids of the shoppers.

Defining improvement opportunities—retailers are normally not aware of the opportunities existing and hence cannot analyze to find out the areas where improvements are possible, or may be he is too preoccupied with his work to find time for the purpose. To be really useful the improvement opportunities must be definable, big enough for the efforts to be made, and realistic for improvements. RC must ensure improvement in performance takes place to keep his own credibility with the retailer as also with his own firm. For this purpose the RC must gather relevant facts, evaluate them and then only define improvement opportunities. For example, if the outlet is not having enough parking place and many, say fifty per day, as per actual count, customers go back because of this fact then, building underground parking facility could be the answer, with the provision of valet parking. If the small children, say thirty families with children, do not let the shoppers buy in peace, then a children's park, or play area could be answer.

Let us discuss why facts are important. Because:

- Retailer tends to accept the hard facts only
- Retailer would also agree to the improvements suggested if they are based on facts.
- Facts are time savers, as from well-accepted facts wrong calculations, trail and error methods are avoided, and the retailers' confidence in the plan is fortified.
- If several facts have come to light, RC should concentrate only on important facts only to ensure retailer's interest and immediate improvement impact. And the effort comes to fruition quickly.

Let us see what could be the important facts for a retail outlet. They are given below:

- Retail gross profit for the firm's products
- Quantity of major product sold per annum, decline or increase taking market growth into account
- Labour cost
- Other expenses like power, rentals, entertainment
- Worker morale

These factors can be found out by looking at the retailer's monthly/yearly balance sheet, talking to the owner, his staff and his customers. It is better to find out the facts from more than one source to achieve accuracy. These results can then be compared with some yardsticks as given below:

- Firm's objectives
- Retailer's historical figures
- Retailer's objectives
- Competitive performance

It can be applied as follows:

Result yardstick	Results	Difference
Firm's plan		
10,000 refrigerators per annum	9,200	800
Retailer's plan		
11,000 refrigerators per annum	9,200	2,200
10 lacs /monthly gross profit	8.2 lacs	1.8 lacs

These can also be expressed in ratios as given below:

- Labour cost as percent of gross profit
- Other expenses as percent of gross profit
- Rentals as percent of gross profit
- Total operating expenses as percent of gross profit
- Retailers net profit as percent of gross profit

These figures provide the guidelines for identifying the improvement opportunities (weaknesses), which figures exceed and which fall short of standards of the firm. It is worthwhile going into details of the opportunities, which would enable the RC in diagnosing the real problems/weaknesses. Vague ideas can lead the RC into avoidable traps of irrationally simple approach to some complicated problems. At times observing the following can be a real eye-opener:

- Outlet's exterior-entry and exit points, parking areas
- Outlet's façade
- Salespersons attitude towards the customers and towards each other
- Economic standard of the area being serviced by the outlet
- Competitor's outlets in the vicinity
- Mystery shoppers experiences (to be sent by the RC)
- Credit provided by the outlet and credit outstanding with age analysis

CASE STUDY 26

ABC Ltd. A Food Product Company

The firm was started in 1978 and in 1980 it had a market share of 60%. However, by 1994 it went down to 30%. In 1989 the firm was in the red and new management took over in 1990. In 1993 there was no loss only a marginal profit, which was achieved through cost cutting and increase in price.

Price increase did not reduce the sales. However, the firm has been facing problems from 1982, as Small Scale firms got better of ABC by lowering prices, giving dealers higher margins up to 100% and in 1991 some medium size firms entered the field. The facts of the case are given below:

- In 2002 the total market is of 1,200 crores with annual growth of 6%.
- ABC product awareness is low. In fact low for most products as buyers have been buying mostly unbranded products or servants in affluent homes where brand awareness is more significant and either the sellers take the buying decisions or the servants make purchases ABC products are bought mostly out of habit.
- ABC quality has been maligned by competition and packaging is of suspect quality
- ABC product is price sensitive in low-income groups if the increase is more than 5%. Middle income is sensitive at 10% price increase. High income is not sensitive to price changes.
- ABC uses Clearing and Forwarding Agents rather than distributors, and dealers
- ABC marketing team is low on motivation and high on turnover of junior staff
- Corporate office and regional office are far apart with distance control and lack of coordination

Task for the Students

Should ABC stay in business? If yes then how?

CASE STUDY 27

Windsor Shoes Ltd.

Windsor Shoes Ltd. (WSL) was established in 1960 as dealers of Bata. In 1972, they diversified into manufacturing canvass shoes, children's shoes and in 1980 they added chappals to their range. They sell in the entire country, especially in metros where they have their own shops also.

While north is a good market for shoes, south favours leather chappal. WSL is well known in the north for shoes along with Bata, Liberty, Baluja and Flex.

Chappals' Market

Market in the north picks up during summer months. Chappals are well known footwear in the south with 70 per cent market. Production and price indices of leather chappals are given below:

Year	1991	1992	1993	1994	1995
Production index	140	190	220	240	250
Price index	150	160	200	205	210

Chappal sales in the north in lac pairs in 1995 is as follows:

Year	1993	1994	1995
Bihar	30	42	64
Delhi	49	60	86
UP	40	55	75

Competition: WSL faces competition from Bata, Baluja and Flex besides local brands. WSL boasts for their stylish lifestyle chappals and they are worried if their chappals would succeed in the north, where Bata is well entrenched. North market share is as follows:

Brand	Bata	Flex	Baluja	Others
Years in the market	75	45	30	
Market share	70	10	5	15

In the north there is preference for Kolhapuri chappals, Bata is popular as family chappal, while Balujais for rich traders, Flex is for the masses. Brands are not very useful as a sales tool. No real niche market yet.

Tasks for the Students

Should WSL introduce their chappals in the north with plans for 25 per cent share of the market? Is generic strategy useful for WSL?

CASE STUDY 28

Gillette Co.

Gillette's vision is of being a world class firm with world class people, products and brands.

The firm's mission is to be a global leader in the products marketed by them.

They operate in 200 countries with manufacturing facilities in 56 countries.

The firm's core businesses are given below:

- Blades and razors—Gillette, 7O'Clock, Wilkinson Sword
- Batteries—Duracell
- Personal grooming products—Braun, Silkipel razors for women
- Oral care products—Oral B
- Writing Instruments—Parker, Papermate, Waterman

Strategic Marketing Plan for Success

Gillette makes a five year rolling plan, which is reviewed three times a year and modified as required. Every six months sales forecast is made.

Philosophy of Gillette can be summarized as follows:

- Keep introducing new products and fifty per cent of their business must come from products, which have been introduced less than 5 years ago.
- Technical superiority in every product and they consider competition as a spur for customer retention.

Gillette's game plan is as given below:

- Keep the user/customer at the centre of activities
- Provide improved products–gain increased net sales
- Have pricing options by improvement in products

Gillette considers the following as their key growth areas:

- Value addition in existing products
- New product speedy launches
- Distribution network
- Display and merchandizing
- Advertising and promotion
- They keep a close watch on standard direct costs and post-marketing expenses, which can be considered controllable overheads
- Synergy for efficiency and effectiveness
- Profits through IT driven TQM and people's involvement

Gillette has developed a marketing strategy for facing recession in the market. They view the impact of recession on the different segments of the market as follows:

Consumers—their demand reduces for non-essential articles and they switch to value for money products.

Trade—they suffer from inventory blockage of non-essential products and they end up with heavy stocks of a variety of products.

Firm—it loses customers as also trade/distribution channels who show little interest in the products.

Gillette's policy for marketing during recession is that of Pause! They believe in operating in the following manner:

- Basic marketing strategy does not change
- They organize better management of resources and plan tactical moves
- They provide value addition; when consumers downgrade, Gillette provides added value to the product; they reinforce the advertising messages; improve the product package
- They arrange new product launches to increase user share and also upgrade the users
- The result so far has been that Gillette has grown even during recession periods.

Task for the Students

The firm justified in upgrading their products and charging more when the customers find it hard to pay their existing prices? Discuss their policy for success.

CASE STUDY 29

Microsoft Inc. USA

Start any computer around the world and more than ninety per cent you will find it running on Microsoft Windows operating system. The firm is as controversial as it is successful and influential. It touches the lives of billions of people and it has changed the way people manage and work in offices, homes, factories and how they correspond with others.

It is a firm, which evokes intense feelings of love or hatred it is Microsoft! Its founder Bill Gates is already a cult figure, worshipped and idolized by millions of young and old in the world. From a middle class family he inherited his acumen from his mother and shrewdness from his father. In just twenty years he is the richest man on the planet.

Where do they go from here?

Microsoft strives to produce innovative products to meet the evolving needs of the knowledgeable customers.

Mission – Microsoft started in 1975, with a mission to create software for the personal computer that empowers and enriches people at home and at their workplace, at schools and in the laboratories.

Vision – Its early vision was to see a computer on every desk, every home and it is now coupled with a strong commitment to Internet technologies expanding the reach and power of PC users.

Values – Microsoft's values are enshrined in the following tenets:

Customers – helping them achieve their goals by listening to them and quickly delivering new innovative products; building relationships based on trust, respect and understanding and service support.

Innovation – moving with the speed of light for bringing new products in the market to remain competitive with reduced costs as well

Partners – helping them grow in their business

Integrity – acting with utmost integrity Microsoft's team is guided by what is right for their customers

People—the team must have an exciting challenging career with growth opportunity and well balanced home and work life

Entrepreneurial culture—the team must remain passionate about the work, contributing to evolution of technology to remain competitive

Diversity—the team is encouraged for diverse activities, with equal chance of promotion and increments for the members.

Community—Microsoft feels responsible to the community in which they operate and wants to make a meaningful difference in its life.

- Finance as on June 1999
- Net revenue- $ 19.75 billion
- Net income $ 7.79 billion

Microsoft headcount and revenue growth is given below:

Year	Head count	Revenue $B	%Growth	Income $ M	%Growth
1990	5,635	1.18	47	279	63
1991	8,226	1.85	56	463	66
1992	11,542	2.78	50	708	53
1993	14,430	3.79	36	953	35
1994	15,017	4.71	25	1,150	20
1995	17,801	6.08	29	1,450	27
1996	20,561	9.05	49	2,200	51
1997	22,232	11.94	32	3,450	57
1998	27,055	15.26	28	4,490	30
1999	31,575	19.75	29	7,790	79

The head count is in the vicinity of 40,000.

Microsoft has been living in the shadow of its illustrious founder. While Bill Gates has many friends his opponents believe he is shrewd and manipulative and wants to dominate the world. Microsoft needs to improve its image to come out of the predicament it faces today.

In 1995 the firm almost lost the battle of Internet to Netscape and Sun Microsystems and Microsoft was caught napping. Microsoft needs feedback from marketing to their R&D to get the latest customer needs. MICROSOFT MUST MAKE MORE FRIENDS THAN FOES. It should not consider that it is a Know All firm. It could consider splitting into several small firms with independent decision making under one over all umbrella.

IBM is reeling under competitive pressure and does not know what hit them. Microsoft must not fall in the same trap. If they do not learn from history than history is likely to repeat itself.

Task for the Students

Discuss the strengths and weaknesses of Microsoft and recommend a marketing strategy which would help them in retaining their leadership position.

CASE STUDY 30

Infosys Technologies Ltd. (ITL)

ITL is a leading Indian firm in software services and packages for exports and the domestic market. Its clients include several fortune 500 companies. Indian software industry is fragmented with several players in the field. India's USP in the global market is that there is a large English speaking trained workforce, which is still relatively available at low cost.

IL has grown in strength with special products development like, In 2000 for Y2K solutions, IntERPryz for ERP, and InEuro for Euro banking services. It is the first Indian firm to be listed on the US Stock Exchange NASDAQ after its successful issue of ADR in 1999.

Management of ITL is totally inspired by its CMD Mr. Narayan Murthy and it is characterized by the following qualities:

- Technically qualified professional management
- Having rich experience of large export orders
- Stakeholder friendly approach
- Positioning in high growth areas
- HR policies for merit recognition
- Focus on core areas

India's Position

Till 2000 Indian industry had a boom time in software. Only the events of 11th September 2001 have brought the industry down at least temporarily. India's competitive advantage lies in the following areas:

- Cost effective software
- World class quality
- High reliability

Rapid delivery. India's position can be seen from the following matrix:

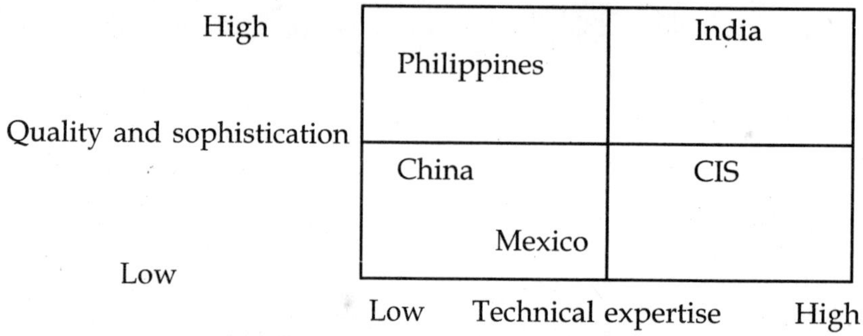

Software industry in India is given in the following table.

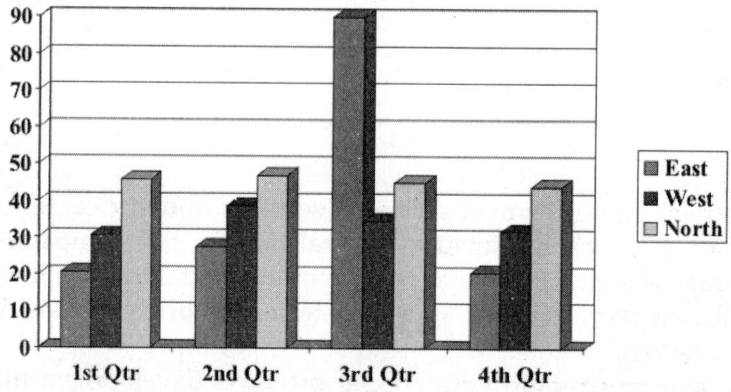

Year	1997	1998	1999	2000
Exports US M $	1755	2700	3900	5700
Domestic M Rs.	63100	100400	158600	245000

In 1999 the growth of the industry was 46% and it was expected to grow at 50%, but the USA catastrophe of 11 September, 2001derailed the momentum of growth.

Top ten firms of India had the following turnover in million rupees in 1998:

1.	TCS	10836
2.	Wipro	4816
3.	HCL	3455
4.	NIIT	3254
5.	Pentafour	2845
6.	Infosys	2576
7.	IBM Global	2428
8.	Tata Infotech	2117
9.	Satyam	1784
10.	Patni Group	1375

Infosys has focused on providing software services with branded products and has moved on to software products.

- Services—revenue is 74% of total revenue of Infosys
- Branded Services—their share is 22%
- Products—account for just 3% of the revenue

Infosys' vision is to become a globally respected firm, which provides best of the software solutions by the best in class people.

Its mission is to grow with protected margins by focusing on horizontal applications and vertical industries.

Infosys goals are to have development centres for software in different parts of the world to provide quality speedy solutions at affordable prices

Its objective is to restrict revenue generation of any division to less than 25%.

Infosys' competitive position is given below:

Market share	Market growth: High	Market growth: Low
High	Infosys Wipro Satyam	TCS Rolta
Low	NIIT	Pentfour

Infosys is in the Star position of the BCG Matrix

Infosys track record is envious, with its shares surpassing the industry norms, including the ADR, which is also performing well in the market. Infosys could be planning on the following lines to keep its growth rate.

Geographic expansion-Infosys gets the major share of business from the north American market as can be seen from the table given below:

Revenue area	1999 in lakh Rs.	%	1998 in lakh Rs.	%
North America	41,739.11	82	21,224.46	81
Europe	4,753.03	9	2,317.20	9
Rest of the world	3,533.27	7	1,552.10	6
India	1,248.43	2	942.81	4
Total	51,273.83	100	26,036.57	

Europe and Japan are almost not there, which came in focus after 11th September, 2001. Infosys would do well to open its markets in untapped areas so far.

As a cash rich firm Infosys could be planning joint ventures in India and overseas to utilize its cash profits and zero debt status.

Infosys could extend the services offered. Its present portfolio includes the following services:

- Apparels
- Commodity trading
- Customer management
- e-business
- Financial services
- Insurance
- Logistics
- Manufacturing
- Retailing

Infosys could plan entry in the following fast pace areas as well:

- Aviation
- Healthcare
- Tourism
- Transport
- Security industry
- Telecom
- Training in software development
- Retailing in the country

Tasks for the Student

Please do the SWOT analysis of the firm and plan out the best marketing strategy for Infosys.

CASE STUDY 31

Exhibitions India P. Ltd.

Exhibitions India has an outstanding reputation for organizing international and national exhibitions and conferences. Under the EI umbrella it has the following other firms:

- Comnet Exhibitions P. Ltd
- Comnet Advertising P. Ltd.
- Comnet Travels P. Ltd.
- Comnet Publishing P. Ltd.

EI's genesis starts from the idea of providing a forum for Business-to-Business interaction. From small beginning of being an agency of international organizers now it has become one itself.

EI's present portfolio includes the following:

- Convergence India—International exhibition and conference of broadcast, cable and satellite equipment
- Commsindia—is comprehensive event for the telecom sector
- Bank net—it is for banking sector
- Space'99 an exhibition on the space technology
- Captech 2000 for the capacitor industry
- Build India/Environment India/Water India
- Pride of India an exhibition held in Vietnam.

Vision—EI's vision is to be leader in B-to-B interaction with total transparency, honesty and ethical behaviour

Mission—statement is crisp and to the point, "Committed to Excellence"

Goals—to increase trade between different areas through B-to-B interactions

Objectives—to maintain high level of excellence for providing neutral platform for business, industry, government interactions through exhibitions and seminars

EI manages its value chain efficiently, which involves the following activities:

- Government approvals and support of the ministries
- Support of industry associations
- Corporate world for participating in the events
- Bringing out brochures and pamphlets
- Setting up of stalls
- Opening-day inaugural functions

Marketing at EI—as per the norms of service industry they have nothing tangible to offer, other than space in the exhibition. The marketing tasks includes communicating the benefits the exhibitor will obtain from taking part in the exhibition.

Among its clients are public sector, government bodies and the private firms. Private firms take much less time in deciding to participate. The governmental bodies take much longer to decide necessitating the need of differential time approach by the EI.

EI uses telemarketing as one of the initial tools to familiarize the clients with the event, which is going to take place. They have generated a database of over 5000 firms as prospective clients for their events. The phone calls gives an idea of interest generated in the client's mind regarding the event. Personal meetings to solicit participation follow the calls. These visits are carried forward by mails, phone calls, e-mails with the details of the event and participation entry forms with rate card.

EI believes that Direct Mail is a good beginning of sales campaign. This is carried out through teaser mail, brochures, pamphlets, and reports of previous exhibitions with their results.

EI believes that after the event management of the clients is as important as managing the client for getting his consent for participation in the event. This is one through post exhibition reports, which gives the order bookings, effective business dialogues and some photographs of the dignitaries from the business world, the government and the media coverage of event.

EI has competition; major one's being the following:

- CII-Confederation of Indian Industries
- ITPO-Indian Trade Promotion Organization

EI is comparatively small and enjoys the benefits of a flat structured firm with fast decision making. It is also competing as a cost effective firm as it can offer competing rates for stalls in the exhibitions.

EI's shortcomings are the following:

- Services provide are common to other competitors with no differentiation
- Low manpower affects the performance at times
- No venue of their own for exhibitions
- Low brand equity, which is surely but slowly improving in the area, which matter to them.

In order to overcome the shortcomings EI could arrange the following:

- Buyer-seller meets—both national and international

- Organize general purpose fairs for both, the public and business
- Try to get better rates from the exhibition ground owners
- Arrange exhaustive market survey in different areas of current business interest
- Communicate with major clients through focused information, which would be of interest to them rather than sending the general brochure
- Increase worldwide geographic coverage

Task for the Students

Do a SWOT Analysis of the firm and give detailed recommendations for improving its marketing efforts.

CASE STUDY

32

Maruti Udyog Ltd.

Maruti Udyog Ltd. (MUL) is the largest auto manufacturer in India. It has 70% share of the small car segment and 40% of the luxury segment. It was set up in joint venture of the government of India and the Suzuki Motors of Japan. Today the government has reduced its stake and it is purely a Suzuki firm. It has a vendor network of nearly 450, nearly a third of these have ISO 9000 certification. It also has joint ventures with some of its vendors to ensure quality and timely delivery. Firm has about fourteen models of cars, vans and jeep. In small car segment it competes with Santro of Hyundai, Indica from the Tatas, and Matiz from Daewoo Motors. Matiz is facing problems because of Daewoo's problems worldwide and its sell off.

Maruti's vision and mission statements are given below:

Vision—to be competitive worldwide in products and services; retain leadership in the country and aspire for a good market share internationally.

Mission—to sell a variety of cars, modern, high technology, fuel efficient for Indian and foreign markets.

The firm's values are as follows:

- Growth oriented organization ready to change to meet customers demand at short notice
- Value for money for the customers
- Stakeholders involvement and satisfaction
- Responsible corporate citizen.

Competitive Analysis of Maruti

Maruti had a good run till 1998, when several international players challenged its supremacy. In small car segment, Matiz of Daewoo Motors, Santro of Hyundai, and Indica from the Tatas have posed major problems for Maruti. In the luxury segment, its

Esteem faces competition from Honda City, Opel Astra, Ford Escort and Ford Ikon. Its jeep Gypsy faces competition from Mahendra's jeeps, and Armada, Sumo and Safari.

Threat of new entrants is real as the segment of middle class cars is growing rapidly. Volvo, Volkswagen, Toyota are planning to enter the market.

With Maruti brand image, economies of scale and marketing and service network, new firms have to spend a lot of money and efforts and that could be the entry barrier in the case while there is barrier now from the government side.

Critical Success Factors of Maruti:

- Suzuki technology
- Economic scale of production
- Strong R&D
- Timely market feedback as a result of continuous research
- Large range of models
- Strong dealer network
- Large service network around the country with trained technicians
- Quality programs Kaizan
- Design expertise
- Brand equity
- Provide leasing options, hire purchase schemes

Realizing the imminence of competition in 1998 Maruti planned to have relationship marketing, with an idea of selling the Maruti cars to its existing customer base and upgrading the product purchases. Maruti brought out Zen, Alto, Wagon R, for this purpose.

MUL is having competitive advantage in the segments they operate. To counter the onslaught of competition they even reduced the price and went for volume business.

MUL has maintained the competitive advantage in the following manner:

- Superior Suzuki compact car technology
- Value for money
- Low on maintenance cost
- Reliable quality
- Largest network of dealers and service centres
- Large product range for various needs and pockets
- Easy availability and attractive finance schemes
- ISO certification, even for a large number of dealers
- Technology transfers to important vendors for ensuring quality supplies

Maruti is a household name not only in India but in a number of countries of the west as well. With a modest beginning in 1997 when they exported 102 cars, now they export to more than 74 countries of the world and the number of cars exported has gone up to 30,000. The countries include Italy, Holland, Chile; with around 70% sales are to Europe.

Maruti looks to future with confidence with the following agenda:

- Commitment to customer satisfaction/delight

- Expansion and modernization of the facilities
- New models as per market demand
- Model upgradation
- Market research to remain proactive in the market place
- Emphasis on overseas markets
- Finance for the customers

Task for the Students

Do SWOT analysis of Maruti and give your marketing plan for Maruti which should enable them to remain market leader without compromising too much on revenue gains, Maruti's MOTTO "Build Trust Worldwide".

CASE STUDY

33

Whirlpool of India Ltd.

Whirlpool vision is to have a presence in every home of the country—with Pride, Passion and Performance. They believe they create the world's best home appliances to make people's life easier and more enjoyable for people around the world.

Pride in the work and in the employees. It is measured by vigorous process of determining the commitment, capabilities, and contribution of the employees.

Passion for creating unmatched customer loyalty for their brands, which is measured by growth in revenues, market share and market position and brand loyalty.

Performance -results should excite and reward the global investors with superior results and other stakeholders. The results are measured by calculating the economic value additions and not just the return on investment.

Whirlpool is committed to achieving global leadership by creating value for its three major stakeholders as follows:

Customers—the firm has customer focus in all their markets, products and services and it continuously measures the customer satisfaction to ensure that they prefer Whirlpool brand. Through their worldwide excellence system they achieve improvement in their results and attain breakthroughs in lowest defect levels, low supply cycle time. It enables them to exceed customer expectations and outperform competition.

Employees -the firm creates culture for high performance that encourages the employees to contribute to the tasks fully as individuals and as teams. In dynamic environment diversity and pursuit of world-class performance is obtained from the employees.

Shareholders—with the aim of global leadership the firm delivers great shareholder value to stay in the top twenty-five per cent firms in the field.

Worldwide Excellence System (WES) is the blueprint for Whirlpool quality management. It constitutes the operating system for achieving its objectives as follows:

- Leadership and people—at all levels people must act to reach the excellence.
- Strategic planning, fact based management and quality of process and products are the major internal processes for achieving excellence.
- Measurement and results set out for meaningful quantifiable measurements, which can be tracked down for improving quality.
- Customer satisfaction constitutes commitment of the firm, customers' expectations, service standards, relationships and satisfactory resolution of complaints.

WES also provides a feedback loop where the response of customers to the products and services is fed back into the system, driving further process improvement and refining the direction of effort.

Whirlpool Corporation of the USA is a leading manufacturer and marketer of major home appliances. The firm manufactures in 13 countries and markets in 170 countries under brand names of Whirlpool, Kitchen Aid, and Roper.

Whirlpool India is a subsidiary of Whirlpool Inc. it has acquired majority stake in Kelvinator of India in 1996. It started with the following four products under Whirlpool brand:

- Refrigerators
- Washing Machines
- Air-conditioners
- Microwave Ovens

Keeping core businesses of white goods they have discontinued unrelated and not core lines. As a result it has divested from compressors and automotive division.

Management Strategy

The firm is following expansionist strategy to avail the opportunities in the Indian market. The strategy has the following thrust areas:

- To register growth in the market through brand leadership to make Whirlpool a dominant brand
- To make external focus of satisfying customer needs
- To achieve business growth through high volumes, high quality and low costs
- To focus on core competencies and to have the best capabilities in the industry
- To have high profit and most efficient cost structure in the industry

Strategy Industry Analysis

Consumer durable industry is characterized by the following:

- Formidable entry barriers, in terms of brand equity, distribution and service network
- Manufacturing of most durables is neither capital nor technology intensive, the need for constant product innovation, makes R&D a key factor
- Rationalization of duties and opening up of the economy has attracted a host of global players

- Increase competitive pressures and over-zealous capacity creation have resulted in lower margins, which are expected to aggravate
- The market for most consumer durables are in the nascent stage and penetration levels are low
- The sector is price sensitive and each durable is a lifetime purchase
- Sale of refrigerators and washing machines are seasonal. Peak periods for refrigerators are the summer months, and for washing machines monsoon season.

Consumer durables market in India is estimated at Rs. 100 bn. The rural market, which has fifty percent of the target group, has lower levels of penetration. Favourable personal tax, politics and increase in credit financing are expected to increase spending capability on durables. Realizing the potential of annual growth rate of 24% is predicted over next three years and helped by the liberal foreign investment politics most MNCs have either established base in India through tie-ups.

The refrigerator market has two segments, the direct cool type and the frost-free type. Its penetration levels are given below:

- Urban 32%
- Rural 10%

Installed capacity in country is 3.2 million units per annum while the demand is 2.8 million units only.

Whirlpool is selling refrigerators both as direct cool, and frost-free types in different sizes, and have introduced the first CFC-free no-frost refrigerator. Its campaign, "ICE ICE BABY" has helped the firm in achieving great success.

Market share in percentage of refrigerators in India is as follows:

Whirlpool	Godrej GE	Electrolux	Videocon	BPL	Others
21	31	24	10	5	9

Refrigerators installed capacity in million units in India is given below:

Whirlpool	Godrej GE	BPL	Voltas	Electrolux	LG	Samsung	Daewoo	Others
1.4	1.3	0.3	0.55	0.3	0.4	0.2	0.2	0.5

Washing Machine Competition

In washing machines Whirlpool competes with the following firms:

Firms	Market share in %
Whirlpool	18
Videocon	35
Godrej GE	12
BPL	22
Others	13

Whirlpool marketing strategy can be summarized as follows:

- To place whirlpool washing machine with every customer in every price segment
- Marketing only top loading machines
- Started with top of the line front loading machine
- Whirlpools creative campaign 1-2, 1-2 has been a big success

Plans of Whirlpool

It is planning to bring a new range of refrigerators in the near future. This would be known as OPERA consisting of the following:

- 180 liters -4 models FUTURA, Home maker, Master piece, Break the barrier
- 210 liters -2 models Futura and Home maker

These brands would be common to India, Brazil and Mexico, which is part of the policy to position the global products in India.

Whirlpool believes that there are three types of competitors in India as given below:

- Basic trading instincts of buying and selling low value products. This is going to continue for a while. Some large competitors with high brand awareness in the country, which is not built on a strong platform of differentiation
- There are the South-East Asian types, not just the Koreans. A number of technology driven firms, pack their gizmos with features and some are good with futuristic plans
- The best products and technology do not build big business or brands, which depends on consumer perception. There is competition from the developed countries of the west. They have a different approach involving clear differentiated product for the firm and its brand. Who is going to succeed will depend on the policies and plans the firms have for India. Whirlpool wants to place its strategy on the third category.

Whirlpool's growth will depend on the following aspects:

- The industry's phase is of consolidation and the number of players will reduce in a few years, which would have a positive impact on sales
- Possible decline in commodity prices in international market for steel, copper could lead top procurement savings for lower manufacturing costs
- Phasing out of CFC products is to benefit Whirlpool as it has launched an array of CFC-free products conforming to Montreal protocol
- Four per cent levy on import duty and rupee depreciation is likely to affect firms cost structure, as a large proportion of raw material are imported. The firm is on an indigenization drive for sourcing components to overcome dependence on imports.
- Whirlpool keeps more than one supplier for its components
- Most Global majors are competing in India, due to its vast potential market. Indian firms also compete.

Task for the Students

Organize SWOT Analysis of Whirlpool and give your own marketing plan for the firm.

CASE STUDY 34

Price Waterhouse

Traditionally an accountancy firm, it was started by Samuel Price and Edwin Waterhouse in 1849 in London UK. 1930, the partners fanned out across the world, establishing semi-autonomous practice for accountancy investigations, liquidation and other financial services.

It was only from 1980 PW started management consultancy in a big way as several firms started accepting consultancy as a useful profession. PW has added technical research to their portfolio, an advance technology centre in Artificial Intelligence in the US with a $410 million Development Centre in London for IT Skills.

PW's USP comes from combining the roles of a consultant and an implementer.

PW's vision reads as follows:

The firm is committed to turning strategic insight into tactical action (strategic implementation), for our clients. In doing so we provide them with high quality, leading edge, and industry focused services and solutions, wherever they do business.

Their mission statement reads as follows—to be the global consultants to TOP-LAYER firms by solving their complex business problems.

The international growth phase of PW began the two world wars, where partnerships were set up in different parts of the world. These were mainly offices to serve audit clients in the first instance. Tax consultancy services were added in the large offices. Today, PW has 434 offices in 119 countries.

The highly regarded Emerson Research firm rates PW as simply one of the best in its 1998 clients' satisfaction survey of high technology firms PW ranked first, in eleven of thirteen client satisfaction categories among 293 audit clients of the big six firms. PW earned five-star status in four categories and it bagged more number one ranking than any other big six firms.

Category	PWs ranking
Overall client satisfaction	1*
Responsiveness of the partners	1* five star
Understanding clients' needs /expectations	1
Audit and accounting services	1 five star
Information technology services	1*
Corporate finance	1*five star
Tax services	1*
Contribution to success of the client's business	1*
Staff responsiveness	1*five star
Proactive contribution	1* five star
Consultancy services	1

Clients have singled out PW among the big six in serving high technology firms as can be seen from below:

"They have a high degree of responsiveness and professionalism"
"Overall they are exceptional"
"I think they do mergers and acquisitions very well. It is a specialty of PW"

Auditing is a competitive area and therefore the firm has diversified its management consultancy to cover such industries as entertainment, media and high tech. To keep abreast of industry trends PW has formed a new consulting group on electronics and on-line financial services.

PW is restructuring itself along product lines, as opposed to territorial divisions to serve the full range of its multinational clients. The purpose of the renewal efforts is helping firms in implementing strategies to improve business performance and shareholder values. Affecting organizational and strategic change using IT for competitive advantage and meeting audit and tax requirements with greater speeds with improved software packages.

Price Waterhouse, the Indian Profile

PW was established in India in 1880 as a part of the worldwide network of Price Waterhouse. PW has access to worldwide resources in terms of experience and expertise. If has the largest professional resource based in India enabling it to have a greater subject and sector specialization with 41 partners, around 1500 professional staff and supported by a panel external technical or professional experts.

Various disciplines include the following:

- Audit and business advisory services ABS
- Tax
- Management consultancy services (MCS)
- Corporate finance recovery and disputes (CFRD)

Clientele includes large and prestigious organizations in the following areas:

- MNCs
- Indian private sector
- Public sector or government
- Bilateral donor agencies/foreign embassies
- Multilateral funding/development agencies.

PW is registered with WORLD bank, ADB, UNDP, UNESCO, IDBI, and FIEO. Besides, it has regular working and consultative relationship with various Indian ministries.

PW has over the years acquired specialization in the following industrial sectors:

- Agro-based industry, including food processing
- Banking, finance and insurance services
- Engineering and electronics
- Finance and insurance
- Hotel and leisure
- Informatics including software
- International funding/ development agencies
- Mining
- Manufacturing and allied industries
- Retail trade-consumer goods
- Transportation
- Telecom
- Petroleum utilities including power and water

PW has other divisions operating in India as follows:

- Price Waterhouse Associates
- Price Waterhouse & Co
- Choksey &Co
- IPAN

Price Waterhouse India is a separate profit centre for the parent firm; it is their SBU-strategic business unit. Partners of Indian operations have stock options in the parent firm. The parent firm does regular internal audit in order to ensure that they conform to their strict guidelines.

In order to scan the competitive environment Porter's Five Force Model is used as given below:

Bargaining power of the customers is moderate as the customers have choice to select from the consultants, but it is not high as most of them are providing certain specific and specialized services.

Bargaining power of the suppliers—they include the business schools and the Institute of Chartered Accountants of India. Their bargaining power is moderate as consultancy is a refined form of business dealings - an aspect highly appealing to intelligent experts. The managerial talent of business schools prefers to join the consultants.

Threat of new entrants is high as it is growing and profitable business.

Threat of substitute products would come from internal experts of the clients. The threat from them is low as the internal experts may not have the vast resources, which are with the consultants. Firms generally prefer to go the consultants.

Competition among rival firms is high. The major players include the following:

- Anderson worldwide
- Vooz Allen
- PA Consulting group
- PE consultants
- Mackenzie
- Boston Consulting Group
- KPMG
- Critical Success Factors for the consultancy firms like PW are as follows:

Consultants form the backbone of the firm. Two basic characteristics of consultants are high intelligence and expertise in different areas as needed. John Foden CEO of PA Consulting group identifies three characteristics of an ideal consultant, which are (a) ability to listen, (b) capacity for analyzing the situation and capacity to come up with creative knowledge base solutions.

HR Planning—they employ meticulous care in recruiting management trainees from the best of the schools.

Career development opportunities–the promotions are performance related
Pay package
Continuous training and skill upgradation
Establishment of relationship with clients
Uniqueness of ideas
Development of new ideas
Experience
Latest management ideas
Efficient management information systems

The dictum is that the firm is as good as its clients.

Task for the Students

Do a SWOT Analysis of the firm and recommend strategies for marketing to combat the competitive forces.

CASE STUDY 35

Asian Paints Ltd.

Mr. Choksey of Andhra Pradesh belonged to the laid-back business community of India. Yet his vision was to "See Indian homes painted in a variety of colours from a truly Indian company."

His mission statement was 'To provide Paints as per Market Demand ensuring desired level and quality of Customer (Dealer) Service, continued availability of Right Product Mix of Right Quality at Right time.

With near servile attitude of their dealers, MNCs took pride in serving metros and large cities through dealers who also supplied the products to semi-urban markets, they were however concentrating on metros and found rural market non-existing. Business environment was hostile to Indian paint industry and more so to a new entrant.

Suppliers of raw materials were favouring MNCs because of their money power. MNCs kept the metros satisfied with their service goal of Asian Paints was, " Setting up manufacturing facility for paints in a large variety."

Strategy was to build a paint company as a role model of outstanding performance.

The poor and rich divide continued. The lot of farmers in Punjab , Haryana and Andhra was improving. In East of India, Bihar youth took to guns to combat poverty by robbery and Mafia started to thrive in Orissa. Environment in 1970s was such that for the first time political changes were taking place. The people had rejected imposition of emergency and the government changed hands. Business climate however did not change much. Entry of new foreign companies was severely restricted through government controls. Population was growing again at around 23 per 1000 as compulsory family planning had failed. Most citizens remained poor with pockets of excessive wealth. Migration workers from Bihar, Orissa to Bengal and Punjab continued. Bengal and Kerala industries suffered due to Marxist role in labour unrest.

Competitive Environment : Market for paints was at dead end. It was totally dominated by MNCs and Indian companies were looked down upon. MNCs had a cartel approach and had dealers with long-standing relationship in an oligopoly market. Entry barriers were not there as paints were low tech and low capital projects. Brand loyalty was remnant of Raj days. Alternative products were lime based low cost used by most in poverty-ridden India. In rich homes and offices wood panelling was being used increasingly. Market was largely controlled by MNCs.

Mr. Choksey found that to fight MNCs he had to look at the market segment so far neglected by them. He surveyed the market and found that near vacuum exists in semi-urban and rural market. They however had special needs. "Low cost paint in small containers." The segment needed a new distribution system as well.

Asian Paints value for the customers was to build through innovative package (size), Distribution, Communication. In 1970s they decided to computerise and network their 30 depots round the country to provide proper feedback of market needs resulting in quick response to meet the needs.

They planned new distribution structure, smaller packages and computerized communication network.

Mr. Choksey did not have any animus towards MNCs who had shown hostility and created entry barriers for him.

Asian Paints differentiation strategy starts from market segment, distribution and packaging.

With increasing volumes in chosen segments Asian Paints achieved economies of scale for cost leadership.

With dominant position they diversified in product range as also market and geographic segments.

1. They diversified into manufacture of raw materials for Paints.
2. Product diversification also included Industrial Paints. Now with large market share they have strong distribution network even in metros.

Asian Paints strategy of quick response translates as having 95% orders supply in 48 hours and is appositive competitive advantage. Their R&D has developed new products to cater to industrial and scientific segments. Paint Industry is in growth stage in India as Construction Activity has a high priority.

In order to maintain market leadership (With 27% market share they enjoy double the market share than their nearest competitor), they have drawn up the following strategy:

1. Backward vertical integration

Mr. Choksey's style of functioning was informal as he kept friendly relations with Depot staff, sales team. He started overseas operation to expand his horizons further.

With liberalized economy international brands are likely to enter the market, as entry barriers are low in paint industry.

To keep their dominant position Asian Paints should do vigorous R&D for innovative products, increase the number of depots for covering the entire country, advertise separately for each market segment and arrange continuous market research to their competitive advantage.

INDEX